Praise for Phoebe Eng
and

WARRIOR LESSONS

"Phoebe Eng has used the knowledge and credentials of her legal training to battle the stereotype of the super-feminine, subservient Asian woman."

—*The New York Times*

"I recommend this book to all those interested in women's efforts to find their true selves."

—Mary Pipher, *New York Times* bestselling
author of *Reviving Ophelia*

"Phoebe Eng lifts the silken veil of stereotype from the marginal world of Asian American women."

—*Pasadena Star-News* (CA)

"An important book for all women, *WARRIOR LESSONS* does more than remind us that to change the world, we must change ourselves; *WARRIOR LESSONS* shows us how."

—Helen Zia, contributing
editor, *Ms.* magazine

"With unflinching clarity and heart, Phoebe Eng offers validation, hope, and a path for authenticity, transformation, and action for Asian American women. Beyond that, she gives all readers a soaring sense of possibility as she gently provokes us to become truth-tellers and troublemakers in the most exemplary and honorable ways."

—Harriet Lerner, Ph.D., author
of *The Dance of Anger*

"In a clear and true voice, Phoebe Eng sings of the power that flows from self-knowledge. The universal lessons of *WARRIOR LESSONS* will awaken women and men alike; Asian Americans and all Americans."

—Eric Liu, author of
The Accidental Asian

"Unique. . . . In a natural, intelligent voice, Eng provides excellent advice while serving as a superb role model for younger Asian American women striving to come into their own."

"Exhilarating in its honesty, like those first acts of defiance against family and tradition. As Asian women, we need to thank Eng, master cartographer, for the map of our lives."

WARRIOR

LESSONS

An Asian American Woman's

Journey Into Power

PHOEBE ENG

POCKET BOOKS

NEW YORK   LONDON   TORONTO   SYDNEY   SINGAPORE

POCKET BOOKS, a division of Simon & Schuster Inc.
1230 Avenue of the Americas, New York, NY 10020

Library of Congress Cataloging-in-Publication Data

Eng, Phoebe.
   Warrior lessons : an Asian American woman's journey into power / Phoebe
Eng.
      p.   cm.
   Includes bibliographical references.
   ISBN 0-671-00958-3
   1. Asian American women—Social conditions. 2. Asian American women—
Social conditions—Case studies. 3. Asian American women—Conduct of life.
4. United States—Race relations. 5. Eng, Phoebe. I. Title.
E184.O6E54   1999
305.895073—dc21   99-11234

First Pocket Books trade paperback printing May 2000

10 9 8 7 6 5 4 3

Front cover photo by Gasper Tringale
Book design by Jessica Shatan

Printed in the U.S.A.

For my teachers,
MALLIKA DUTT
ELAINE KIM
HELEN ZIA
PEGGY SAIKA
SHARON HOM

and for my mother,
MEI-HUEI

and my father,
HARRY KUO-FEI

Acknowledgments

This book belongs to the hundreds of women that took the time to share their most intimate stories with me over the past three years. I am grateful to my editor, Nancy Miller, and assistant editor Kim Kanner, whose insights have molded this book and whose patience was tested regularly as I found I couldn't stop adding new ideas to its chapters. This book would also not be possible without the prompting of my close friend, Don Fehr, who first suggested many years ago that I consider taking on a book project. Geri Thoma, my most wonderful agent, guided me with humor and care through the process of a first book and through much more. President and publisher Gina Centrello and editorial director Emily Bestler at Pocket Books gave me their enthusiasm from the first day we discussed this book, as did Tina Bennett, Sandra Dijkstra, Janet Goldstein, Phil Friedman, Will Schwalbe, and Doris Cooper. Toko Serita, Phuong Do, and my sister, Donna Eng, entrusted so much of their lives to me, and their influences are felt throughout these pages, as are the voices of the women from the National Asian Pacific American Women's Forum and National Asian Pacific American Women's Leadership Institute. Sabrina Silverberg, Mallika Dutt, Scott Wolfman, Wayne Marquez, and Karen Cole have always been there to lift my spirits in the worst bouts of writer's block. My thanks go to The Writers Room, which provided the quiet space I needed to finish this project, and to Hope Edelman for first suggesting it to me. Warren Scott, Martha Glessing, and Les Edwards, all mentors from past parts of my life, were also very important in my writing of this book, as were those whose writing and teachings have had a lasting and eclectic influence on the way I see the world: Cornel West, Gloria Steinem, Alice Walker, Michael Eric Dyson, Thich Nhat Hanh, Clarissa Pinkola-Estes, Edward Said, Susan Taylor, Derrick Bell, Sherman Alexie, Naomi Wolf, Joseph Campbell, Shawn Wong, Maxine Hong Kingston, and the love of my life, my husband, Zubin Shroff. I hope that the ideas in this book live up to all of their visions of healing and hope.

Contents

PART IV: THROUGH THE FIRE

THE NEED FOR A COMPASS

Over the last few years, as I made my way across the country as a lecturer and writer, I have met many hundreds of Asian American women who have shared with me their stories—how they see their lives, whether they feel in control of their destinies, and, if not, what they needed to get there. Whether they were American-born, recent immigrants, professionals, students, or workers, and regardless of where in Asia their families originated, it became clear that they often shared common yearnings for connection to each other and advice as to how to take a middle path between family expectations and realizing their own hopes and dreams. They talked of being strong and knowing their worth, yet still they felt misunderstood and sometimes isolated. Often, especially if they were the American-raised daughters of immigrants, they were trying hard to resolve their feelings of "being in limbo" or "falling through the cracks" of the often divergent cultures of East and West. What they asked for most was a compass or a road map to guide them into a more powerful, more grounded view of themselves.

Perhaps that need comes from what Filipina American writer Karin Aguilar-San Juan referred to recently as "the complicated relationship [that we have] to the idea of 'home,'" which to each of us can mean so many things. Where is "home" when our extended families span multiple generations and many continents with intricate social bonds? And, as Aguilar-San Juan suggests, is America truly "home" when even those of us who claim four and five generations born in America can still be perceived as foreigners? I look at my own extended family as an example. In America, the Engs are teachers, we are merchants, some of us have worked in sweatshops, and some of us own them. Among us there are artists, ad executives, waiters, and millionaires. Some speak stilted English; some can't read a word of Chinese. Yet as different as we might be from one another, "home" for each of us is fluid and multiple in its definition. Comfortable enough in America, Chinatown, and even Hong Kong or Taiwan, we seem to belong everywhere. And because of this, we might also belong nowhere. "Home," it seems, ends up being a mixed-up notion that must be redefined if it is to have meaning for many of us. No wonder we need compasses. Without knowing where we stake our ground, it is difficult for us to know where we're going.

With a knowledge of our past that is often shaky at best, and a cultural future that remains uncharted, we have had to figure out by ourselves what it means to live with confidence as Asian American women. How do we learn how to stand up for ourselves? How do we learn to accept ourselves, our weaknesses, doubts, as well as our strengths, and know that we are still worthy? When do we let perfectionism and expectation fall away so that we can finally live truer, more powerful lives? Without road maps and compasses, we have grown accustomed to defining our experiences and our validity individually, through blind trial and error, often without mentors, often without hearing the stories of others that might help us understand our own lives. In my life, I have often found myself swinging back and forth, alone and searching for a stabilizing center.

Call it a blessing or a curse. I was the first of two daughters born in America to the Eng family, in the Chinese Year of the Tiger, a year, it is said, that yields girls who grow up to be trouble. Like tigers, the Chinese horoscope says, such girls are too unruly to control, too confident in their own power, too dangerously unpredictable and rebellious. And so, with kicking and fighting in my stars, it was my uncanny good fortune to have been born outside of China, in Philadelphia, home of the Liberty Bell. In America, where rugged rebellion is sought-after and rewarded, I was raised true to my tiger calling. Within one generation of stepping off a steamship onto Ellis Island, the Eng family of my father (a lineage of hardworking Cantonese railroad workers and laundrymen) and the Liu family of my mother (Presbyterian evangelicals from Taiwan) had an American-born daughter who grew to embody the fruits of their hard work. A lawyer in the family! And one who spoke such good English!

By the late 1980s I had become a young international attorney, a Chinese American yuppie (aka "chuppie') in training. The Pacific Rim was booming, and I was to be stationed at the center of it all in Hong Kong. Finally, I thought, my hyphenated Asian-Americanness, which had always been a cross to bear in my younger years, might give me some advantage. What I didn't understand then was that in Hong Kong, as an American woman with an Asian face, with one foot planted in America and only my pinky toe planted in the land of my distant ancestry, I would have even less advantage, even less a sense of belonging than I did in the States. In a Hong Kong law office, I would learn the hard way about the complicated intersections of gender, class, and nationality in Asia. I would learn how reluctant the older Chinese secretaries would be to work for me, a young Chinese American neophyte lawyer. I would learn that when Asian clients retain an American law firm, they prefer their counsel to be the tall, blond, blue-eyed men that happened to speak better Chinese than I. I would learn that our Asian clients, as traditional Chinese, Japanese, and Korean men, were even more apt than American clients to presume my subservience, asking me to whip out my steno pad and take dictation. The difference was that, unlike at the Park Avenue law firm where I was often the coffee girl, in Hong Kong, I served the tea.

My American roots would earn me the dubious label of *jook-sing*, a foreign-born, literally a bamboo hollow brain (which, by the way, is *not* a Chinese compliment). With a faltering, American tongue that tried in vain to sound truly Chinese, and a western swagger that hardly fit within the rules of how a good Chinese woman ought to walk, I fell through the crack of an East-West divide. In fact, it was more like a vast, gaping crevasse. I didn't belong in Asia, so I came back to America, resolved to accept it as home.

But back in America, I found that being an Asian American woman means living hidden behind layers of imagery—that of dutiful daughters and mothers, straight-A students and diligent workers, silent and exotic seductresses, tragic and self-sacrificing Madame Butterflies. With these images of marginality, Asian American women as a group have, until now, been excluded from the core of most American dialogues. Even within a women's movement that is striving to be inclusive, we are an afterthought, an embellishment, if we exist at all. We struggle with our invisibility and we share desires to be treated seriously, past stereotype.

I decided to try to do my part. I left the law and joined a team of like-minded souls in creating a magazine that aimed to reflect more realistically the experience of Asians in America. *A. Magazine* served as a voice for people like myself, caught in that East-West divide and eager to articulate a new future of our own. And now in *Warrior Lessons,* I want to etch out a message of hope and power for Asian American women, continuing the path of one of my personal heroines, the writer Maxine Hong Kingston.

In 1976, Kingston's *The Woman Warrior: Memoirs of a Girlhood Among Ghosts* was published, a book that is considered the cornerstone of every young Asian woman's coming of age in America. The story was about a young girl like me, with a family like mine, who evoked and experimented with the stories of her past in order to create a viable future. In *The Woman Warrior,* Kingston talks about her cultural confusion and offers beautifully poetic stories that left us with a starting point from which to venture out into the world. To complement those stories, she told tales of the mythic heroine Fa Mu Lan, a woman who took her father's place in battle in order to save her family's honor. In an interview with Bill Moyers, Kingston tells the rest of that story, which she had chosen not to include in her manuscript. After returning victorious, Fa Mu Lan was able to relinquish her armor and resume her life at home, without internalizing the brutality of war. As Kingston explained to Moyers, "She was not dehumanized or broken by war. And so it's important to figure out how we can do that. How do you come back from a war and then turn back into a beautiful woman? And give that beauty back to your family and community?" Years later, her book has become the most widely taught work by a living American writer on college campuses today, its author telling us that the real power of the warrior lies not only in her willingness to fight, but also in her choices after the battle. In *Warrior Lessons*, I want to explore that transformational, humane side of her strength. The power I describe in these pages is the ability to build legitimate communities and trust, and the courage to be accountable to ourselves and one another. In *Warrior Lessons,* the practice of power for Asian American women becomes the act of connection.

The Woman Warrior gave young Asian American women a voice. It legitimized our issues. We learned in *The Woman Warrior* that each of us has the ability to fight when aggression is needed, and to create when life is good. But *The Woman Warrior* offered only a starting point. We learned how to be young girls then, but now, we need to talk about adulthood, with all of its issues and choices.

Many of us now find ourselves just as concerned about the present as we are about reclaiming our past—we are looking for better ways to communicate and negotiate, how to build our families, our jobs, and our futures. While we struggled with identity issues as young girls, those issues have become even more important to us now, as we decide how to raise our children, whom to choose as partners, and how perceptions and stereotypes affect our chances of achieving our goals.

By voicing our common experiences, *Warrior Lessons* takes us one step further on our American odyssey. It explores the lives and memories of Asian American women across the country, women who have guided me in my own search for strength and identity, and who have been generous enough to spend hours with me during interviews or filling out questionnaires. These are the lessons about our families, our goals, the risks we take, the skirmishes and battles we fight, and the importance of commitment and creative activism in life. Told for their common ground, these stories have helped me to piece together that road map I've sought for so long but could not find, and may help others to steer through the issues that they face in their own lives.

As I write this book, there are still relatively few works that take the measure of Asian American women's perspectives with the aim of finding the common ground among them. Psychological texts such as *Working with Asian Americans* by Evelyn Lee, and *Asian Americans* by Laura Uba, offer case studies and statistical backup to show the trends in our mental and emotional health. Collections such as *Making More Waves*, edited by Elaine Kim, Lydia Villanueva and Asian Women United of California, *Leaving Deep Water* by Claire Chow, and *Dragon Ladies,* edited by Sonia Shah, preserve the diversity of experience among us and demonstrate our great resilience of spirit. *Warrior Lessons* recognizes that diversity while striving to keep the common ground, because that is where I am convinced that our potential for transformative power lies.

In my conversations and from the several hundred written and E-mail interviews submitted over a three-year period from Asian American women across the country, some patterns emerged strong and resonant. I found that regardless of whether I was in Boulder, San Francisco, New York, Chicago, Dallas, or even Honolulu, whether I was speaking with a factory worker, an investment banker, or a community activist, women expressed many of the same concerns and posed the same questions, including:

- How can we deal with family expectations?

- Why don't our daughters understand us?

- How can we work past stereotypes at our jobs and in our relationships?

- Can we be feminine and sexual in the face of "geisha" stereotypes?

- Why do we distance ourselves from one another?

- How do we begin to build connections among us?

- Can we really trust one another?

- Where are our mentors?

- How can we vent anger, and why is our anger most intense when it is directed at each other?

Warrior Lessons speaks to these questions, and proffers that the answers lie in deep, sometimes painful, introspection that leads to a strengthened emotional grounding. It includes narratives that we are often reluctant to share about our doubts and conflicts at home, at work, and in our relationships. Its themes break down myths that hold us back. Most important, it puts us on a road to a much more powerful view of ourselves than we might have had before.

This book comprises twelve lessons, which start by exploring personal roots and patterns and progress to our interactions with the world around us. In any true transformative process, one starts by looking within. And so Part 1, "Inner Work," begins with the lessons of the self, how we might approach parental expectation, family patterns, and even our sources of anger and where we might have found a sense of power up to now. Part 2, "Ourselves With Others," delves into sexuality, desire, and the intimacy of friends. Why do we love whom we love? And why do we sometimes choose distance over closeness with one another? Part 3, "Survival Skills," includes hands-on suggestions for how to handle tension and conflict creatively and constructively, how to seek out our mentors, and become teachers. Part 4, "Through the Fire," is about creating accountability for ourselves while cultivating a greater sense of an Asian American women's community. Here we'll consider the necessity of risk at key points in our lives and the altering of ingrained beliefs, which will ultimately allow us to grow. In the final chapter, I suggest ways to approach leadership that can bring our issues to the table more inclusively and efficiently.

Trying to give voice to commonality can be a risky business, and there were two pitfalls that I worked to avoid. The first was that generalizations about experience can lead to stereotyping, threatening the individuality that we cherish so dearly. Many of us have also been raised on the idea of success through assimilation, and perhaps because of this, we have learned to resist categorizations that lump us together as "otherly" Asian people. To address these concerns, I have consciously incorporated the voices of many Asian American women, across generations, geography, class, and ethnicity.

I am less concerned with terminology and the boundaries of "what constitutes an Asian American?" than I am with showing the fluidity of our identity. Well aware of the political and philosophical considerations that surround this issue, I have nevertheless chosen to use the terms "Asian American" and "Asian" somewhat loosely and interchangeably—the first when the person or idea arises predominantly from an

American experience and the latter when it harkens back to tradition or the memory of native homeland. Ethnically specific terms such as "Korean" or "Chinese" will be used when describing a first-generation immigrant or a notion that is specific to a particular culture in Asia. Regardless of my phrasing, I contend that all the experiences described in *Warrior Lessons* are Asian American.

The second pitfall was what I call the "ancient Chinese secret" booby trap—the tendency to justify the Asian American voice by claiming that it is unique. By focusing solely on what sets us apart from others, the Asian American narrative has, in the past, been valuable primarily for its unusual settings, rich imagery, choppy pigeon English, and the authenticity of our ancestors' colorful stories. "Ancient Chinese secret" tendencies can limit the potential of our stories, implying that our exoticism is what gives us legitimacy. If we share aspects of experience perceived as common to others, the thinking goes, our stories and themes are no longer as valid. But, until we can understand the ways we share experience with others across racial and cultural lines, we will not realize our full capabilities for a meaningful, purposeful kind of power. When a Chinese American garment worker can finally recognize that she shares a part of her experience with other low-paid women across America and even internationally, she gains power. When a young Asian American woman understands that the difficulties she has at home with her parents may have their roots in larger causes outside of her immediate household, she derives power from that revelation. When she sees that the competition she may feel with other Asian American women is often a shared, destructive behavior among women in general, she comes to realize that building alliances will always prove more powerful than distance.

Warrior Lessons speaks about and to a specific kind of Asian American woman—one who sees herself at the crossroads of two often-conflicting cultures. She is one who wants to nurture her sense of her own validity, who has tried to develop her own sense of place and home, even when falling between the cracks and boundaries that have been laid before her. She may be a recent immigrant, or her family may have a long history here. Her ancestral heritage is important to her less for its specific geography and more for the common issues of family, honor, shame, and "otherness" it raises.

In her book *Revolution From Within,* Gloria Steinem wrote, "Most writers write to say something about other people and it never lasts. Good writers write to find out about themselves—and it lasts forever." In my attempt to be a "good" writer, I have tried to use this book as a journey and an education for myself as well. I realized halfway through that, in order to be real, I had to bring my own voice and my own experience to the table in as truthful and intimate a way as I could. Only as I revealed the layers of my own contradictions, misgivings, and confusion could I begin to request others to do so with me. And so *Warrior Lessons* is also about my own growing process, my coming-of-age and my coming into power. It includes stories that I was reluctant to tell for fear of being judged, or of not being "correct" enough. Some of the personal stories I share will leave me exposed and vulnerable. And yet all the ways I have found over the years to silence myself and question my voice have had to give way in order for personal change, and eventually connection, to occur. I offer *Warrior Lessons* as the first of many such nonfiction voices, in hopes that others will follow.

The path of the warrior is in front of us. So what are we waiting for? It's time to hit the road.

Part I

INNER

WORK

SHE CASTS OFF EXPECTATIONS

We know very well what it's like to live with family expectations breathing down our backs:

Get married! (and to the right man)

Have children! (meaning more than one)

Make money! (and lots of it)

Can't you be like _____? (Fill in the blank with the name of your nerd cousin, valedictorian friend, or other mother-appointed rival.)

When we don't live up to expectation, we don't need words to know. It's Asian mother telepathy. We can see it in their faces. The downcast eyes, the wistful, concerned look, the deep breath. No matter how much we try to ignore it, it still hits us hard. What do we do with the heavy burden of family honor? And do we ever escape it?
Let's start with a story.

My mother and Rita were like sisters. They grew up together in Taiwan. They came to America together on a lark and found a way to stay here by enrolling in nursing school. They slept in the same bed in a cramped dorm room, head to foot, for a year. *And Rita's feet stank like smelly cheese!* my mother adds. They double-dated and ended up marrying two Chinese American guys who were also best friends. Their children grew up together. And when Mom and Rita hit forty-five, they shared their stories about disappointment and sometimes even depression.

After a while Rita's calls to my mother started to spin out of control. Rita would wail about whether it was worth living anymore until her gentle husband took the phone out of Rita's hard-clenched hand, apologized, and hung up. Rita said that her kids never did what she asked. She didn't know what had gone wrong. Her son was living with a hippie and smoked pot. Her daughter had two babies with her American boyfriend, didn't marry him, and left Rita to take care of her children. Rita told my mother that she had started to take Valium to calm down. And then her calls got wilder. She'd call my mother sounding drugged and crazy, again saying that her life had been worth nothing.

One spring about ten years ago, we got a call from Rita's

husband, telling us that Rita had died. It seems that her nightgown had caught on fire while she was making tea, and despite her husband's desperate attempts to smother the flames that engulfed her body, Rita had burned to death. My mother and I often wonder if Rita killed herself, or was so drugged with Valium that she fell asleep on top of the stove. My mother ends the story sometimes by saying that Rita's tormented soul is really what killed her.

Rita's death showed me in a heart-wrenching way what can happen to a woman who is isolated and desperate and whose cries for help go unanswered. It showed me how our self-destructive sides can get the better of us, no matter how happy and carefree we might once have been. But for me, Rita's death carries even more of a punch. It has become for me a parable about disappointing one's Chinese parents. That is how deep expectations run. Don't live up to them and you run the risk of your parents going mad and dying of disappointment and shame.

Expectations: A key word in the Asian American coming-of-age lexicon that I have come to know so well. As the older of two daughters, I became the stand-in son that my parents never had. In those shoes, I received the windfall of their expectations and, to the detriment of my very deserving younger sister, the greater part of their attention. I also had to bear the crushing weight of their hopes. So what did I do with all that expectation? I did what any self-preserving person would do—I tried as hard as I could to duck it.

At eighteen, I chose a college clear across the country and left my suburban New York home, ending up in the San Francisco Bay Area, home of the counterculture, hot tubs, and acid parties, the place where I pushed through some very important rites of passage and finally came of age. My choice to attend school three thousand miles away wouldn't be the first time that I would perplex my parents, and it certainly wouldn't be the last time I would disappoint them. When it became clear that I was not, in fact, going to Harvard (through no choice of my own, although filling out my application with a fat, blue Magic Marker pen probably didn't help my chances), I think they finally realized that they would have to begin to accept compromises in their American Dream daughter. So for the next twenty years, I have pushed the envelope of their willingness to compromise, pushed them to accept progressively more incomprehensible choices, like my decision to write these stories. That choice will mean having to deal with the fallout that will no doubt accompany the decision to write them as true stories, without the safety net that fiction can provide. Take it from this well-seasoned prodigal daughter: There is often nothing worse than not living up to parental expectation, *and yet, when on a path to self-discovery, there is absolutely nothing better.* That must be the tiger blood in me. Always stirring up trouble.

WHAT ARE YOU DOING WITH YOUR LIFE?

"Aiyo! Ah-Phee! Why do you write those bad things? People will think you are either stupid or crazy!"

That's Mom talking, the relentless voice of reason. She has just read the past few pages and is justifiably freaking out about her daughter airing dirty laundry.

"I want to connect with women that I care about; that's why I'm writing this book, Mom." I'm trying to explain a philosophy to her that I can already feel she won't understand. It's an American idea, this truth-telling process, probably grounded in some Christian notion of absolution. To my mom, truth is pretty useless unless it helps you get ahead. She believes in images, specifically, the image of her successful lawyer daughter, and that my salary and status should pave the way to a life free of problems. Certainly free from the necessity of writing what she surely views as a scathing tell-all, like something Roseanne would write.

"We have to have the courage to talk truthfully—to admit that we have questions and that we're fallible. Saying so can be an act of power." I'm still not getting through to her. I give her a publisher's legal waiver and ask her to sign it.

"I am trying to create a special language of activism for people like you and me who need it, and to do that requires honesty."

"Let someone else connect and do activism," she says. *"You worked too hard, you have such a good résumé. You're throwing it all away! Oh, and by the way, if you're really going to write this book, I hope you're not going to write bad things about me, too. Are you?"*

I begin to get a sinking feeling that we are in for one of our long discussions that pits me against her. It is the same dynamic that has kicked in every time I have reached a turning point in my life, where, instead of choosing the path of least resistance she lays out before me, I choose a dusty road of questionable adventure, strewn with rocks and potholes and thieves.

I have made a life out of defying Mom. She wanted me to go to a college close to home, so I found one as far away as I possibly could. She thought that I should go straight to law school after college, so I took a backpack and went around the world on five dollars a day for two years instead. When I hit twenty-five, she thought it was a good time to settle down with a nice Chinese boy. I decided to move in with a guy from southern Italy who chain-smoked. Now I was about to defy her one more time, by leaving the legal profession, the coveted prize for a mother's job well done, so that I could join a bunch of young writers with little in their bank accounts to publish a magazine for Asian Americans. I thought it was the opportunity of a lifetime. My parents thought I had gone off the deep end.

The struggle to meet the demands of fulfilling family expectations while still living lives of our own choosing causes a great deal of stress for many Asian American women and often creates situations where compromise is impossible. Yukiko, a Japanese student who has spent the last four years attending a rural college in Illinois, brims with energy and self-confidence. She shared this story with me over the Internet one day, exhibiting the ever-present guilt that comes along with choosing independence over family responsibility:

> After I graduate from college, I probably have to go back home to be near my family next year. I know I don't have to go back, but I feel like I have to look after my grandmother and parents. I know they want me to be near them, but will I really be able to help them just because I'm near? I want to travel and experience other cultures around the world (and I haven't told them yet, but I already bought a ticket to Guatemala!). I feel guilty myself somehow. I really love my family. But if I have to stay close to home, I could not satisfy my life. So I will probably go my way even if my family doesn't accept it. THAT IS ME. I'll never ever regret my life. I wish to live with satisfaction.

The ache of striving to be oneself amid all the noise around us telling us to be something different can be wrenching. For many of us, one of our first opportunities to follow a self-defined path comes when we select our college majors. Our decisions to pursue our studies in art, literature, communications, or philosophy, may not necessarily generate the most positive feedback from family. As Phuong, a Vietnamese American community worker told me: "They don't understand what 'social work' is. My uncle says, 'What are you studying, and why does it take such a long time to study that subject?' The expectation of me is to be the emotional support of the family, not the intellectual."

When I casually mentioned to my mother that I would be majoring in English literature, she took a deep breath and then threatened to pull the purse strings. *"What's this English literature? You don't have to go all the way to Berkeley to read novels. You can do it closer to home. You study business or engineering or something useful, or you come home!"* was her ultimatum. So I studied business, took the least number of courses possible in that major, and loaded up on as many English classes as I could handle. Yes, I can have my cake and eat it too, I insisted. But it meant that I would have to work twice as hard as everyone else, doing what was expected while pursuing my own path, at the same time.

Expectation pressures follow us into the workplace, as increasing numbers of us choose career paths off the beaten track, as was the case for Carolyn, a poet from Hawaii: "My mom once asked me, 'Why you spend three thousand dollars on a computer for? You can't make money on poetry.'" Others, such as Prema, a lawyer-turned-funder, have explained their unpopular choices in terms that her family can respect and understand: "I told them I'm not a lawyer anymore. I do fund-raising. They said, 'Fund-raise? What's that? Is that a job?' So I told them, 'Okay, I do charity work,' which they understood. Luckily for me, charity work is seen as a very noble 'hobby' for a woman of status and wealth in India."

And when we start families, some of us are exasperated yet again that we are not living up to mother-standards, as was the case for Monique, whose mother is Chinese and whose father is Caucasian: "I thought my mother would be overjoyed at my pregnancy, even more so because I was expecting a baby boy. Instead she said to me, 'I'm a little disappointed. I wanted a girl.' Go figure. When my Chinese American friend told me she was pregnant recently, also with a boy, I told her not to expect her mom to be elated. She called me later and told me that her mom had the same reaction as my mom did. She couldn't believe it!"

In a 1987 study by psychologists Robert Hess, Chih-Mei Chang, and Teresa McDevitt, marked differences were found in the ways that Chinese American mothers accounted for their children's successes and failures as opposed to European American mothers. For instance, while the study found that European American mothers were more likely to attribute academic success to good school training, Chinese American mothers were more apt to credit good home upbringing. If Chinese American children fail, however, their mothers were more likely to attribute it to poor home upbringing than their European American counterparts. While success is not praised or outwardly acknowledged, failure is personalized and attached to family honor. It can create a feedback loop that conditions us to see success as a minimum standard.

Cheryl is Korean American, a publicist in the fashion industry. She tells a story about her childhood that many of us may remember well:

It seemed that I could never do enough. I always got A's in Catholic school, except for that one B I always got in religion. That B was all my parents ever focused on. I'd tell them, "But look at all the A's I got!" and they'd say, "Of course you got A's. That's what you're supposed to do." So the message was pretty clear. Instead of getting excited about my successes, I learned instead to fear not meeting their almost impossible expectations.

As my survey responses bear out, the pressure of expectations in our families comes almost solely from our mothers. For better or for worse, our mothers generally define our family spiritually and serve as the main communication link to their daughters, passing on to us their own ambitions. And while our fathers may cheer their children's accomplishments from a distance, the raw pressure to fight and perform is our mothers' turf.

Generally, our mothers are more willing to give us their blunt, if not imprecise, advice on how to lead our lives. Lora, one of San Francisco's most prolific labor attorneys, remembers working in a garment factory with her mother every summer since she was eleven. From dawn to dusk, they would sit behind sewing machines to earn the money the family needed to pay the rent and put food on the table. There were times when Lora would work during the school year as well. Working at that young age allowed her to understand the powerlessness of being used as cheap labor, as her mother would remind her constantly. At home, Lora again confronted her powerlessness as, night after night, she witnessed her father's gambling addiction. He'd raid her small savings and steal from her piggy banks when he had no money of his own. Lora remembers her mother's advice to her and her sisters when they were young:

My mother used to say, "Don't let yourself be treated like a girl-child slave. If you were in China, your father would have sold you a long time ago for money." She used to say that to us when we were seven, eight, nine years old. Basically, my association with being a girl and a child is with being a slave.

But how was Lora to figure out how to avoid this "girl-child slave" predicament? How was she supposed to fight for herself and be strong? Her mother had told them the situation to avoid. Yet as a young girl, Lora was faced with the problem without a clear way out. Lora, like many of us, was well aware of the goals that had been set out for her. What our mothers usually don't provide, however, are the step-by-step instructions on how exactly to get there or where exactly we should be going. Their expectations, though ominous, end up being imprecise, and daughters can wind up grasping at straws, understandably frustrated in trying to fulfill them.

When asked why we frequently forgo our own wants in order to fulfill our parents' expectations, many of us respond with reasons that incorporate notions of filial piety and reverence for our elders. I was taught at an early age the nature of that exchange. My parents worked hard to ensure that I'd have the good life I now enjoy, and I was to repay them by concurring with their wishes. "Be a good daughter, marry a man who can control you," my mother once said. "Have children and get a good job that won't take you too far from home." And what she implied: "In exchange I will give you everything I can— all my attention, my money, my being, my honor, and my dignity. Your performance will be linked to my very life, and because of this, I know you will comply."

Women such as Hoai are familiar with this exchange. Her parents have worked for decades in their grocery store in Colorado, and much of what they've earned has been put into their four children's college educations. Recently, Hoai found out that her parents' store had once again been robbed. Even after several robberies in the past, and even after Hoai's mother had narrowly missed a bullet in one of those incidents, her father refused to install a security camera because he felt it was too expensive. "I somehow feel responsible for their situation. They've worked their whole lives for us, and so when I told them that I quit my job to become a filmmaker, all she could say was, 'Now I'll never be able to retire.' This was supposed to be a major joyous decision in my life, and all I could feel was guilt. By trying to be myself, I was letting them down." For weeks, Hoai was racked with violent nightmares where rage, dismemberment, and chaos were recurring themes.

"Filial piety" is often synonymous with payback—daughter's guilt and obedience in exchange for a mother's undying but tacit support. Our guilt can come in many currencies. Guilt for having the privilege, choice, and mobility that she deserved but never had. Guilt because her talents were never fully recognized and rewarded due to her heavy accent, because she had to make compromises, because she was seen as a little Asian woman. Guilt for feeling that she might be jealous, not of us, but of our opportunity. Guilt for telling her that she has no right to feel proprietary over our lives.

We need not fall into a cycle of guilt and dependence that locks us into aspirations, lifestyles, and dreams that are not our own. But to avoid this requires that we take responsibility for our choices. Reverence for our elders does not imply a blind obedience to their wishes. Respect, if genuine, must be mutual, even in Asian families. *Filial piety cannot become a cultural excuse that absolves us from having to determine who we are and what our lives stand for.*

I realized that I could no longer rationalize my own fear of self-determination and risk taking by blaming the heavy expectations of family. After all, they have always wanted only what they thought was best, given their own experiences. How could I have expected them to know what more was possible? Had I lived in lock-step compliance to their wishes, I would have grown resigned and resentful. Instead, I took the chance of losing approval and followed the paths that spoke most powerfully to me. And for that, I can now live the life I have always dreamed of, with a fluid schedule that allows me to travel and work when and where I want to, and a relationship with a man who doesn't feel he has to control me as much as share his life with me on equal terms. Through it all, I have learned a valuable lesson—if what our parents want for us is success, then they will grow to understand that our best chances for succeeding will lie in doing what we truly want to do.

The truth is that if family bonds are loving and true, they are also unconditional. Our parents will learn to understand this, even if it may require our defiance and heartache to get there.

As much as she has tried to dissuade me and disapproved of the many choices I have made, my mother always ends up, albeit reluctantly, as my staunchest supporter. When I became the publisher of *A. Magazine* and had no money to hire staff, she would come into the office on her days off and stick stamps on envelopes, alphabetize my Rolodex in some very odd ways, and organize the office. She would get lunch for me and clean the office, saying as she wiped the desks in mock disgust, *"This office is filthy dirty."* As much as she grumbled about me and my stupid choices, she seemed happy to participate in my dream, or at least she may have been fearful enough that, if she did not help, my failure would rub off on her as well.

She may still think I'm crazy. She may still question why I chose to join a band of young renegades fresh out of college to start a magazine that had big visions with no budget. She saw no 401K plan, no business card, no secretary—*"and no salary either!"* she adds. For a long time, she probably thought that the word "entrepreneur" meant someone who doesn't make any money. Yet through it all, she brought me Tupperware tubs of home cooking every week, sticking them in the freezer as she murmured under her breath, with love, *"My kids are spoiled rotten. See? They can't do anything without me."* Her thoughts behind these words might be these:

I was trained as a midwife in Taiwan, and brought many babies into the world before I even entered a formal day of nursing school. In my hands I held babies that I knew would be cranky, ones that I knew would be gentle. It is in the way they move even while they take their first breaths. If I can see this in the children of strangers, I must know about my daughter. I held her. I watched her grow up. And she thinks because she is grown up now that I can only see what she wants to show me. I know more than she thinks.

Yet, my daughter thinks that I don't know her. She thinks that I don't understand or believe that she is strong enough to do anything she wants, even if I do think she makes the wrong decisions half the time. She's my daughter after all, even if I do call her a dreamer. We have the same spirit. We trust and we believe in things. If she is the way she is, I must have taught it to her. I must have been responsible for the way she turned out. Crazy. I would never tell her this, but no matter what she ever decides to do in her life, I will always help her out and support her, even if I do try to talk her out of her choices.

That is the irony of expectation. Defy it and most of us will still receive our mother's love and support, because in our willingness to answer to what calls us, we show them the strength that is there for two. There comes a day when daughter breaks from mother and becomes a woman. And as it was our duty to listen and learn when we were young, so it becomes our duty to catch the wind and fly out on our own. Our lives are ours to learn from.

How to Open Up a Dialogue

We know that it's never that easy. Dealing with family expectations can be oppressive, regardless of our age. We may be convinced that our families will disown us for making unpopular choices. Or, despite knowing that the outside world treats us as adults, that we will never escape the role of "child" to make our own decisions. The intensity of the family bond and "our-daughter-must-pay-back" mentality can make our choices very difficult. But to the extent that we can move *toward* as opposed to *away from,* the emotional issues of family, we move toward a more solid self as well.

"You'll Always Be My Daughter"

Psychologists refer to the intense period of self-definition and self-imposed distance from parents as a process of individuation. Among Asian families, studies show that individuation processes may not take place until we are thirty or even older. "My children will always be my children," is how one Korean great-grandmother put it. As a thirty-four-year-old Filipina American told me, "I thought that when I had my first child, my mother would finally see me as an adult. No chance. Now she's got a new set of instructions for me—how to bring up my baby the *Filipina* way."

"In my Hmong community, a woman is not seen as valid until she marries. I am over thirty and I am still not married. My Hmong community still treats me as if I am a little girl," one respondent wrote. Until we are viewed as adults (or at

the very least, not as children), it will continue to be difficult, though not impossible, to begin an honest, equal
dialogue about what we want from life that may differ with
our family's expectations of us.

We need not wait for our parents to decide when that time
will be. We can begin to develop that dialogue for them. Find
a calm time when you are feeling good, or set up a
specific day or activity for a talk between you and your parent, one on one. There need not be an agenda. All that is
important is that you try hard not to be reactive when your
buttons are pushed, listen without judgment, and express your
opinions confidently without reverting into a child's role. As
psychologist and author Harriet Lerner advises, "When we
define a new position in a relationship we need to focus on
what we want to say about ourselves, not the other person."
According to Lerner, we need to be less focused on the other
person's reaction or countermove or on gaining a positive
response. You are beginning to establish a new dialogue that
welcomes you in as a fully capable and responsible adult.

Considerations for Daughters and Their Families

When a daughter claims her status as an adult member of the
family, power dynamics will begin to shift. For daughters,
being treated on par will mean taking on certain responsibilities for ourselves, including recognizing and then letting go
of younger patterns of behavior—sulking, withholding participation, complaining that we are treated like children while
still expecting mothers to cook our meals and do our laundry. When we are the daughters of immigrants, we can have
such control over our parents, holding them hostage at times
to American Dreams and to links to the future, and it can be
difficult not to use that control to manipulate. Can we begin
to give as adults, rather than to receive as children?

For parents, letting go of the role of nurturer can be very difficult. As parents, we see our children as extensions of ourselves. They are what our lives have stood for. They represent the hope and promise of all our work and sacrifice. Our generation provided the sweat that gives them opportunities that we never had. Our choices were made for their benefit, not ours. "How is it," one mother asks me, "that my daughter can be so ungrateful?" Is it possible that as parents, we may have given away too much of ourselves in the bargain? Or that the hopes we place on our children might have absolved us of our responsibility to wage our own battles? Can we take a step back and refrain from feeling that we will always know what is best for them? Can we let our need to control fall away so that our children can grow?

The Other Person's Shoes

When Jennie Yee, a psychologist from North Beach Asian Mental Health Services in San Francisco, mediates intergenerational conversations, she helps families to find common ground: "Daughters and sons have to understand that in most cases, parents only want them to be happy. They just come from a very different set of experiences." According to Yee, nonsympathetic listening can lead to all sorts of miscommunication: "Parents may goad us to do well in school and enter traditional jobs because they see these as insurance policies for our futures. Their children might interpret this as their parents' lack of confidence in their judgment or abilities. In another example, parents may push their daughters into dating relationships that 'preserve their Asian culture' because they feel their daughters will be more comfortable in the end. Their daughters might read that as 'prejudiced.'" Yee attempts to have family members acknowledge their concerns and speak from their own point of view, without assuming the response of other family members. If parents are concerned about their daughters' future, those daughters might have to prove to them that they can provide for themselves. If they are concerned about their daughters' choice of person for a relationship, daughters might invite their parents to spend individual time with their partner so that they can begin to know one another, on their own terms. As Yee points out, "Sometimes, all parents need is to understand."

Dialogue is a beginning, and results are never immediate. In some cases, a family member's mental health or behavioral patterns may require professional intervention, and dialogue alone cannot solve much. Even in the most open of Asian American families, changes in stature and shifts in family power dynamics will be accompanied by anger, frustration, and feelings of futility. Asking and answering the questions that matter will entail moments of miscommunication, the dredging up of memories, and accusations. So it is important to anticipate them and to know that good results will be gradual. Slowness, deliberation, and patience are all part of the process of developing a new level of relationship. The more intense the issue, the more slowly one should move. Keep in mind that big proclamations or sudden emotional cutoff are destructive to this communication process. As Lerner advises, "You cannot learn to swim by jumping off the high dive."

It may help to set small goals together. It may help to develop an understanding of what our personal boundaries are, and hold fast to them. We may have to assure our families that the distance we need does not imply abandonment or disrespect. Inevitably, yet gradually, truths emerge that will allow change to occur more easily. When we take the time to let our families know who we really are, we begin to move our family stories forward in the most remarkable of ways.

SHE BRINGS THE FAMILY FORWARD

DAUGHTER: *My immigrant parents can be so conservative! They do things I just can't understand. They react in strange ways. It's as if the clock stopped as soon as they set foot on American soil. They've been living in the ideas of that time ever since.*

PARENTS: *And American-born daughters can be so . . . American! They just don't understand how hard life can be. Why do they dress like that? Why don't they take our advice? And why do they make their lives so complicated?*

When immigration experiences enter the picture, the next generation bears the yoke of ushering in great changes in the family. As daughters, one of our greatest roles may be to test the family's limits and challenge its premises of honor, respect, and reverence.

How do we uncover a past and understand family themes that can help us thrive into the future? How do daughters reconcile the generations?

My mother is either in extreme denial, or she can't tell a story for beans. I found myself grasping at any details of her past so that I could develop my themes about mothers and daughters for this book,

"So, Mom, tell me about your journey to America," I ask. We might as well start with something easy. The coming-to-America theme may have been done to death, I thought, but we've all got to start somewhere.

"I came to America with my friends, and we partied. Rita and Ah-Deng and me, we had so much fun, especially during our two-day stopover in Hawaii."

"Okay . . . that's a start. What happened then?" This is going to be like pulling teeth, I think to myself.

"Oh we went to nursing school in Baltimore and partied and danced and had a great time. Here, I'll show you how we did it."

She takes my hands and starts to dance.

"Cha cha cha, turn, cha cha cha. Hey, Ah-Phee, not like that! You don't know how to dance!"

"And then you came to Philadelphia where you met Dad and married him, isn't that right?"

"Oh, Philadelphia and New York City had great dances for the Chinese students. They were fun. We knew where all the good parties were."

"And then you met Dad . . . ," I interrupt, trying to lead her into the story I really want to hear.

"Oh, yes, and then I met him [She looks at my father, who is reading the paper but listening intently.] *and I was trapped."*

My mom and dad look at each other and start to giggle like five-year-olds.

"Yup, she was trapped all right," my dad says, his eyes crinkling up as he smiles. For years that little dig used to irk him. But since he's retired, he seems to have found some hidden humor in life in general, and he lets the comment roll right off his back. Both approaching seventy, Mom and Dad have finally learned to love each other dearly, even if they still can't agree on anything, including how to light a barbecue or back the car out of the driveway.

"Party" seems to be the operative word in my mother's recollection of her youth. She has this tendency to paint rosy pictures with vague words and big general ideas that lack specific details, reflecting the straightforward, no-nonsense way she sees the world. She's a pragmatist who has no room for sentimentality, not the artist seeking to create finely tuned pictures that my father is. In telling her short, proclamatory stories, she comes off as light and flighty. Try as I may, I cannot make her go into more detail about her past. Sometimes in my frustration, I have condemned her as shallow or selfish.

But perhaps she really can't put her past into words. Perhaps her gift of storytelling is not refined enough to paint the kind of pictures that I want her to. She has already told me that she can't imagine pictures in her mind's eye when she reads a good novel. She can never remember any of her dreams.

I want her to tell me her own juicy version of *The Joy Luck Club.* I hoped for some ponderous stories of reflection and color of the kind that I have come to equate with the rich and powerful legacy of Asian women in the literature I've read—the stories of Asian women who have been wronged, women who have killed themselves, or drowned themselves in wells, or gone crazy because of the strict rules that kept them tied to hopeless situations. Instead she laughs at me for being so "second generation." *"Forget about it, Ah-Phee.* Joy Luck Club *was not my life, it was someone else's. Those mothers were not me. Keep your Kleenex for yourself. I just liked to party."*

And maybe she is right. Why did I consider it so impossible that my mother in fact did just enjoy herself? Maybe my need to picture gray stories about her past had more to do with me, my need to fit her into a pigeonhole of sacrifice and self-effacement.

I remember recently talking to a student from mainland China one day who could not understand why Americans loved movies with dutiful Asian women who always looked as if they were about to cry. "You know, in China there are so many famous movies about strong women who have attitude and confidence that most Americans never get to see." It made me think about how my own perceptions have been influenced by what Western tastes prefer here in America—the tragic, sad images of Madame Butterfly and Miss Saigon. The books that I have read and the films that I have seen inevitably helped to form a picture of my particular culture and history. My picture of Asia is reimagined, the result of what has been made available to me to see, read, and hear. If the only images of Asian women that I had seen were ones of submission and sadness, wouldn't that have a powerful impact on the way that I interpreted my history?

Stories about Asian mother-daughter relationships are mired in myth and romanticism and tearful regret. They seem stalled in themes of self-sacrifice and silent resilience in the face of outer torment. But while those are the themes with which we are familiar, they are not the only ones that exist. Strength among Asian women does not always come hidden behind masks. There are among us the mothers and daughters who are bringing our families forward and changing the way we live our lives. Sandra, a sansei (a third-generation Japanese American) from Chicago, realized that few books existed for Asian American children to help them reconcile the conflicts between Eastern and Western cultures. So in the early nineties, Sandra founded Polychrome Books, devoted specifically to publishing for Asian American children. Her books include *Nene and the Horrible Math Monster,* about a Filipina American girl and her confrontations with Model Minority myths, and *Blue Jay in the Desert,* about the Japanese internment at the end of World War II.

Dan Hoang is a first-generation Mien woman, from a more recent Asian immigrant group from the highlands of Laos, Thailand, and Vietnam, whose primary communities have settled in the Midwest and in California. Dan Hoang was the first in her family to go to college and now works as an office manager in Minneapolis. In her free time she teaches Mien women to organize their communities and to pass on from mother to daughter the history and songs of their indigenous culture.

Both Sandra and Dan Hoang are giving an Asian American women's community a face and a voice that will allow their future generations to be confident and outspoken. Why is it that so many of us remain unable to tap that reservoir of advice and power from our own mothers? Instead we often distance ourselves from them, believing ourselves to be markedly different from them in temperament, ambition, and behavior. We often see our American lifestyles as distinct and severed from their immigrant stories.

Most Asian American women that I have interviewed agree

that their approach to life is very different from their mothers'. The tenor of their explanations was similar: "She is submissive. I am not." "She believes in lying low. I cannot do that." "She allows things that I would never allow." These were some of the differences that were offered. When given the choice to identify the Asian American women who have given us our most positive senses of power, few women replied with "my mother." The most frequent response was "my friends."

The mothers that I have talked to understand the cultural and generational rift that threatens to pull their daughters away from them. Connie Chan, a clinical professor of psychology at the University of Massachusetts in Boston, says that in her research and private practice she has talked to a number of parents in their fifties and sixties who "exhibit a great deal of poignancy and sadness. They say, 'We came to the U.S. to provide a better life. And our kids clearly have a better life, but in the process we've lost them.'" According to Chan, "There is an innate sense of disappointment and loss, and a question about how to reach their children."

WHEN MOTHERS TEACH DAUGHTERS

Despite the generational and cultural gaps that can threaten our mother-daughter relationships, there are also many potent stories that show us the power of knowledge passed from mother to daughter. Nguyen, a college student, whose mother is Korean American and whose father is Chinese American, recalls her own upbringing with parents who were active in the sixties' antiwar protests. Her story demonstrates how some Asian American mothers have instilled in their daughters a sense of visible empowerment by actively encouraging certain skills, as she describes in a collection of essays called *The Conversation Begins:*

My parents gave me a lot of freedom to grow on my own. With that flexibility, I didn't feel the need to rebel. I don't really understand the kinds of relationships my girlfriends have with their mothers. Usually their mothers are over-protective, making my friends want to defy them even more. Although my mom and I are not equals, we are best friends. I can talk to her, confide in her, laugh with her, and cry with her.

Nguyen was born two days before International Women's Day, on March 6. When she was young, Nguyen resented the fact that her mother was always so busy during her birthday, going to meetings and organizing IWD events. But when she turned eleven, she was asked to participate in one of those programs, and it changed her world: "I gave a speech in front of three hundred people to raise money for a child-care center in Angola. My mother coached me and bought me a purple jumpsuit for the occasion. For the first time, I was actually doing something that might make a dif-ference on the other side of the world. I think I grew more during that five-minute speech than I had during the previous year. That's when I realized why my mother did what she did and why it was important."

But not every mother is able or equipped to pass on the skills that Nguyen's mother did. After all, she had been in the United States since she was very young and had already trav-eled a great learning distance in terms of American accultura-tion. When our mothers are more traditional, chances are that we will be learning most of these skills on our own. *In fact, in many cases it is we who will teach our mothers about what it means to be empowered and to question convention.* Oftentimes our mothers have inherited a legacy of silence and oppression that requires a daughter's strength to confront and override.

WHEN DAUGHTERS ARE THE TEACHERS

On a spring day sometime in the 1970s, Mrs. Yee looked out of the small window of the garment factory where she worked to see her daughter, Jennie, picketing her employer, as shouts of "Decent wages! Decent pay!" drowned out the neurotic humming of the sewing machines. As Jennie tells it, "My mom would call me her 'Little Communist Girl,' because I was really into community work and was involved in a lot of protests. She didn't really understand why I chose to put so much time into this. I guess she thought I should be studying more. Then one night she came home and told me that she wasn't being paid the minimum wage. She told me that she had asked her boss for three years to raise her wage, and he always promised her that he would, but never did. Then I told her, 'Listen, Mom, you go up to him and tell him that he better pay you at least the minimum wage because that is your right under the law. You've got the law on your side.' She walked away and didn't say anything about it again until one day she told me that she followed my directions and, what do you know? She got her pay raise! I think that's when she began to understand why my activism is important."

Tina, a Korean American woman in her twenties, had always perceived her mother as weak, a pushover, and some-one who had given in so many times that, in Tina's opinion, she probably deserved the mistreatment that she received from her husband. "She was always giving in when my father went into his crazy rages. And when she did that, my brother and I also had to suffer. I remember hating her weakness and resolving to myself that I would never be like her." But now that Tina is in her late twenties, she looks back and realizes that every serious relationship she has ever entered has had an element of terror and abuse in it. She can't believe how her situations are so similar to her mother's, and it scares her. No matter how much she has tried to be exactly the opposite of her mother, she finds that she is living the same kind of life with the same kind of themes. "I try so hard not to be like her," she says. "I actively do things opposite from what I think she would do. But I end up in about the same position. Maybe it's ingrained in me that this is the normal way men and women act with each other."

When Tina decided that she didn't want to live her mother's life, or enter into another bad relationship, she sought the advice of her friends, who recommended that she talk to a therapist. "It was hard, because seeing a therapist is a sign of weakness in my home and I know it's dishonorable to share personal stories that shame the family," she said. "But going through a process of therapy seems to be helping me get my life in order. Now I am trying to get my mom to come with me. I want her to feel better and to fight for herself. And if she can't bring herself to come with me, at least I can try to teach her what I've learned at my sessions so that both of us can talk together with a little more perspective."

When KaYing was given the post of executive director of a well-known Hmong service organization, her parents didn't realize what an honor this was. They never realized that serving their Hmong community could create the possibility of status. It wasn't until they attended large Hmong gatherings that they realized that their daughter KaYing had become a very respected member of their community. "Before, the elders used to address me as my father's daughter. Now, instead, my parents are often introduced as 'KaYing's father' and 'KaYing's mother.' In my community, the way we are recognized and identified is all about status. My parents are finally beginning to appreciate the honor I bring to the family."

As Hope Edelman wrote in *Motherless Daughters,* her contemplation of mother-daughter relationships, "Every daughter's experience is one of identifying with and differentiating from the past, and both processes are equally important. Finding the generational similarities connects us to our origins, while moving from them allows us not to blindly repeat our parents' lives." It's when we feel the pull either to reject all aspects of them or to become identical versions of them that our ability to develop our own identity is impaired. We might spend so much time either creating contrasts or creating spitting images that we lose sight of our own big picture—pursuing what *we* want. Psychologist and writer Kim Chernin talks of the possibilities created by a daughter's ability to rework or even shatter what is habitual and limiting between mother and daughter. In that moment, the daughter creates the mother she feels she has always needed and deserved. "'Giving birth to one's mother,' a woman takes responsibility for the relationships and circumstances that will advance her development. What she is becoming matters more than what she has been." If circumstances are not right for her development, she will create them by making the solid relationships she needs to see her through.

We are our parents' daughters, complete with strengths as well as flaws. Accepting this without having to react positively or negatively allows us also to accept ourselves, and to work in the name of progress, as opposed to judgment.

FATHERS AND DAUGHTERS

Strong women tend to have strong fathers, but the quality of that strength can be shown in varied ways—from stubbornness and rage to inspiration and drive. To gain clarity about what motivates us, we have to begin to understand our fathers, the way they view themselves in the world, the roles they have played while growing up, and the pressures they have faced as Asian men. In short, we have to begin to consider them with the distance required to be fair.

Ever since I can remember, there has been a big blue box that sits on the top shelf of a closet in my parents' bedroom. I am not supposed to touch it. When I was young, I tried many times to yank it down, prodding with chopsticks and broom handles to dislodge it from behind a clutter of shoe boxes and purses. Inevitably, my mother would catch me in the act, scream that it was covered in dust as if dust were a form of bubonic plague, and that I'd better put it back because it wasn't my business to go peering into her closets anyway. Thirty years after that admonishment, I shamefully find myself climbing up on a chair again, sneaking behind my mother's back, trying yet again to see its secret contents. This time I am insistent, even though she tries that old dust excuse on me again. But now, it doesn't deter me. Woman to woman, there is little she can do to stop me this time. Besides, I'm bigger than she is.

Inside there are hundreds of old photos, miniature ones that record a lifetime. Some show my mother as a schoolgirl with fat cheeks. She must be no more than seven or eight years old. I sift through more, and there she is picnicking in Taiwan with her church friends, eating apples and, of course, dancing. I don't ask her about the white guy in the army uniform with the Buddy Holly glasses who keeps cropping up in her pictures, and she doesn't volunteer a story.

But it's the pictures of my father that are most intriguing. Before me lies a treasure trove from his young life—the long-sought missing chapters of his past. I am dumbstruck at what I see. There he was, looking so dapper in his first art studio—the epitome of fifties Brill Cream–cool confidence. Another picture with his friends—and they were black friends and white friends. Who would have thought that my dad was a multiculturalist? More photographs of him, in army barracks, museum-touring, in a carnival funhouse, strumming guitars, smoking cigarettes, being goofy with a giant sombrero. And who was the Caucasian girl with the long hippie braids smoking cigarettes with him? My father had such a handsome, innocent face, like an Asian Cary Grant. By the looks of these pictures, my father and I should have been best friends, with similar ways of seeing the world and living in it. How did things turn out so differently?

According to counselor Claire Chow in her book *Leaving Deep Water*, when Asian American daughters speak of their mothers, it is usually in terms of guilt and manipulation. However with fathers, the issues are more about power and control. This was certainly true for me, as I remembered how I railed against my father's volatile temper that could escalate within seconds. At the dinner table, he'd shake his head at my pie-in-the-sky political ideas. We'd lock horns in arguments that would send me storming out of the house, vowing never to return. We were probably too alike—recognizing and criticizing each other's weaknesses too readily because they were our own. Fighting with him was my defense against the chaos he presented. And it was my ruthless way of telling him, "Just because you are the man of the house doesn't mean you will always be right." The irony is that he is the one who taught me always to question authority.

Like an adulating son who suddenly sees that his father is merely mortal, I had so many expectations of my father. I would search constantly for the information that he could impart about how to get along in the world. And as I grew older, I realized that he did not have all the answers. I was on my own and too young to empathize with the possible reasons for his angry tirades. All I knew was how fathers were supposed to be—happy like Robert Brady on *The Brady Bunch,* or Mr. Cunningham on *Happy Days.* It was too early for me to understand how sensitive and resilient my father was.

Expectations can run two ways. A daughter's can often be the harshest.

OUR FATHERS, WHO ART IN SILENCE

With mothers, communication and exchange may be acceptable, but getting past silence with our fathers can prove difficult if not impossible. The cultural legacy of the male-dominated Asian family plays a large role in our interactions with our fathers and, in many instances, has led to communication with them that is more "telepathic" than forthright. Reading the other's mind and predicting the other's actions become the basic method of family survival. It can result in a daughter's frustration at not being able to be open or honest.

Sociologist Henry Trueba describes how conversation dynamics are dictated and viewed in Chinese culture: "In the culture of the United States, verbalization is extremely important. In the Chinese culture excessive verbalization is seen as bad manners. There are rules governing the discourse patterns: when to speak, who speaks first, what to talk about, what not to talk about, what is considered appropriate, what is considered rude, what is considered complimentary or insulting." Communication will be difficult enough given those parameters, but if our fathers lean conservative, honest or emotional communication will be very tricky indeed.

Though many of our fathers don't speak readily or willingly about their pasts, there are ways to coax out their stories. We can ask him about his childhood. And what his family life was like when he was young. And if he has ever perceived or encountered discrimination, what was his response? Who gave him support and who didn't? How did he feel about the obligations of being the breadwinner, the patriarch, or strongman? Does he ever dream of doing some crazy project? If he could live his life over again, would he live it the same way? Questions like these can help us to accept him for who he is as opposed to what we imagine him to be, and to understand his actions. We owe it to ourselves to attempt a discussion.

The results can be tremendous. Confident, tenacious women who have breached the generational divide with their fathers can count them as a primary source for advice—at school, in business, and for life perspective. "He's just much easier to talk to. Not emotionally vested like my mother," says Annie, a Vietnamese American from Mississippi. Se Ri Pak, the young U.S. Open golf champion, was coached from the age of nine by her father. Vera Wang, the well-known fashion designer, has often credited her father for helping to launch her business, as has Dineh Mohajer, the twenty-five-year-old CEO and president of Hard Candy, one of the trendiest cosmetics companies targeting young girls. Many interviewees also remembered that their fathers were their most avid fans, telling them that they could do as well or even better than any boy. While not every father provides those resources, skills, or words of support, *each of our fathers does have some core of strength, an insight that can be passed down so that we can begin to see them not just as our fathers, with all the expectations that the role implies, but as a link to our family history.*

It has taken time to get the stories out of him. In the late 1930s, my father and grandmother came to America to help my grandfather in his laundry business. Mother and son sneaked away in the middle of the night from their Toysan village, leaving my father's two sleeping sisters behind. On the ocean liner to America, my father befriended an old Canadian man who taught him the alphabet over the long transpacific journey. It must have been strange when my dad met his father for the first time. Did my grandfather shake his hand? Did my father run away? What were my grandfather's first words to his son? In America, my dad knew that it would be a different ball game. From then on, he would have to share his mother's attention, as she fulfilled her duties as wife and worker. His life as a young boy would be more difficult, too. Enrolled in kindergarten at the age of eight because he didn't speak English, he somehow learned to endure the taunts of the kids in his class, who wondered why such a big boy couldn't understand them. For the next decade, my grandmother was constantly pregnant, with a new American-born child every few years. My father must have been his parents' souvenir of the old world, counted on as the Number One Son to help them earn the family income of fifteen dollars per week.

Iron! Wash! Fast! Fast!

Unfortunately, my father was a dreamer and a dawdler. Instead of sorting the laundry, my dad would open the packages of dirty clothes and read the newspapers they were wrapped in, to practice his English. *"Reading isn't going to help us make money and put food on the table. Stop daydreaming!"* my grandfather would yell. He called my father lazy. At sixteen, my father left home, with his American-born brothers and sisters screaming around the crowded apartment above the laundry.

Two years later, he enlisted in the army, forcing him to live a "real American life with real American people." He practiced his English, and he never looked back. Under the GI Bill he studied art in Italy, where he painted and went to the Uffizi Gallery in Florence every day, lodging at the Pensione Bartolini in the Oltrarno. Not bad for a laundryman's son with little support from home.

Now I watch my dad in the garden, the verdant haven that he has worked so hard to afford and maintain. He is practicing his tennis swing, intent on getting that forehand precise, like everything else he does. As an architect, my dad has learned to be meticulous and painstakingly thorough. He has done everything by the book, including learning how to bowl, plant peonies, buy a stereo, and now, how to play tennis. This is how he has learned to be truly American, through books and television, so that his actions are not so much natural as much as rehearsed, as in a play. He has adapted by learning not to trust his instincts, because intuition for so long proved him wrong. By following books, he'll make no mistakes, sacrificing a certain instinctive flow for near-perfect predictability. That is how he has also become the best ballroom dancer at the Long Island Chinese Community Center. Through books and videotapes, my dad has learned to dance an excellent tango.

Now he swings at the air with the intensity of a zen master—forehand, backhand, overhead smash!—like swatting at imaginary flies in slow motion, but with perfect, focused concentration. In an America where physical difference once brought him ill treatment, his form and appearance now mean everything to him. It doesn't matter whether he wins his tennis games (which he usually does anyway), as long as his strokes *look* right.

It is the first time that I am able to stand back and look at my father's life and see him for his great resilience of spirit. I am in awe at what he has been able to accomplish in his lifetime, past the anger, past the negativity, past what I once considered a want of self-esteem. In order to become what he is now, he had to break away from the strict confines of a family that would have kept him bound by duty as a first-born son. But to do so, he had to sever the ties that held him back, forsaking his responsibilities to family. Important things often carry high prices.

I didn't realize how similar our coming-of-age stories were. Insolent and proud of being so, I thought I was being such a maverick when I tore three thousand miles away to college. Who knew that I was repeating history? Like my father, I needed room to grow. Just as my father's breakaway fulfilled his search to make America his home, my own breakaway to Asian-steeped California allowed me to take back pieces of culture and pride that had been thrown away too hastily.

He must have thought it amusing that his first daughter followed in his footsteps, even though she thought that she was being such a rebel. He must have remarked how ironic and funny life could be that his Number One Daughter was bringing the family one step closer back to the Asian roots that had caused him so much pain in the first place.

Each time I visit my dad, his list of pills has gotten longer. I have to speak to him a little slower and louder now, since he's having trouble hearing me. We had a big scare when the doctor found a blur on his chest X rays, even though it ended up being nothing at all. Still, mortality has become an important issue. Recently, my husband helped my dad carry home a fireproof safe from Home Depot to store all of his important documents. And to set the record straight, my dad also wants us to know finally who he is and who he has been. He begins to tell the stories I have always wanted to hear—about the third-grade teacher who chose him as her favorite and gave him a memorable compliment, telling him that he could draw like Rembrandt and presenting him with his own box of crayons for encouragement. How he enjoyed weekend picnics with his mom and dad in the country, where, free from the claustrophobic laundry, he could roll down the grassy hills. A few months ago, he drew a map of his Toysan village, showing us where his house was in relation to the other five houses. He tries hard not to judge me too quickly now, knowing that I might walk away, hands thrown up in the air out of exasperation. Instead, as I describe some latest thought, he will say to me, "Sounds interesting. Maybe the next time we see each other, we can have a long discussion about it." And both of us can look forward to that time.

Have I grown older and more accepting? Has he?

Honor, respect, and reverence. Freedom, choice, and movement. I've learned that it isn't necessary to choose between them—because the way we live meaningful lives is never about either/or choices. My father and I have found the balance, by finally having the courage to be gentle with one another.

Lesson Three

SHE LEARNS TO SHOUT

Maybe this has already happened to you:

You kept your self-control in some situation until your words could be contained no longer.

Then all of a sudden—BAM! You couldn't believe your own ears. Those words, that anger, was that really you talking?

They called you a bat out of hell. The dowager that swiped out an eye with her sharp dragon claws. "She must have been in a bad mood. Must be that time of month." And in one broad stroke your rage may have been marginalized.

No use worrying about the opinions of others right now. What counts is that you've voiced a pent-up side of yourself and by doing so, you've entered into a whole, new world.

By looking your rage squarely in the eye, you have brought forth a warrior.

What does it mean to shout?

"You're going to talk," I said, my voice steady and normal, as it is when talking to the familiar, the weak, and the small. "I am going to make you talk, you sissy-girl."

—Maxine Hong Kingston
The Woman Warrior

He was just having a bad day. A three-hundred-million-dollar real estate deal, the Japanese buyout of the Regal Empress Hotel, was his biggest in years, and it was falling through before his eyes. And so Robert's mood was bound to be bad. With his reputation, partnership status, and the seventeen thousand dollars he required each month to maintain his quality of life and his kids' tuition payments at Trinity, who could blame him for his behavior? After all, being a partner in one of New York's top international law firms was a tough and tense way to make a living. Every partner, even the nicest of them, falls into tense moments like that. It was part of the job. I felt sure that when I became a partner in a few years time and some big deal began to spin out of control, I'd have my bad moments, too.

I was always finding excuses like this for Robert, my boss. I had to make myself feel better somehow. I had to justify why the hell I was staying in that snake pit, slaving away like some church mouse, unnoticed, and unappreciated. When it came right down to it, I really hated this job.

It was the holiday season, and I knew that, like last year, I would be spending Christmas Day at the office, reviewing documents I didn't care about and spell-checking merger agreements, while the firm's partners and our clients would be skiing in Aspen or Mont Blanc with their families, as, in the great scheme of things, I felt they ought to be. And by some strange reasoning process, I had also accepted that I was also where *I* ought to be, sacrificing my precious holiday time with family and friends by paying my flesh-equity dues for a crack at becoming a partner one day.

In retrospect, I now realize that Robert was just a bad boss and that none of his antics should have been taken personally. But at the time, all I knew was that I was the young lawyer he was using instead to be his very highly paid secretary. His form of training was to dig his red pen into my drafts, berating me for missing my commas, saying that I was not careful enough, always looking for errors in meaningless minutiae. If I drafted a cover letter for him that read, "Please find enclosed . . ." he would slash it out like Zorro and write, "Enclosed please find . . ." Maybe small tyrannies gave him pleasure. He was, in short, a troubled soul who felt power in controlling tiny things, and here I was stuck in pencil-pushing hell with him.

Unfortunately for me, Robert also had a volatile temper. When in the wrong mood, Robert would insult and ver-bally annihilate those he felt he could terrorize, including neophyte associates, like me. I lived in a constant state of fear of him. I learned to tiptoe around his office, put his tiny proofreading projects at the top of my priority list, forsaking the legal work of other partners that would have taught me more. Somehow, I thought that if I ingratiated myself, Robert would stop insulting me.

Needless to say, it hardly ever worked.

Robert was having a bad day, for sure. So when I heard him screaming and stomping through the halls, my heart started beating fast as my survival adrenaline kicked in.

Robert barged into my office. Bingo, I had hit the jackpot.

"What the hell did I tell you to do last week?" Robert looked crazed. He obviously wasn't looking for an answer, just a little of my blood. He slammed a one-page document onto my desk and told me that it should have been three-hole punched and that the signature should have been signed in blue.

"What are you doing at this firm? What are you, STU-PID? Why can't you just do what I asked for JUST ONCE? CAN'T YOU UNDERSTAND ENGLISH? READ MY LIPS," he enunciated. "A CHILD COULD DO THIS!" He slammed my desk with his fist and my pile of papers flew to the ground.

Is it clear yet that Robert had a bit of a temper problem?

He was screaming into my face. I could hear other associates kick their doors shut to block out their own stress and wage their own passive but audible protest against his absurd tantrum.

"WE DON'T PAY YOU PEOPLE ALL THAT MONEY FOR NOTHING! Fix this document RIGHT NOW. IN FRONT OF ME. I WANT TO SEE YOU DO IT."

Running through my mind were the biting insults I wanted to hurl back if I could only open my mouth and stop shaking. *Bing!* There went my Guilt-Over-Salary button. ("Yes, indeed, Robert, I know I'm overpaid, especially since all I'm asked to do is type and proofread!" I thought.) *Bong!* There went the I-Can't-Stand-Being-Ordered-Around-Especially-by-Older-Presumptuous-Men button. ("I wish I could give you a swift kick in the balls right now, Robert,

but somehow right now I can't seem to move," I thought.)
Bing bong! There went the Why-Me? buzzer, as my face grew
hot and a lump started forming in my throat. And "Can't you
understand English?" What was *that* supposed to mean? Like
a well-trained sadist, Robert was hitting all my buttons. And
like a well-trained victim, I could only sit there shocked, saying nothing.

"You know, Robert, I think you are a *bit* out of control." I
tried to fake a smile to be polite. It was one of my typical
reactions, coming from a combination of charm-school
teaching from my gracious Chinese mother and my gut fear
of being fired. Both of them had taught me well that "Save
the job" was the bottom line. A quick strategy assessment:
Yes, well, maybe everything would turn out fine if I just
nodded and spoke in a calm, sweet voice. Maybe I could
appeal to Robert's sense of reason.

I must really have been living in la-la land.

Robert was treating me this way because experience told
him that he'd get away with it. Even if I *was* a lawyer who had
passed the bar exam with flying colors. Even if I was just as
smart as my fellow associates, even if I could spot a loophole
as quickly as any of them. And even as the other partners told
me that I had a shining future with the firm. Why did Robert
assume that I would gladly do this drudge work?

As Robert slammed and cursed at me, I felt something snap
inside. I suddenly realized how tired I was of lowering my
voice and taking two steps back so that Robert could feel
more comfortable, more in charge, less threatened. I was tired
of laughing off his tantrums as the silly ravings of a neurotic
boss. He was being offensive, no matter where his words were
coming from. And I suddenly understood how much energy
it took to stifle myself all the time. These thoughts swirled in
my head, free associations that were finally clicking into place.

Now this maniac was still yelling in my face, ranting on now about how I would thank him later for teaching me a lesson.

That was the cue I was waiting for. I, the little church mouse, began to roar.

"Robert," I interrupted. I cleared my throat to stop my heart from falling out of my mouth. "Don't you *ever* talk to me like that." My shaking voice had slipped back into my throat midsentence, but I swallowed and forced myself to go on. "In fact, I never want to hear you talk to *anyone* like that in front of me. You are embarrassing yourself."

Robert looked at me stunned, and pounded his fist on the wall.

"GODDAMMIT, YOU WANT TO ARGUE WITH ME? WHY CAN'T YOU JUST DO WHAT I TOLD YOU TO DO! JUST LISTEN TO ME AND DO WHAT I SAY!" His six-foot-two frame towered over me, the sitting church mouse, and he pounded my desk so hard that I jumped up at the impact.

This was it, I told myself. Trust the moment, Phoebe, and go with what you feel for once. If you're going to lose your job, you had better go out fighting. I hit cruise control.

I finally let go with the anger that had been gnawing at me ever since I had set foot in that law firm and its wacky, illogical processes. And as I yelled back at Robert, my words found a natural, poetic flow, finally liberated from the stiff clip of legalese. They expressed the natural thoughts of a confused associate who was only trying to find some core, some anchor of meaning and dignity in an otherwise tortured situation. Still, to eke out each word required me to transcend the present and its dire consequences:

"THAT'S IT, ROBERT. I'm taking this straight to the management committee. I HAVE HAD IT WITH YOUR

BULLSHIT." My voice shook, and steadied itself only when I forced it louder. As a reflex, he stepped back as if I had pushed him.

In my mind, all I could picture was my mother's face, horrified and ashamed at my outburst:

Aiyo! Good Chinese girls don't curse in public, Ah-Phee. It's not very attractive. Very shameful. Keep quiet, Ah-Phee! He will go away if you just ignore him.

It was too late to invoke Chinese common sense. It had come time for a good old American fist-in-the-face battle. So I drew in a deep breath and delivered the sledgehammer.

"NOW GET OUT OF MY OFFICE!"

Who was this woman talking? It couldn't have been me. I could almost hear the whiplike crack of my words as they slapped against his face.

As his volume level rose in response, so did mine, so that the two of us, shouting over each other, lost all communication. But connection wasn't what I was looking for then. I had no need for that. I just needed to shout. Without realizing it, my voice had become resolute, indignant, *loud*.

In the halls, they were listening. The soothing computer tap of secretaries typing and the murmur of business deals being made had suddenly and disturbingly stopped. That silence gave me the time I needed to finally realize that this was serious. I was telling off my assigning partner for all to hear. For a brief moment, my first since becoming a lawyer, I felt myself rising to my own call. And I was probably going to be fired within the next few minutes.

Robert snatched away his one-page document and stomped off.

And in the silent aftershock of the next few seconds, I started to hyperventilate, as if the truth of my words and the power of my own voice was too much to handle. Those vocal cords hadn't been stretched like that since God knows when. What had I done? It took no time for the faces to emerge from the offices.

"You showed him."

"You were brave. I never could have done that."

Where were all these people before? None of them, not even my office mates, my comrades-in-arms only a few minutes ago, had offered to help or intervene. Was everyone really that fearful? Did they think that I deserved to be berated? Was I wrong to have kicked up a retaliatory fuss? More sympathetic attorneys came in.

"It wasn't you; it was his deal falling through."

"An asshole, isn't he?"

But I had already entered a hyper-heaving stage when I realized that, despite my verbal pyrotechnics, I was hurting from Robert's stabbing remarks. Like a homing missile, they struck their target of a self-doubtful place deep inside. Maybe I wasn't good enough. Maybe Robert was right. I had no right to work here.

I relaxed my strongman guard for only a millisecond, and immediately collapsed into tears of disbelief. I gulped and gasped uncontrollably like a drowning victim in trauma, but refusing to die. Someone handed me a tissue. How very humiliating, I thought. How utterly . . . *uncorporate* and *distasteful* to reveal emotion.

Embarrassed by my weakness, I excused myself and headed straight to the ladies' room. It's the one place where women attorneys and secretaries have been known to hide themselves in fits of frustration and tears when confronted with the identical kind of situation. I stayed there within the safety of calming beige walls for what seemed like an awfully long time.

I told you, Ah-Phee. You should have just shut your big mouth. Haven't you learned yet? Don't be so American loud! It will just hurt you in the end. Can't you just understand that silence can be your strength?

I imagined my mother's disappointment and the way she'd shake her head. Once again, I thought, her homespun advice was so completely useless in my world.

TURNING POINTS

There are times in our lives when we are faced with a fork in the road that presents us with two distinct choices. These can be moments of opportunity, when the choice that we make will impact who we will be, what we will achieve, and how we find what is meaningful to us.

In my conversations with hundreds of Asian American women, I found that many of us will have in common at least one fork in the road. The election to claim and outwardly express rage will be one of our pivotal life choices. That rage might emanate from family pressures and expectations for us to be dutiful daughters. It might be the rage of having to deal with false stereotypes and biases of an outside world that keep us from realizing our full potential. It may be the rage of having to put up with those who disempower us by disrespectful behavior. If we choose to recognize it, explore it, and channel it constructively, that rage can lead to a new sense of power. Deny it, and we are thrown back into situations that continue to wear us down.

While my run-in with Robert may seem like an ordinary confrontaton with a maladjusted boss, it wasn't so for me. The outburst with Robert signified a fork in the road. At that point I was no longer willing to endure the path of a painful situation in order to fulfill my family's expectations or my sense of honor as a gracious Chinese daughter or as the first lawyer in the Eng family. Not on these terms. Not when Robert's tirades called my self-esteem into question on a daily basis. For me, it was a defining moment when I recognized that, in fact, I *was* being treated and perceived differently, and that it was going to be hard, damn hard, to be taken seriously as a fighter, as an equal on a professional level, but that I was willing to do what was required. It was the first time, after almost thirty years and some of the best education money could buy, that I finally understood that life was nothing like what school or my parents had prepared me for. I thought that good performance, good grades, and efficient turnaround would get me what I wanted, as they always had in the past. *I now understood and accepted the reality that unless I started using my voice to stick up for myself, no one would be doing it for me.*

When called to the table to explain his behavior, Robert was at an uncharacteristic loss for words. He had no justifiable alibis, and I won the moral victory. The partners that supported me gave me pep talks in the months that followed. They cared about keeping me, they said, because I showed promise as a fighter.

In their book *Female Rage*, Mary Valentis and Anne Devane write that rage can be used to empower women's lives. But upbringing and social codes can make it difficult to allow that rage to create change in the situations around us. Valentis and Devane talk about a "geisha" complex, not necessarily limited to Asian women, but named for the icon of submission that we all know so well. According to Valentis and Devane, the "geisha" as an archetype is a woman who is "constantly pleasing others and putting herself in second place. Unable to separate her thoughts and feelings from other people's, she lacks self-confidence and boundaries and is prone to tolerate abuse. Her aim is to maintain the status quo at any cost." In her hostile dependencies, her anger remains unexpressed. Instead it is unconsciously captured in her body before it escapes. The result, the authors write, may be chronic fatigue, a locked jaw, panic disorders, or irrational fears, such as agoraphobia. The rage of the "geisha" is like a powder keg. Once ignited, it explodes with a shocking boom, in a rash response that may not be a reaction to the immediate situation, but is instead the result of the long-term suppression of anger.

How much of the geisha was in me? As much as I thought of myself as strong, resilient, and outspoken, I felt that every word of that definition fit my own actions to a tee.

I chose to unleash my anger on Robert that day, but it could have been anybody. So much of my life had spun out of control at that point. I was confused about my career choice, pursued to please my parents. I knew that I didn't enjoy the practice of corporate law. When I returned home drained to the bone near midnight on a regular basis, I was greeted by the cold shoulder of the man with whom I'd been living, who felt that I should have been home to greet him with dinner. Then on weekends, I would visit my family only to listen to my mother tell me why I shouldn't be living with a man from Italy because he was just using me and had no intentions of marrying me. Squeezed to the hilt at work, ignored at home, and disapproved of by family, it was no wonder that I blew my fuse one day when the world stopped making sense.

It seems that sudden explosions of anger have been part of Asian culture throughout its modern history. In fact, the outburst of wild rage called "running amok" is derived from a Malay word, *amoq,* which originally meant "engaging furiously in battle." In a 1990 study described by Aurora Tiu and Julian Seneriches, this behavior was documented among

Filipino women who felt that they had been shamed or had experienced an act of disrespect, much in the same way that I had. According to Tiu and Seneriches, angry outbursts are common in cultures that impose heavy restrictions on aggressive behavior and stress concepts of honor, hierarchy, deference, and etiquette. Their cases describe women who had experienced a series of belittlements and a sense of being undeservedly disregarded. They suppressed their anger until they could no longer keep it in. And then they hit the roof.

Because the tendency to express anger or to engage in conflict is frowned upon as either unattractive behavior for women, or dishonorable and shameful behavior because we are Asian, we have found subtler forms of playing out our anger. Instead of lashing out, we may avoid confrontation by getting back at people through gossip. We might use sarcasm or imagine elaborate revenges. We might grind our teeth, use alcohol, or bury ourselves in work. "I write my anger down on paper, and usually I don't show it to anyone—it is just for me to vent frustration," one Vietnamese American woman, an executive director of a large national organization shared. "Or I'll close the door and scream alone just to release it." "I cry in my car, because it's the only private space and time I have," was the solution for one of the young women I spoke with. Yet if we are able to reframe rage as a positive experience, to connect it back to the situations that caused the rage in the first place, we can use it as a powerful tool rather than as a source of anxiety. *Anger tells us and those around us where our innate boundaries are, what we instinctively feel is tolerable or intolerable, and can signal when those limits have been trespassed. Most important, what causes us to rage most wildly is also what we fear the most.* Anger is a built-in alarm system. As is only sensible with alarms, it makes sense to acknowledge and respond.

LETTING IT OUT

When I was young I knew I could sing. I'd want to test this out, but I didn't want to make too much noise. I didn't want anyone to hear me. So I would take a pillow from the sofa and put it over my face and sing as loud as I could. That way I wouldn't bother anyone, but I'd be assured that I was exercising my voice.

I was an eccentric child.

My mother was a fine soprano who used to sing over the airwaves of Taiwanese radio, and I had the good luck to inherit her fine vocal cords. By the time I was fifteen, I was taking voice lessons to learn how to project my voice by mentally bringing the sound from my stomach, up past my chest, and into and over the top of my head, the way opera singers do. But I felt that I had to contain my voice, that it was too powerful to be projected fully. I wouldn't allow myself to just belt it out like Ethel Merman. I never stopped to think about what would happen if I just let go.

So with all that muffling in my past, where did I find the courage to talk back and say, "Enough is enough. Now you're going to have to deal with me, front and center, and with all the strength that you never thought I had!"? Maybe the accumulation of tiny insults and my soft, round countenance that announced to the world that I must be a sweet, silent, submissive, and obedient people-pleaser became too farcical and surreal, so that my only recourse was to top it off with the most surreal reaction of all. To talk back. To say, "Fuck you."

But such outbursts don't get us much more than shock value, and maybe a little bit of a cathartic purge. What creates real change is our willingness to understand why we have chosen to rein ourselves in, in the first place. In

Women Who Run With the Wolves, Clarissa Pinkola-Estes suggests a ritual called *descansos:* "To make *descansos* means taking a look at your life and marking where the small deaths, *las muertes chiquitas,* and the big deaths, *las muertes grandotas,* have taken place." To do this, Estes suggests that we draw a time line of our lives, from birth to present, marking all of our experiences of loss, all the times when roads were not taken or paths were cut off. For many women, the "big deaths" may be traumas such as betrayal, harassment, sexual abuse. The "little deaths" will be more subtle misdemeanors—wounding slights, belittling comments, and painful rejections. The rage of many Asian American women lies in *las muertes chiquitas,* the small, eroding deaths that, taken singly, are so imperceptible to friends and peers and so easy to dismiss as small. But years of small deaths can take their toll if we do not bring ourselves to address them as they occur. They build inside of us until we cannot contain them any longer. The process of *descansos* allows us to lay those angers to rest by remembering, forgiving, and moving on.

There is a particular type of reserve and humility that has come to be known by various names within Asian cultures and has made its way through the generations to Asian American women. According to Laura Uba, in her book *Asian Americans,* in Japanese American communities, the phenomenon is referred to as *enryo* and can be manifested in several ways—as in a hesitancy to speak up or to openly contradict a person in a position of authority. *Enryo*-ing stems from a cultural tradition against loudness, aggression, and dominating other people in social situations. *Enryo*-ing individuals might gently disparage themselves, their children, or their possessions so that others do not feel inadequate. There is an aesthetic beauty and irony to the concept of *enryo*. In Japan, family honor can be maintained because the listener is not actually expected to believe these negative remarks. In Japan, the listener is expected to assume that the persons making such disparaging statements are in fact just playing through a kind of *enryo* charade. But in a country where cross-cultural dissonance exists, the *enryo* code gets scrambled. In America, *enryo*-ing is not often perceived in the way that may have been intended. Actions that have signified deference and respect in Asian countries, particularly when used by Asian American women, have been mistaken in Western culture by both men *and women* for indications of passivity and weakness. Yet, if *enryo* is an indelible part of one's upbringing, it is easy to forget that graciousness can be taken wrongly.

Miscalculated *enryo* used to work against me in school, at work, and in my early relationships, when I didn't know any better. In high school, I would sit in the back of the classroom, wanting to be brave enough to sit in the front but feeling uncomfortable about being noticed by the teacher and the rest of the class. On my first jobs, I was too modest about my work, interrupting my bosses' praises by aggressively pointing out what I thought were its weak points, only to have my bosses end up agreeing with me. In my early relationships, young boyfriends called me their little China girl, which made my stomach turn, but I never said a word.

Enryo-ing tendencies might convince us not to apply for jobs with intimidating titles and important-sounding duties. They may stop us from disagreeing because it might seem rude. They stop us from expressing dissatisfaction because we might offend someone. *Enryo*-ing tendencies like these can sabotage us, creating potential situations of rage by the time we become adults. Jackie is a Japanese American friend who works at a large corporation. On weekends we try to see each other over a *dim sum* lunch in Chinatown, spending hours picking at tiny baskets of spinach dumplings and shrimp noodles. And every Sunday following *dim sum*, Jackie goes into the office to put in a full day's work. One Sunday, she told me:

> There is so much work to do! My desk just keeps getting piled higher and higher because I just can't say no. In a way, I don't want to refuse new projects because I believe that if I do them, I can make a difference, but everyone else in the office seems to be able to turn down extra work and enjoy their weekends. I can't seem to do it. Why am I the person everybody runs to at five o'clock on Friday to assign a project that is due on Monday? I know that if I don't start putting myself into the equation, I'll start to resent my work. But thinking about myself is not something I was ever taught to do.

In addition to the powerful pull of *enryo,* other experiences can lead to the appearance of silence, as Vanessa, a college student from Connecticut who came to the States from the Philippines at age eleven, not speaking a word of English, describes. She arrived in America during the summer, giving her the time she needed to learn English by watching television and listening to the radio intensively for three months before school started.

> On the first day of school, I was excited about trying out my English. But it turned out to be a bad experience. The teacher decided to introduce me as the new

kid by making me come to the front of the room and asked me to tell everybody who I was. When I answered her, she started to correct my English. In front of everyone! I was so humiliated, I didn't speak much for the rest of the year. I was so afraid of making a mistake. All I did was answer with as few words as I could, and never in complete sentences.

The theme of traumatic silence is echoed by KaYing, a strong-willed, thirty-year-old Hmong woman from Minneapolis:

When I was younger, I wasn't allowed to go out with friends. I would let out my frustration when I practiced violin. I'd press really hard on the bow and it made an awful noise. Now, as an adult I still don't know how to deal with anger. I turn to friends mostly, and ask them, "Am I crazy? Why do I feel so bad?" I never share these things with my family.

In grade school, an American girl kept beating me up every day. She'd pull my long hair and say things that I couldn't understand. I tried to fight back, but I'm pretty weak, so she was a constant terror in my life and I couldn't understand why she was doing this to me. It made no sense. Then in the eighties we moved, and that was where I really withdrew. I didn't speak to anyone. Some people thought I was mute. In the small town of Manitowoc, I lived in a housing complex full of Hmong like my family. The white people would throw eggs and make crank calls. I kept wishing I knew how to do kung fu so I could kick those guys' butts. Always keeping quiet, keeping things in. I think a lot about what I should have said after the fact.

DEMONS THAT CAN'T BE NAMED

Like many Asian American women, I couldn't identify what constructive rage actually felt like. I was so afraid that if I allowed rage to surface, its power would destroy me. As a consequence, I was unable to use its energy. During my first few years at the law firm, I worked round the clock because I accepted every project that was given to me. Like my friend Jackie, I could never say no. I would second-guess every statement I uttered, every move I made. Was I doing things right? Was my behavior correct? My rage and confusion came out in a highly competitive streak, in my constant, overzealous need to please people, and in feelings of powerlessness over situations around me. I felt as if my gears were out of whack, grinding against each other and wearing me down from the inside.

Channeling rage is a difficult process that takes time and concentration. The first step is to identify its source. For some of us, the originating stress emanates from a faint but relentless sense of inequity or of being viewed as powerless, easy to control, or inconsequential. In these cases, our anger will be based in a profound sense of predetermined invisibility.

Yet it is difficult for many of us to tie our anger to concrete notions of racism or sexism, two words that we have learned are "fighting words," and may carry too much of a punch to describe the discriminatory behaviors that we face day to day. As a defense, we may deny the existence of these forces within our own lives, because recognizing them would make us feel insecure or anxious and because the racism directed at us is not usually overt.

Laura Uba offered this anecdote from an Asian American woman in Los Angeles as an everyday example of how some of us might react to such disparate treatment:

At a gas station, a Euro-American man, in pulling up to the pump, hit the car of an Asian American woman in front of him. He got out of his car and walked over to the cashier to pay in advance for his gas, completely ignoring the woman whose car he had bumped. A likely explanation is that he was arrogantly disregarding her because of a racist assumption that Asian Americans can be taken advantage of and will not even complain (or because of a sexist assumption that females can be similarly abused). Recognizing the reason for this man's behavior could be anxiety provoking for an Asian American in this situation. She might unconsciously feel that if she recognized his racism, she would feel vulnerable or angry—and she does not want to feel that way. As a result, she may unconsciously make the decision not to see the racism. Instead, she may tell herself that maybe he did not hit her car—maybe it was a little earthquake that shook her car. Or she might tell herself that he is so stupid that he did not realize that he hit her car (even though he clearly hit the car hard enough to know what he had done). Neither of these alternative explanations makes her feel vulnerable or angry. At the same time, though, she fails to see his racist (and sexist) behavior for what it is.

This is the tightrope issue for Asian American women. Already aware of the positive Model Minority stereotypes and images that cast us as highly desirable, sexy, ultrafeminine women, we often can't process our confusion about these notions to formulate a fitting response. We are not members of a minority group that is generally seen as downtrodden and exploited. And yet our stories of subtle disparate treatment have much in common with other minority groups that experience negative stereotyping. Sexist and racist behavior can be cloaked in filters of nuance and language, making it very hard to decipher and to react appropriately.

As I travel around the country on my lectures, I hear countless stories of almost imperceptible slights and subtle dismissal by bosses, waiters, clients, classmates, or strangers we might meet across a conference table or at a cocktail party, who will assume that we have nothing to say or do not want to speak. We might be mistaken for one of the wives or girl-friends, as a marginalized guest who may not even be able to speak English, but who spices up the crowd with exotic ethnicity. Women have also shared with me stories of:

- A boss's or coworker's overwillingness to "construc-tively" criticize our work when that criticism would not be given as freely to other coworkers.

- A taxi driver who cannot seem to hear us, or under-stand us, even as we are speaking as loudly and as artic-ulately as anybody else.

- A professor who refuses to understand simple ques-tions once he detects a slight accent.

- A subway teller who makes us wait while she takes a short break, assuming that an Asian girl won't complain as others might.

Situations like these create dilemmas for us. All of a sudden, we have to decide whether to respond to or dismiss the questionable behavior. Knowing that there might be reper-cussions, we may hold back and second-guess our intuitive responses, thinking that the slights could not have been intentional or perhaps did not occur at all. In the end, it is *our own choice* to ignore or to act. Do we make our lives easier for the moment by allowing the offensive behavior to go unchecked, or do we raise a fuss and risk embarrassment by appearing overly sensitive or paranoid?

"What am I supposed to say when a man says to me, 'I love Asian women'?" asks Jeannie. "Should I say, 'Thank you,' and accept it as a compliment," she suggests, "or do I call him a bigot for lumping me in some Suzie Wong category?" In another example of the ambiguity of so-called positive stereotyping, Sandra remarks, "I am told that landlords in Manhattan think that Asian women make the best tenants, so as an Asian American woman, I've never had a problem finding an apartment, even in a tight housing market. The word is that we are quiet, neat, and always pay the rent on time. So I guess that's good for me, even though I play my music very loud and have my friends over till all hours of the night." She stops to think about the irony. "I guess I'm not being evaluated as an individual in those cases, and yet I *benefit* from the stereotype. So should I keep quiet and let the stereotype work for me, or do I open my mouth, tell the truth, and make things harder for myself?"

I think about her choice of words: "make things harder for myself." I begin to understand how easy silence can be in so many situations, because it does not challenge us to take responsibility for ourselves. Silence is expected of us, and if we perform to expectation, all goes smoothly. The toll it takes on our self-esteem remains hidden and only slowly corrosive.

"Sometimes," says Celine, "we can use our silence to advantage, don't you think?" Celine is my sounding board. We talked for hours over coffee as she gave me a smart young woman's view. She tells me to get real. That one should admit that the passive-Asian-female stereotype can be turned on its head and used, even exploited, for all it's worth.

"I mean, come on. Can you really say that you have *never* played into that role even when you knew you could get what you wanted through doing that?" I sit back and think. Maybe I cannot admit to myself that I have, so Celine gives me an example: "Don't you see? It's so much easier to get things from people if they don't feel intimidated by you. Silence lets us have all the choices we want. No commitments, you know?"

Hot on this track of analysis, she continues with another example: "And how about this? Take me and my boyfriend, for instance," she says. "If we ever get into a fight, he knows that I can't be too mad if I'm yelling. Now, when I'm quietly seething, well, that's a different story. He knows to stay clear of me because he's in the danger zone. He's seen my real Korean tantrums and tries very hard to avoid them. See? He learns to *fear* my silence."

While Celine has a good point, I can't help but fear what happens when we grow to love our silence. *When silence becomes our means to power, we avoid a responsibility to participate actively. It places the power outside of ourselves to determine the outcome.* And if Celine's pent-up silence is ultimately what fuels her sudden, fearful bursts of rage, in effect it also prevents her from using her anger for more constructive, communicative purposes.

When we are silent, we can allow so much to pass unchecked that it becomes hard to discern when our boundaries have been crossed. When we are not practicing our vocal skills, constantly assessing aloud what is and is not acceptable, we can tend to freeze, even if merely out of a lack of practice. Our silence can often surprise us, showing again that the pull of *enryo* can be strong, even in the face of obvious aggression. Betty, a journalist who knows that she is powerful, even though she is sometimes silent, discovered this in what she recognized in hindsight as a situation of sexual harrassment, although she could not name it at the time. She described it in an editor's note in *A. Magazine:*

A man who frequently came to my office had invited me to go out with him several times over a period of five months. At each of my refusals, he became increasingly aggressive, and on the last occasion even grabbed my arm and backed me into a door. And I—who have always believed myself to be a liberated, strong-willed woman— suddenly felt transformed into a quivering, voiceless victim.

After that last incident, a complaint was made to his company and the problem, thankfully, was solved. But I still haven't gotten over the fact that, when confronted with the situation, my knee-jerk reaction was silence. It's scary how suddenly childhood conditioning reared its head despite my years spent in a women's college learning to take pride in myself.

How many ways have been given to us to silence ourselves and our natural impulses to rage? Have we heard these words before? Have we been asked:

"Why are you complaining?"

"Stop being so sensitive."

"You must have done something to deserve it."

"You're being disrespectful."

"Don't you have other things to think about besides
your own concerns and insecurities?"

"Don't you understand that other people suffer more
than you do?"

"You are spoiled rotten."

Learning to turn rage outward is just the first step of many
in gaining a personal sense of power. Wendy Mink, a professor
at the University of California at Santa Cruz and the daughter
of Congresswoman Patsy Mink, in recalling her childhood
experiences in *The Conversation Begins*, wrote about how she
channeled her early rage into constructive action:

At first we lived in Arlington, Virginia, and I went to a
public school there. . . . The white kids called me "Chink"
and told me to ride in the back of the bus and made fun
of me. . . . Once, in high school, I agreed to accompany a
friend on a blind double date, and when the guy showed
up he threw a tantrum, saying, "I am not going out with
any damn Filipino." Other people treated me as an exotic,
asking me when I learned to speak English or if I wore a
grass skirt all the time in Hawaii. To some I was a Jap; to
others, a Chink. As Vietnam heated up, the word "gook"
was added to the arsenal.

I spoke out against the prejudice. I answered it. But that
is what you live with if you're not part of the dominant
culture. You find ways of coping by learning to direct your
anger in creative ways like politics or the arts, or you
repress it, or you explode. I chose the political path, attending my share of civil rights marches and anti-war marches
not only to express my feelings but also to participate in
some process of public political education.

TALKING BEHIND CURTAINS

I am sitting in a room, in a circle with twenty students, many of whom are Asian American women, who have come for a fireside chat. We gather after an intensive lecture where I have shared stories that could have been theirs as well. Those young women remind me of myself in college fifteen years ago, curious to hear what it's like "on the outside," eager to tap into each other's experience about what we've been through, how we've made the choices we've made, and what we can do to make our lives less dissonant. These are the times I relish, as we are all seated in comfortable chairs that allow us to stay in each other's company for as long as the conversation lives. It is in these more private chats that I glimpse the potential of connection beyond self-imposed silence. Women who, because of either culture or courtesy or personal choice, did not choose to speak in the lecture hall, now participate effusively and confidently.

This particular setting is in Richmond, Virginia, and the young women around me have just completed a leadership program called Women Involved in Living and Learning led by a warm and committed organizer, Holly Blake. The WILL program has taught these young women some vital skills—how to hold themselves out with confidence, how to defend their ideas, how to face creative conflict in order to reach meaningful resolutions. I notice the difference between these lively women and the other students I've met during my two-day stay. These women have a curiosity and light in their eyes. They engage in discussion confidently. They laugh freely and share with trust. They inform my own perspectives about how rapidly the culture of Asian American womanhood is changing. When talking with them, I am reminded of the other young, dynamic Asian American women I've met, like Cathy, a junior from Houston, who has organized a high school mentoring program for younger Asian American women, and Yuan-Kwan, a freshman from Maryland, who puts together her own photocopied 'zine called *Meniscus,* or Swaty, a sophomore in Illinois, a student leader who asked if I had any suggestions about coping in the small rural college town where she was the only South Asian resident.

In these groups, I assume the role of storyteller, recounting parables and situations that are drawn from real life, to offer a way of seeing the world that helps them understand power. I talk about how the worship of secrets has often inhibited the lives of women in Asia, and that by honoring them now, we do an injustice to ourselves. I tell them about the architecture of ancient Beijing and the mazelike streets in Tokyo, where high walls signified the level of privacy and mystery that separated outside community from inside home. I show them how that same mind-set, when brought to America, can allow the mistreatment of Asian women to continue undetected within our communities to this day, despite laws that are there to protect us. I ask them to analyze the concepts of shame, "saving face," and "family honor," to understand them for what they are, silencing devices, control devices, that inhibit the free flow of stories and ideas.

Through venues like these that are created in small pockets around the country, Asian American women are creating a venting and mentoring process where we are learning to progress past anger and fear. Through these group gatherings, in regular dinner get-togethers, church and reading groups, and local community organizations, and on the several Web sites that are specifically for us and our concerns, we are sharing intimate and personal stories that just one generation ago we might not have allowed ourselves to tell. They are stories about the frustration we feel, but also the pride we have in ourselves, both of which were seldom encouraged. With our stories, we are piecing together a history that is truer than anything we have heard about ourselves to date. And those shared experiences are the proof of larger patterns.

Within the circle of a fireside chat, I cannot help but think: within those patterns lie the latent powers of the warrior.

SHE QUESTIONS HER POWER

CURIOUS PERSON: *What are you writing?*

ME: *A book about Asian American women and their notions about power.*

CURIOUS PERSON (jokingly): *Oh, so it's a thin book?*

In this fourth lesson, I want to prove that curious person wrong. But to begin to talk about power, we will have to question its very premise. What does power mean to you? Is it influence over others? Praise for a job well done? Your family's love?

And when have you felt most powerful, most validated? As I'll explain, I had grown accustomed to finding my power, what made me feel valid, in four main ways, each of which proved limited. Only after living and thinking through those times was it possible to find a truer power—from within.

In the dog days of July, when we were overcome with boredom and scorching hot temperatures, my sister and I would fight. Sometimes it was more than our mother could bear, and so she'd banish us to our cousin Shirley's house, a small apartment on Mott Street, deep in Manhattan's Chinatown. It was like being sent to an amusement park. While Chinatown adults slaved long hours in the restaurants and garment factories, we kids did anything we wanted almost all of the time.

In Chinatown, we'd spend long summer afternoons at the Pagoda Theater, a sticky-floored movie house where we'd watch the best double-feature kung fu films that I can remember. That's where I learned to read as fast as a Model Minority bullet, speeding through the English subtitles that flashed across the screen with a few seconds left to see the pictures. My favorite fighting women in their fine medieval Chinese costumes would somersault from roof to roof, their gossamer layers of white billowing as they brandished weird-looking weapons, sticks and swords and fireballs, against evil forces. They could harness the wind and make worlds collapse. As in all great kung fu movies, they'd shout out their maneuvers so that their opponents would know, moments before their demise, the debilitating blow that would deliver them into oblivion. *"Double Snake Whirlwind!"* she'd scream, and a gale would blow with such force that all her opponents would be sucked into the abyss. *"Ladder Technique!"* she'd say, and she'd fly up onto two ladders, using them as makeshift stilts, to gain fighting advantage. Kung fu warrior queens knew they were hot. They never tried to hide. They never screamed in those sissy high-pitched voices the way women in the American movies did.

Those movies would leave Donna (my sister), Shirley, and me crazed and adrenaline-charged and ready to test out those new moves as soon as we got back to Shirley's cramped apartment. We would erect barricades with Shirley's plastic-covered, peacock-embroidered sofa cushions and create hidden rooms by draping sheets over her lower bunk beds so that we could reenact the movie scenes. Nerf balls made great fireballs, and chopsticks did well as improvised daggers. We'd fashion our warrior hair so that it flowed like fountains from the top of our heads. We'd leap from the top bunk bed down to the double bed only inches away, imagining that we were flying around in the small bedroom where Shirley's entire family of five slept. And when Shirley's older brother Steven came home from school, we would attack him in cleverly engineered surprise ambushes.

I thought of the Pagoda Theater recently, when I watched a movie called *Wing Chun*, starring my favorite karate-kicking diva, Michelle Yeoh, a former ballerina turned movie star who does her own stunts. Wing Chun was a woman fighter who knew how to turn her physical weaknesses into advantage. With her slight stature, Wing Chun knew that using direct force would be her downfall, since most of her opponents were men and physically much stronger. So Wing Chun came up with a different way of fighting, using quick, delicate flicks of her wrists to steer away oncoming blows.

She became a master at anticipating her enemy's movements, not so that she could meet them with greater force, but so that she could sidestep them more quickly. She learned how to bend like a reed, forcing her opponent to overextend and lose his balance. Then, like a rubber band, she'd snap back with a strike that would knock him over, as he tried to regain position. He'd grab a long stick, but Wing Chun would draw him into small spaces and corners so that the bulky weapon would be blocked by the walls and ceiling. Then she would use her short dagger to draw the combat nearer. Having brought the battle in closer, she knew that his staff would prove useless. *She was so smart!*

Wing Chun knew how to turn big, obvious power against itself. She understood that efficient fighting had less to do with strength and more to do with knowing her opponent's weaknesses. Wing Chun could vanquish her opponents and have the humanity to spare their lives. And like so many modern-day warrior women, she could perform so many duties at once. After conquering evil villains, she even had a day job, selling tofu at her aunt's lunch stand. Wing Chun took multitasking to an admirable extreme.

If power was what I was looking for and found in fictional characters like Wing Chun, where could it lie in real life? My young suburban life was not full of evil characters that had to be vanquished. It wasn't realistic to think of power in Wing Chun terms, in terms of how well we can wield a sword or punch someone's lights out. I had as a model only physical demonstrations of power set in superhuman terms, so what did the notion of practical power mean to me?

As a young girl and perhaps even now, to me power meant getting by on as equal footing as I could. No more than that. To most of us, power concepts are not about winning large battles or influencing large numbers of people, or gaining elected office, or winning a Westinghouse science award. They are about the day-to-day events, how we survive the ordinary bouts of teenagehood and then adulthood, full of the pressures of keeping up and staying in the game.

We develop temporary methods—in this chapter I call them Power Myths—to help us rationalize the world and help us through.

On Saturday nights in Westbury, four girlfriends and I would pack ourselves into our parents' borrowed cars to go clubbing in big, bad New York City. I loved Saturday nights, going into the city on a fake ID, my hair big as Farrah Fawcett's, set hard with half a can of hair spray, decked out in my black-and-purple sequined camisole that would catch the light of the mirror ball as I got down to Blondie's "Heart of Glass." My lips were coated too thickly with bubblegum roll-on lip gloss that made me look as if I had just kissed a bottle of Mazola corn oil. My eyes were carefully done with black kohl eyeliner that gave my eyes that "smoky" look, just as the Revlon ad promised. As juniors in high school, Bonnie Lavnick, Geri Rosenthal, Ilyse Nayor, Jane Oberwager, and I called ourselves the Meshuganettes, an all-Jewish girl tag team (with one honorary member, me) that could plow through honors math and still look great on a dance floor. In 1979, we were sneaking in on the tail end of the baby boomer's excesses, gawking at the grown-ups in their gold chains and aping them as effectively as we could, feeling as if, at seventeen, we were one of them. To us the city was a series of dares, a giant, heaving party that went on round the clock. We big-haired girls would brashly and confidently push to the front of lines at Studio 54 and Danceteria, batting our Maybelline-coated lashes at the bouncer, who would always let us in, for no other apparent reason than that we were five unaccompanied girls. So what if we were part of the bridge-and-tunnel crowd, suburban girls who had to pay a toll to get there? We were underage and having a great time.

POWER MYTH #1: THE POWER OF FITTING IN

In the 1970s, in the Long Island suburb where we lived, multiculturalism and diversity were pretty simple concepts. The motto was simple and basic: "Do whatever you can to be like everyone else, and you'll be absolutely fine." As in most suburban enclaves then and even now, "belonging" was the goal, and that meant differences had to be hidden at any cost, no matter how patent and indelible those differences might be. Deny your differences and they won't exist, my father would tell us back then. "You're just as American as anybody else," he'd say. And in enlightened times, perhaps he'd have been right. But back in the seventies it didn't explain why we were called Chinks or why parents voiced polite concern at a PTA meeting when I was given the female lead in our high school bicentennial production of *Oklahoma!*, implying that Asian Americanness was actually un-American.

I thought the rest of America, like my own town, was Jewish, and so Jewish was what I aspired to become. Our family must have been good at the assimilation game, since we were eventually jokingly dubbed the "Engsteins," a term of endearment and acceptance that must have meant: You are an honorary one of us. And because of this we do not notice your differences (really, we swear!). Even if we don't always understand your mom's heavy Chinese accent.

Our parents' regimen for ensuring that my sister and I became American allowed us certain privileges. We were in essence the first Chinese American slackers. We didn't go to Chinese school on Saturdays like our cousins did, and we ate as much McDonald's as we wanted. We hardly ever ate Chinese food two days in a row, knowing that telltale clinging smell of Chinese food would be the scarlet letter of Chineseness once we stepped out of the house.

Jane Oberwager pulled into my driveway in her parents' wood-paneled Ford station wagon, packed already with Ilyse, Geri, and Bonnie. With the Bay City Rollers blasting on WPLJ, Jane honked for me to join them, and like someone in a scene out of *Happy Days*, I threw on my coat and hopped into the car, having just gobbled up the last mouthfuls of dinner that my mom had flash fried. We shot toward the city and Danceteria. It was Saturday night again.

The flash point came on the Long Island Expressway in the form of a harmless sentence. It was Bonnie, in her trademark follow-the-moment, don't-think-before-you-talk, endearing way, who blew my world apart.

"I smell Chinese food!" She took a short sniff to confirm it. The carload of us fell stone silent, as if Bonnie had said something vulgar and ugly and unmentionable, as if someone had farted or as if she had called attention to a friend's withered arm or a growth in the middle of my forehead. All eyes turned to me in my big rabbit fur coat.

It became very warm. I looked away and slowly rolled down the window to let out the warm, greasy smell of oyster chicken that clung to my coat and cut through the brittle winter air. I might wear the same clothes, paint my eyes larger, and have hair as big as any of them, but with Bonnie's tiny, innocent statement the truth had been set loose. On a level so basic that the limbic sense of smell would suss it out, there was difference in me that I had learned to be ashamed of.

University of Chicago sociologist Robert Park used the term "racial uniform" to describe the indelible qualities that immigrant communities cannot hide and that give them what he called "a status on the margins"—the shape of their eyes, the color of their hair, the complexion of their skin. Park used this notion to explain why it is that certain ethnic groups in America—no matter how willingly they may shed the language, customs, dress, and culture of the old country—will still be sidelined in a dominantly white culture. Although Park had written that paper back in 1928, he could have been talking about Westbury in the 1970s.

Contrary to what many of us may think, "fitting in" is not an exercise in self-hatred. Instead it is a coping mechanism, a protective sap, that allows us to go on with our lives, to raise our families, get our promotions, and live life free of the annoying daily reminders that things may be more difficult than we care to admit. It's always easier to wear the right clothes, drive the right car, talk the right way, and keep our conversations light than to ask ourselves why we feel we have to, or even want to. To figure out how to be Asian in America without resorting to the Power of Fitting In is hard work. It involves searching for the nuances, the compromises, and sometimes the hypocrisies in many of the events in our lives. For many of us, assimilation becomes an easier, short-term solution. But it comes with a profound sense of psychological loss. In an America that defines immigrant success so heavily in terms of conformity to norms, our cultural psyche has suffered.

Don't go against the grain. Practice smooth interpersonal relationships. Maintain face. Themes of fitting in are etched in cultural memory, going by different names in many languages. In the Filipino language of Tagalog, for instance, they go by the names of *utang ng laab*, "reciprocal obligation," and *hiya*, "shame." Guiding social principles like these teach us to sublimate self in favor of the community, to avoid what might be embarrassing, and to keep the best face forward in public. They are principles that were meant to preserve order in a community, which, when transposed into American life, continue a needless forfeiture of the past and all its knowledge.

POWER MYTH #2: THE POWER OF THE ONLY ONE

And still after all that work, something was not right. You were like that piece people jammed into thousand-piece puzzles, shoved into the corners of other perfectly fit pieces, regardless of what shape you were. Sure, you blended in pretty well, wore the right colors, did your best to look the part, but you were part of the sleeve, the shoulder of the puzzle, and you were placed somewhere in the torso.

—M. Evelina Galang
Her Wild American Self

Fitting in was not the answer. It didn't feel honest or empowering. And maybe because I knew that, I found myself in wandering mode going to college in California, where roughly one-third of the students were Asian American just like me. They had been born in America and spoke English just as well, since it was their first language, too. They wore T-shirts and jeans. They ran for student government. But at Berkeley one thing was different. These Asian Americans had a strong sense of belonging and place.

Many of them, having come from California schools like Lowell High in San Francisco and Berkeley High, and having been surrounded by other Asians their entire lives, took for granted their privilege of multiculture. Many of them had social lives that revolved around mini "Asian scenes" that were almost exclusively Asian. One would assume that for a Chinese American freshman who was already beginning to question her sense of belonging, a whole new world was opening itself up for me and that I had found my people.

In fact, it wasn't the case at all. I had never been around so many Asian faces, so much black hair. Berkeley seemed like China to me. It took me a full year to learn how to distinguish one Asian face from another. Traumatized at the difference of my surroundings, I resorted to what I call the Power of the Only One. It was the notion that I, as the only Asian face in a crowd, would remain important only as long as I remained the lone one.

I joined a sorority, one of the last bastions of white life that had not yet fully opened its doors to the promises of racial diversity.

The Power of the Only One allowed me to bask in my differences while being innocuous enough to fit in at the same time. I baked chocolate chip cookies and followed sorority ways. I dated white fraternity guys who were more right-on than the Westbury guys, since California boys seemed to have no problem with Asian girls. I began to understand the power I had as a token.

I hadn't yet thought about what real power was, so I accepted that role of the token and felt that I was privileged. Doors open up for Only Ones. We add color to otherwise monochrome cocktail parties. We get to be the one-stop-shop on any subject that seems to fall within our ethnic category, ranging from what kind of sushi to order, to kung fu, to the rise of Pacific Rim economies, to the proper way to hold one's chopsticks. When I came back to New York as an attorney, I found that being the only Asian face in the crowd worked well for me in a New York law firm. In my newfound legal circles, where the lawyers were so unlike me in background and upbringing, I found an odd comfort in my exotic Asian status while also trying hard to mimic the corporate ways.

I thought of the strange predicament that befalls those with Only One status. What do we do when several of us are in a room together amid others? Purposefully avoiding one another seems unnatural, and yet that is what tokens do. The other choice, gravitating toward one another, carries another set of consequences. Only Ones know instinctively that congregating can cut them off from the general flow of a gathering, forming a social boundary that only the most enthusiastic Asiaphile would want to transcend. Congregating, as seen by an Only One, therefore becomes a form of exile.

POWER MYTH #3: THE POWER OF THE GOOD LITTLE MODEL MINORITY GIRL

At the age of eight Sarah Chang played a Paganini concerto with the New York Philharmonic without rehearsal and on one day's notice. Midori, the other prodigy violinist that people always confuse with Sarah Chang, had her debut at the age of eleven, when conductor Zubin Mehta invited her to be a surprise guest soloist at the Philharmonic's New Year's Eve party. At seventeen, Japanese American whiz kid Matt Seto could outperform ninety-nine percent of the mutual funds, capturing the hearts of Wall Street. At thirteen, Indian American Bala Ambati became the youngest person ever to become a doctor, like Doogie Howser. Se Ri Pak, at twenty, won the U.S. Women's Open, spurring on a wave of Pak-mania as the "hottest woman golfer in two decades," according to *Newsweek*. And as my mother says about America's favorite Olympian ice skater, "Everybody loves Michelle Kwan. She's just the top." I celebrate each and every one of their victories. It makes me proud. They are, each of them, extraordinary and gifted people.

But please, if we're relying on them to legitimate our own personal sense of power and pride, all I can say is, give me a big, fat break. They may be our role models, they may be Asian, they may inspire, but the fact that we share common ethnic heritage has little to do with either their victories or our own personal worth. The process of finding our own sense of inherent value and pride is much more difficult than that.

We seem to love this third myth, what I call the Power of the Good Little Model Minority Girl, as it allows us to think of ourselves as smart and hardworking and better than most. Who wouldn't love it ? The glowing positive aspects of the image seem to cry out for a resounding "Thank you!" for the compliment and make it very difficult to tell a more sobering set of facts. So many of us are reluctant to bring negative attention to the image because we do so well just being quiet. "The myth helped me in countless ways, even when I was very young in school, where teachers assumed that because I am Asian I would be smart," Lisa, a twenty-four-year-old Chinese American from Houston, told me. "I remember getting back grade-school math exams where my answers were wrong, but the teacher hadn't caught the mistakes and gave me a good mark anyway."

The truth is that many Asian Americans, especially later immigrants from northeast and south Asia—Shanghainese, Koreans, Hong Kongers, Taiwanese, Japanese, some Filipinos and Indians—came with class status already intact. For these families, privilege, education, and wealth were theirs prior to coming to America. Immigration, which required the expense of a transpacific ticket and the connections needed for a visa, happened to be the filter that gave entrance to only the most promising. Even many of America's Vietnamese refugees are former professionals and teachers, as are many Korean store owners. For many of them, it is only language barriers that have hindered their opportunity. Tight-knit family structures and a reverence for education have made it easier to preserve or regain their middle-class status in America.

But there is a flip side to that experience, which disproves this myth of a Model Minority. When I begin to describe it, I am often put in the awkward position of being called a complainer, like an ungrateful guest who has treated her gracious host's praises like a proverbial gift horse—as happened to me one day unexpectedly.

"Why must you be so negative about the image? It's a good thing, isn't it?" one PBS talk show host once asked me.

"Because it's a stereotype . . . ," I answered. I tried to continue.

"Why do you insist on looking at the glass half empty as opposed to half full?"

"Whether they are positive or negative, stereotypes have to be examined—"

"You should be flattered by the good press."

It was a live taping, the cameras were rolling, and I, who thought myself a veteran of on-air interviews, couldn't believe my ears. We were stuck in auto-rewind. Stuck in a world where long-accepted notions don't die easily.

I don't feel that my host was being rude or that his questions were intentionally racist. I have to believe instead that his questions were posed out of a genuine need for clarification.

This was probably the first time that he had thought about an issue that for me reveals itself in some way every day.

And so I'll start from scratch. First of all, Model Minority ideas attribute excellence to a broad group based on race, an oversimplification of the experience of an entire racial community. Second, the label of the Model Minority allows Asian Americans to play what sociologists call the "middleman minority" role. We're neither black nor white. Instead, we exist as a buffer zone between the two, neutralizing our potential to add new meaning to important race discussions.

Since the Model Minority myth defines success in financial terms (for example, the Vietnamese refugee turned millionaire), through awards (the Westinghouse scholar), degrees (Harvard and Yale), and job titles (doctor, engineer), it emphasizes the importance of compliance to the most conventional aspects of a dominant culture. That image of our conventional success, in effect, blames other minority groups for a perceived failure to comply as readily with those same expectations. It steers us away from the possibility that we might be average Americans struggling like everybody else, or that common inequities may exist across race lines among all Americans. Model Minority myths support the belief that the racism ethnic groups complain about is the product of their own shortcomings. That is how this myth preserves status quo thinking.

Model Minority news bites also ignore information that questions the stereotype. Census figures show, for instance, that Asian American workers receive *smaller* economic rewards for their education than white workers. This means that Asian Americans need more education to maintain economic parity with white Americans. It also leads many Asian Americans to believe that they have attained middle-class status without realizing that they are underemployed and overworked. Asian American students have the largest proportion of both the highest *and lowest* SAT scores, exploding the myth that we are all supergeniuses. Model Minority myths conveniently point to higher average incomes of Asian American households as compared to whites without also acknowledging that an average Asian family in America has more members in the workforce. Additionally, those higher income figures cast their nets broadly to include incomes of visiting businessmen and company executives from Asia who are here temporarily under foreign work permits.

The myth does not incorporate the hidden face of Asian America, the Cambodians living in San Francisco's Tenderloin district, or the Vietnamese living in San Rafael's Canal district, or the Hmong living in the San Joaquin Valley, many of whom live below the poverty line. Ignoring these communities makes it easier to cut federal and local budgets for the social programs designed to benefit the Asian groups that require them. Nationally, 15.3 percent of Asian Americans live in poverty, and in San Francisco and Los Angeles their rates of public assistance are often twice as high as whites'.

When Model Minority curtains are pulled away, it becomes easier to listen to stories such as Marlene's, which represents a typical Filipino agricultural experience:

I didn't know I was poor. My mom got a cannery job, which was considered good, because it was union. It was better than farmwork, because in farmwork, there is no work for three months out of the year. I remember one year when my family had to go on welfare and how devastating it was to my dad's pride. Even though they tried to hide it from us, I remember hearing them fight about it when we all went to sleep. Then my dad got a job as a cook at the airport.

By the time we turned twelve or thirteen, we had two choices in the summer. Either go work on the farm and earn money for the family or go to summer school. So we chose summer school when we could because working out in the fields meant a ten-hour day and we didn't get to keep the money, since it all went to support the entire family. When I went back to school in September, we were asked to write about what we did for summer vacation and I wouldn't know what to write, since mine weren't very exciting.

The myth of the Model Minority exerts tremendous pressure on young Asian Americans. Overbearing expectations coupled with personal and parental pressures to succeed have led to a rate of suicide attempts among Asian American young adults that is higher than the national average. Recent federal studies reveal as much as a three hundred percent increase in the suicide rate among Asian American children.

There is backlash as well. Model Minority myths have contributed to a skyrocketing increase in racially motivated attacks against Asian Americans, which rose fifty-five percent from 1994 to 1995 and another fifteen percent in 1996, based primarily on the false perception that we are gaining at the expense of others.

Pretty contradictory news? No wonder it's easier to choose to remain in sound bite bliss.

But the most dangerous aspect of the Model Minority myth is not how it shapes the views of the general American public. It is that we have learned to perpetuate these myths ourselves, so that we ourselves grow insular and racist, believing in an ethnic superiority to the exclusion of others. "My father is a doctor, and I am going to Princeton to be one, too. My Korean community is very close, and we help each other. That's why we're called the new Jews," I remember one

American-born young man telling me on a national call-in radio show. He implied that his personal experience was all that counted in his analysis of a larger political world, and that as long as he got what he wanted, as long as Model Minority myths worked for him, he would continue to sing their tune.

Fiercegirl Backlash

Many young women I have met realize the absurdity and destructiveness in playing preconceived roles of the Assimilationist, the Token Only One, and the Good Little Model Minority Girl. They don't want to fit in—they are too confident in their specialness and value. They do not want to bask in the privilege of the Only One because they thirst for a sense of community. They have not accepted conformity to the Model Minority myth as a relevant goal in their lives, even though family, the media, and academia steer them relentlessly toward attaining it, and often reject them if they do not meet its requirements. They sense the larger patterns that affect their lives and can detect where image is not meeting reality. They see their parents working hard to provide for their children, fighting to keep their jobs, and saving scrupulously for the future. These young women know for themselves the obstacles to negotiating through a working world where stereotypes can impede their advancement. They sometimes feel unjustly steered into career choices that do not work for them but fulfill external needs of status or security. Many of them have wanted to lead creative lives, as artists, freelancers, community activists, or travelers, but will feel that they have failed their families and their communities if they choose to embark upon these personal goals. To them the Power Myths are stifling, unimaginative, and infuriating.

These women with brains and a sense of importance are finding it difficult to channel creative energy, with few models to guide them as independently thinking women. We are seeing the energy of frustration rise from these young Asian American women. Encouraged by a Generation X world that has allowed girls to carve out a culture of their own, fueled by rebellious themes of power among girls who feel that they do not fit in or are hemmed in by the confines of family pressure, the backlash of young Asian American women tends to be fierce and uninhibited.

The counterculture that expresses the rage of adolescence reverberates in Asian American families as well, creating even deeper communication rifts because of the cultural tendency to suppress aberrant behaviors that we feel bring shame. In her 'zine, *BambooGirl,* Sabrina Margarita, a multiracial woman who is part Filipina expresses her Fiercegirl attitude in an ad hoc mission statement for her powerfully worded publication:

> At one time I was hearing a lot of "Don't do this, Don't be too loud, Why don't you try out for a beauty pageant? (if you're Filipina, you know why that thought makes me retch) and mostly, "Why don't you try to be more NORMAL?" Now these aren't things people would outrightly say, but it was evident in the way I was treated, talked to, and interacted with, especially from the point of view of an Asian mixed chick who likes to wear whatever I want, like my tattoos and piercings, and loud opinions. Let's just say there was a lot going on, and no way to get it out of my system.

The hard-core punk music culture helped Sabrina get the validation she sought for not wanting to be the "beautiful petite Asian flower" she saw her friends becoming. It allowed her to be comfortable with the fact that she was a young woman with a lot on her mind, that outwardly she was angrier than the rest of her peers, that she could be "some kind of overachiever," using her *own* sense of goals, and that she could discuss serious issues in a confrontational way. In *BambooGirl*, she writes to her subscribers:

> *BambooGirl* is like a big FUCK YOU and validation for myself, and other girls who have found it a bitch to get to the point where they knew they were worth it. And this time I AM NOT BEING QUIET ABOUT IT. This is my personal experience, but I know I'm not the only one who has it. This is my chance to slap people back and say, "I'm not your fucking geisha."

Working in a similar vein, Lela is the producer of a comic series and film short called "Angry Little Asian Girl," featuring a heroine with a Hello Kitty face and her two middle fingers poking up underneath her pigtails in a lewd gesture. Lela likes to depict scenes with Angry Little Asian Girl thrashing out at parents, teachers, and "ignoramuses" who assume her submissiveness.

The Fiercegirl is a role that travels across the globe, resonating with young women in Asia who, through the Westernized music channels of Channel V and MTV Asia, are adopting an irreverence that is giving them new expressive power. They don't need Madonna and bad-girl American rock sirens. Punk bands like Shonen Knife and Super Junkie Monkey in Japan and Abrasive Relations in the Philippines blend their culturally unique messages with raucous, free, and sometimes zany music. One Japanese girl band, Cibo Matto (meaning "food madness" in Italian), features keyboardist Miho Hattori and singer Yuka Honda, along with bassist Sean Lennon, Yoko's son. Their songs, performed live, feature Miho screaming, "Shut up and eat? Too bad no *bon appetit!*" in songs with absurdist food-associated names, like "Birthday Cake," "Beef Jerky," and "Know Your Chicken." To the delight of their audiences, Miho and Yuka kick their microphones to the ground and yell at the top of their lungs, stunning college audiences into shock with the completely unexpected anti-stereotype. Stateside, KMEL's E Fly Girl, Elaine Leung, Austin's deejay Cream, and New York's Hindi pop deejay Rekha experiment with nonconformity through their love of music.

For Fiercegirls, power is synonymous with loud defiance. It is obvious in its gestures, and is worn like a warning sign. Fiercegirls aren't afraid to speak up and talk back. Their language often reaches the powerfully profane and is coupled with a wild, quick wit. It is a raw, restless energy that, if not directed toward a creative activism, can turn in on itself in destructive behavior. Tranh, another Fiercegirl, a Vietnamese American law student from Raleigh, North Carolina, tells her story of having to overcompensate for what she calls "sickeningly sweet images of dutiful Asian American women." Her story is cloaked in the dilemma of having to live up to the positive stereotype of a Model Minority standard, which denies Tranh of her sense of self-determination and creativity in her own life.

> There were times when I acted in an extremely self-destructive way because of the expectations of being a Model Minority. I did what I could to break that myth, going out of my way so that people wouldn't think I was good at math or that I was the quiet, subservient Oriental girl who always obeyed the rules. I only ended up hurting myself.

Tranh, like many creative yet conflicted Asian American women I've spoken to, had bouts of depression, excessive drinking, and drug use, despite the heavy shame factor that those activities might have brought upon her family.

As with bad girls everywhere, the main point of conflict comes most immediately between mother and daughter. Lennie from Seattle, whose mother is Filipina and whose father is Vietnamese, described her physical fights with her mother, who won't allow her to bring home friends, especially young men, from school. As the youngest of five daughters, Lennie is the troublemaker, "the spoiled baby," her mother says. Because of the limitations put on her at home, Lennie has learned to be secretive about her relationship with her boyfriends. Recently she moved out of her house because she and her mother started to fight physically. "My mother is living in a fantasyland. She thinks we live back in the Philippines where she grew up. She calls me no good because I'm not like the Asian girls she sees on TV. My other sisters just listen to her. They have no backbone."

While expressive of honest rage, Fiercegirl backlash can be reactive without being analytical. The women who are Fiercegirls know, in the gut, that something is wrong. As a counter, they are lashing out at everything that meets with their disapproval, from the "Asian airhead good girls" who are abiding by the silly rules, to the overarching "system," to "white men," whom they feel are "stupid" and "deserve to be treated badly." The strong Japanese girl bands may carry Fiercegirl images of irreverence and individuality, but when asked why they do it, they often come up short for answers or offer responses such as, "I don't really know. All I know is that I'm having a good time." Image is beginning to usurp content, resulting in a Pyrrhic victory at best. What Fiercegirls need is a prescription for the power to turn rage into creativity. What Fiercegirls need is the assurance that family is there for them, to support them and understand

and bridge divides, rather than blame or judge them as they experiment with new notions of power.

Merry White, in her book *The Material Child,* explored the concept of teenage rebellion as signifying a necessary period of differentiation and self-awareness. She concluded that this phase of development was peculiar to Western societies, where generations are more apt to be distinct and kept apart. Teenage rebellion occurs more frequently in communities that do not have clearly defined rites of passage to usher its young people into adulthood.

Yet, for Asian American women, rebellion may not be synonymous with adolescence. Instead, our need for self-definition may come many years afterward, since emotional and physical separation from our nuclear families tends to happen later in life. Many of us do not start dating relationships until well into our twenties. Many of us do not move from home until several years after that. As we become less dependent financially and emotionally on our parents, and as we are faced with the inevitability of dealing with life's realities—job, marriage, and child rearing—we finally come face-to-face with the world at large, its harsh realities, and its hierarchies. Fiercegirls, often in their mid- and late twenties, are the embodiment of confidence and a rebellious response to inequity.

Fiercegirl rage later in life may be similar to American teenage rebellion, but family reactions to it can result in irreparable schisms, especially in families that adhere to strict Confucian, Hindu, or Muslim codes that point out rebellion by shaming it, disowning it, or attempting to hide it. By choosing to ignore the fact that rebellion is an American rite of passage that our American-raised daughters will go through, and by resisting the conversations we need to have between our generations, we make it difficult for our young women to find modern roles within our families. The price is often long-term, emotional distance between parent and daughter. In the worst cases, our daughters will choose to cut and run.

POWER MYTH #4:
THE POWER OF THE CONTRARIAN

What do we do when we finally accept that stereotypes exist, when Model Minority myths are exposed for what they truly are, and when our Fiercegirl, in-your-face attitude is yielding less powerful results than we anticipated? The answer seems to lie in being the exception to the rule, the non-Asian Asian, the one who contradicts all expectations and therefore is finally appreciated for the individual that she really is. Overcompensation, the conscious refusal to fall into stereotype, seems to have been the answer for the Asian American Contrarian.

To demonstrate our uniqueness, how many of us have overcompensated in the following ways?

- Perceiving that she was expected to be quiet and soft-spoken, Kay forces herself to speak whenever meeting with new people. She does this even when she is tired, just so that others know that she is articulate and understands English.

- Kim goes out of her way to make sure that her coworkers know that she is not interested in her cultural heritage. "I don't want my coworkers to think I am different from them," she explained.

- Vhu feels she is "math blocked." "I think my aversion to anything related to math is kind of a reflex to this

math-nerd image of Asians I have in my head. I guess I
just decided that numbers wouldn't be my forte."

These are some of the ways we might act so that we place
ourselves outside the reach of stereotype. Some with more
creative flairs have gone even farther. Helen, a gifted young
Malaysian American writer, uses her sense of fashion as a
Contrarian statement. By choosing to wear outlandish
clothes, like her wigs or her orange plastic platform shoes,
not just to parties but to her office as well, she makes people
acknowledge her. "I want to be looked at for my human side
and so my clothes let people know that I have a unique personality. Even though I know I do my job well and want to
be noticed for it, I want people to know that I am a human
being as well, and that I am not just another Asian American
yuppie in a business suit," she tells me.

Like Fiercegirl attitude, Contrarian techniques, even while
self-determining, keep us fixed in a mode of reaction. We still
must keep our eyes peeled for ghosts of stereotypes that we
know are ridiculous, yet we expend tremendous energy fighting them anyway, showing just how deeply those stereotypes
have been internalized. This coping mechanism, just as reactive
as undirected Fiercegirl anger, prevents us from creating power
and defining what we want for ourselves and instead keeps our
focus on telling the rest of the world what we are not.

A ROAD MAP TO POWER

Finding the situations that have made us feel worthy will
require time and a willingness to be honest with ourselves. It
will mean looking back to how your family has rewarded
you and the circumstances that made them arrive at the definitions of success that they passed on to you. It will mean

identifying what made you valid and acceptable to your friends, teachers, bosses, and anyone else whom you gave the power to judge you. Finding a personal sense of power means looking your fears of nonacceptance and possible failure straight in the eye and knowing them for what they are.

To begin to envision our particular notion of power, we need a road map, which might look something like this:

Setting Aside Time

The most crucial step in thinking about power is *making the commitment to do it*. Set aside a block of time when you will do nothing else but think. In our busy lives, time is often a luxury, especially when we are asked to use it for an amorphous long-term goal. It seems that we always have important things to do, with immediate consequences if we don't deliver. Think of envisioning power as something that you must do for yourself—consider it exercise for the soul. Take an entire weekend for yourself and make no plans. Or go on a daylong hike. Lori, a very directed woman who heads her own production company, believes very firmly in five-year plans. She takes two weeks out of every year to go on solitary walks to think about the past year's accomplishments and whether they have fit into her larger life principles. If situations have changed over the year, Lori will fine-tune or re-adjust her sights, but she will always have some kind of target. Lori takes that time to think about the values that ground her and give her guidance, so that every decision she makes is consistent with that "bottom line." This is her way of setting her compass. When her actions are consistent with her values, she knows that she is acting from a place of power.

Clearing a Path

Before we can begin to envision what power means to us, many of us may have to clear away a tremendous amount of static that can block or distort our perceptions. Defining power means trying to let go of past hurts that have made us feel helpless—letting go of recurring memories that make us feel small or second-rate and trying for at least an instant to remove ourselves from the cages around us so that we can imagine outward.

Pam has a giant photograph in her living room for everyone to see. It is a picture of Pam and her sister when they were very young. In it, Pam stands next to her sister looking pained and confused. Her hair, which she had just cut herself, is disheveled and sticking up, as if she had been pulled out of her nap to take the picture. In stark contrast, Pam's sister has dressed up for the picture, with her fancy hat and frilly dress, and she's smiling for the camera in an idyllic little-girl pose, hugging her doll. I've come to understand that this is the way Pam had come to see herself in the world, oppressed and outdazzled by her sister, even though so much has changed in the thirty years that have passed since that picture was taken. Pam is now a stunning woman, with a successful career. In her spare time, she founded a drama group that continues to receive wide acclaim even though Pam considers it just a hobby. Yet for years, Pam has chosen to focus on what she lacks, what needs to be improved, and how inferior she is to others.

While the past is important, we need the promise of the present to bring us forward. Before Pam can begin to explore the power themes in her life, she has to find a way to reconcile the past, the sibling rivalries, the vestige of anger and hurt of feeling less valued as a second-born, and the ways that she has incorporated those themes into her adult life. Only by clearing the air can Pam really discover what is important to her, and where her power lies.

Soo Lee found her legitimacy and her worth as the matriarch of the family. She has given so much of herself to her family and is still the mother who coddles her children, even as they are approaching thirty. She's grown accustomed to her role. Her iron-fist rule of the household has pushed her children and her husband to fulfill her own ambitions and has created such dependencies in her children that they do not yet know how to assume responsibility in their lives. While she assumes the role of the silent wife in public, Soo Lee is very different behind closed doors, telling everyone what to do and how to do it. She is frightened when she thinks of the prospect of her son's and daughter's independence. If they do not need her anymore, then what will she do? She has learned how to use her mother power to manipulate emotionally. Over the years, Soo Lee has derived a sense of worth that is vicarious, avoiding an examination of her own capabilities to achieve a sense of power herself.

To clear the path means having the confidence to look inward and not outward for a sense of value and purpose. It means taking back the discretion we have given others, our family and friends, to assess us and plug us into their needs. While there may be good reasons to fulfill our roles as family members, finding our power means stepping outside of the roles that give us, and those around us, comfort.

Exercise: What Is Power to You?

"You have to stand for something or you'll fall for anything," one of my mentors once wrote. "If you don't know what your position is, if you don't know where to draw your personal line between right and wrong, you'll never see yourself for what you truly are. You'll never have the confidence or drive to do what you have to do to make a difference." Without a sense of what we stand for, the process of power is impossible.

On a sheet of paper, write down a list of situations that made you feel powerful. Since we want to define power that emanates from within, try to turn each "outer-defined" notion you've listed into an "inner-defined" one. Try to avoid pinning your powerful moments onto other people, such as family members. For instance, try to stay away from moments of worth that are defined by your boyfriend's compliments or flowers from your husband, or definitions of success that are derived from your children's success. This list is for *you*.

Add to the list the situations that, if they happened, would make you feel personal success. For instance, if you feel that success is "making lots of money so that I never have to work again," write it down. Next to it, reword the idea in terms of the personal satisfaction it implies to you. What does having money actually represent to you? In this case, it might mean "being more in control of my time" or "doing only what I truly want to do." If there are negatively worded notions on your list, try to make them positive. For instance, if you wrote that success is "not having to answer to anyone," try thinking about what this really means and cast it in the affirmative. It could mean, for example, "determining my own agendas" or "being responsible for my own decisions and my own future."

Think hard about the items on your list. Next to each item, strip away the details, the actual happening, and write what the situation really represented.

Some responses from women I interviewed follow:

Power and Success List:	**What It Really Means:**
I got a major client for my company.	I got a tangible result that proved my work was good.

I graduated college at thirty.	I persisted.
I spoke up to my boss.	I knew when my boundary was crossed and acted.
I left work early, with a full desk.	I decided that some times are for me.
I participated in a rally.	I was part of something bigger than myself.
I got a fan letter.	I affected another person's life.
I have respect from peers.	I am acknowledged for my efforts.
I am in good health.	I take care of myself.
I choose how to spend my time.	I put myself first.
I'm still standing at the end of the day.	I survived.

How different is your list from the examples here? By writing your list down, do your value system and your notions of power become any clearer? Does it become more evident that power is ultimately our ability to determine our futures, whether it be in the everyday or in the long term?

Understanding Two Types of Power

Starhawk, the peace activist and leader in the women's spirituality movement, distinguishes different types of power in her book *Truth or Dare*. She refers to the first type of power as "power-over," meaning domination and control. It is the conventional kind of power that is found in traditional hierarchies, governments, large corporations, and older patriarchal societies. "Power-over" has its source in war and the concept of win-lose competitions. "Power-from-within" is what she defines as a more personal and spiritual power, pertaining to the social power or influence that exists among equals. "Power-from-within" is based on the inherent value in each of us, removed from various signals that represent us to others. "Power-from-within" recognizes that groups are strong and balanced only when each of their members is strong and balanced.

This latter form of power has special significance for Asian American women. "Power-from-within" frees us from the weight of outside expectations, downward pressure, and confining stereotypes. Released, we are free to act genuinely.

Finding the Root of Your Power

Go back in time using the notion of inherent worth. Think back to the moments when you first felt self-determining. Then think of more recent moments when you felt in control. Was it that last promotion or raise you received? Was it the last time you were praised for a job well done? Was it when you were asked for advice or received an unexpected compliment? Was it when you sent a letter to your congressperson? When you spent a wadful of cash? When you organized a conference?

Power can find itself in small gestures, as Mei demonstrates in her story:

> I bought a car, and when I came home, I realized that they had overcharged me. What was on my receipt was not what I agreed to. The salesman explained a financing plan and told me the wrong terms. I didn't want to go back and complain, but I decided I had to stick up for myself

because they cheated me. I went back and asked to see the manager, and they told me to go home. I sat down and said I wouldn't leave until I spoke to the manager. They thought I was a crazy Chinese lady. Then I told them that I had done my homework and called the manufacturer to complain about their dealership's sales tactics. Then they started to listen to me. They heard my accent and thought they could cheat me and make me go away because I wouldn't know any better. I was so happy when I proved they were wrong.

It is important to acknowledge and remember the way you feel when triumphant moments like these occur. By doing so, we can change our patterns of behavior gradually so that instances of self-affirmation and self-determined victory become more frequent.

Part II

OURSELVES

WITH

OTHERS

Lesson Five

SHE TAKES BACK DESIRE

You Chinese girls have such beautiful skin!

Oh, no, I think to myself. Not another Suzy chingchong remark. I can't take it anymore. I know that the woman at the cosmetics counter was just trying to be nice, but she's looking at me as though she wants to know where I bought my Pearl Cream.

When we talk about beauty and desires, what do we think about? Personally, when I think about what makes a woman attractive, I imagine the confidence in her stride, the courage of her personal style, and all the outward signs that tell the world that she's right where she should be, all the time. A beautifully powerful woman is one that causes concern.

How do we talk about physical beauty and seduction in ways that are self-affirming? And when do you feel alluring?

To answer questions like these, let's begin to understand the role of aesthetic and desire in our lives.

I
t began with the dotted line of a felt-tip around her eyes.
Then he put up a little blue tent, blinders, so that all she
could see were his delicate, fast hands.

"Hold still. Hold very still."

Betty sat in Dr. Yoon's surgery chair. She didn't dare move,
as he cut above her eye. Casual, like a filling. In fact, Dr.
Yoon was humming. An hour and a half is all it took, and
she was conscious for the entire operation.

*"You're so brave. Most patients want the general anesthesia.
Knock themselves out, you know?"*

"I'm a nurse. I'm used to these things."

*"It's better that you chose the local. If you're awake you can
work with me and we'll have better control of the outcome."*

He had injected with short spurts, like a dentist injects
Novocain, first around her eyes, then around her temples, then
near her cheekbones. Almost twenty times (with nothing else
to do, she counted) with a twenty-eight-gauge needle.

She could feel the liquid shoot under her skin, puffing it
up slightly as her face became numb. Then came the smell of
burning flesh as he followed the dotted line with a laser-
tipped pen, excising a flap of skin, called an epicanthic fold,
and pulling it away with a tiny scissors. She heard the tear-
ing. Now dangling in his tweezer was what looked like a

117

small specimen of fatty chicken skin. Dr. Yoon flicked it. Not much blood. He threaded a needle and sewed up the open gaps across the muscle.

"Close the right eye for a second?" He checked that his stitches were not too tight. He didn't want her to have that "perma-surprise" look. Some lid jobs did, unfortunately, turn out that way. As he finished up, Dr. Yoon snipped some skin from each side of Betty's nose and stitched that, too (*"Too much fat there,"* he said to her). He also snipped a bit under her eyes to tighten up the bags. He would throw in those procedures at no extra charge. Even though Dr. Yoon was Korean, he knew that his Chinese patients always went away happier when they were given a bargain.

It took four weeks for the black-and-blue to turn to yellow and then to fade, and another six months for the swelling around her eyes to settle completely. During that time, I looked at Betty's swollen face with its cartoon X-mark stitches around the top and bottom of her eyes and nose, shiny from Bacitracin antibiotic ointment. She was happier and felt better about herself, but was it worth all this? I wanted to know. "Getting hard to see, the skin was drooping over my eyes," she said, using age and earth's relentless gravitational pull as her reason for getting a new pair of eyelids.

BODY ALTERATION

Betty had done her calculations. With five thousand dollars saved consciously and specifically for this project, she bought herself what thousands of Asian women buy themselves each year. Wider eyes and well-defined lids where they had never existed before. Eye-lifts are simple snip-and-tuck operations, minor surgery, like a root canal. They are the most frequently occurring plastic surgery procedure among Asian women in America (nose buildups, where a sliver of ear cartilage or bone or plastic is adhered to the bridge of the nose to make it more prominent, are second). Operations like this represent a trend among Asian women around the world, from Brazil, where the operation costs in the neighborhood of five hundred dollars, to China, where it costs an average of eleven dollars, the equivalent of an entire month's salary for an average factory worker. Eye-lifts are so accepted among Asian women in cultural hubs like Los Angeles that it is not uncommon for women who have had them to let friends know proudly where they got theirs done, for how much, and by whom.

In 1990 the American Society of Plastic and Reconstructive Surgery reported that over thirty-nine thousand reconstructive procedures were performed on Asians, making us more likely than any other nonwhite ethnic group to undergo the knife. The figure could be considerably higher if one includes the procedures performed on Asian American women while they travel abroad in Asia ("Better and cheaper," one friend told me) and the procedures performed by American doctors who are not plastic surgeons. It is so common for Asian women to undergo face-altering surgery that many Asian fortune-tellers now ask for baby pictures as they matchmake and foretell futures.

The procedures are more risky and complicated than beauty magazines and friends' accounts let on. Infections can occur. Badly performed procedures can result in permanent scars around the delicate eye and nose area. Jawline-contouring operations, which sand down the jawline to create a more oval-shaped face, can drastically weaken a jaw, making it difficult for many women to chew food. And like any invasive surgery, the months that follow can be uncomfortable and chock-full of antibiotics, as the body attempts to heal.

I tell women about this darker side of body alteration, thinking that it might make them step back and objectively examine the extent to which many Asian American women have gone to adhere to ideal images. First I might start with the cold, clinical details. However, as I describe the macabre procedures, I notice my game plan often backfires. Some of them are making mental notes, registering the information and gauging for themselves whether they could bear the discomfort. They ask how much it costs. After grimacing at the horror stories of body alteration, many of them will admit thinking about it from time to time, imagining which procedures they would have done to their own faces and bodies if they actually went through an operation of their own—if they had the money, the time, and the nerve. Some of them have already thought through the issue, expressing their willingness to have some kind of cosmetic alteration at some point in their lives. Often they will qualify their remarks, though, with phrases like "when I get older, of course, when I start to sag anyway." They feel it's acceptable that women in general can alter their bodies to hold back the effects of time, but apparently aren't ready to admit that altering one's body for racialized reasons is equally acceptable. It might explain Betty's nonchalance, having undergone her own cosmetic procedures at the age of sixty-three.

It isn't surprising that Asian women are flocking to procedures as drastic but attainable as cosmetic alteration, which Naomi Wolf described as "a reasonable reaction to physical discrimination," in her book *The Beauty Myth*. Subtle assaults yield subtle, often internalized reactions. While not all of us would agree that we experience apparent or obvious discrimination, many of us clearly recall the halfway funny remarks or the comments of friends that we learned to toss off lightly, but which lingered with us for years. Listening to many women who were honest enough to share their pasts, I learned that the impact of those comments has lasted longer and been planted deeper than many of us care to admit. Twenty-year-old Min Hui, a Korean American adoptee, recalls her own experiences. Adopted when she was a baby by a Christian family in Tennessee, Min Hui lived on army bases throughout her childhood. "I hadn't ever thought of myself as anything but American, until kids started making fun of my eyes. 'Why can't you open your eyes?' they'd ask me. 'Do you see things smaller?'" Angela can remember boys chasing her, chanting "flat face, flat face," which caused her to dread school recess, when kids were set free to wreak havoc on each other. Julie remembers being told at sixteen by the boys in school that she "had no butt." In Valley Forge, Pennsylvania, Mei tells me that because her hair lies flatter than her coworkers' and friends', she perms it tightly for height and uses a can of hair spray every three weeks to keep it puffy, creating what my friends refer to as "Chinese suburban mom hair."

Body image issues and general dissatisfaction with one's appearance are a serious identity issue for women in America across race lines. In a 1995 study by Melpomene Institute and *Shape* magazine, eighty-five percent of the women respondents said they were unhappy with their appearance. With non-Asian women, however, body image issues are linked most often with concerns about weight and weight control, and most studies and literature on body image are discussed in the context of eating disorders. Asian American women, with the exception of those from the Pacific Islands, are on the average smaller and thinner than the "average American woman" and do not share "weight" as the predominant body image issue. For us the more prevalent issues seem to involve the facial features that make us indelibly and patently "Asian," and therefore different— what sets us most uncomfortably apart from our concept of an American "norm" and links us directly to what is foreign and exotic, and all that this implies.

STUCK IN THE MIRROR

Why the obsession with our physical traits? Some claim that it can be traced to an Asian American experience rooted in what playwright David Henry Hwang once referred to as the Tyranny of Appearances. The definition of us as a group, whether we like it or not, bonds us more by our faces than by any particular shared set of perspectives. We are defined, *and perhaps even define ourselves,* more by physical appearance than by any single set of historical experiences or political agendas. Without an accessible sense of cultural pride, we have become fixated on the only apparent characteristic that labels us as otherly. Our solution up till now has been to obliterate the differences either through attempts at assimilation or, more extremely, by cosmetic alteration, rather than to develop a framework for appreciating physical differences, so that the onus of change is societal rather than individual.

Research suggests that African American culture, with a definition of beauty that is more flexible than the mainstream, instills a more positive body image among African American women. The effects of Asian culture on body image are very different. Anecdotal evidence suggests that, when it comes to physical appearance, Asian women are quite critical of themselves. A study in 1995 found that fifty percent of Asian American women said that how they look compared to others influenced how they felt about their bodies, which was close to the fifty-one percent response rate of white women. Only thirty percent of Hispanic and forty percent of African American women felt similarly, revealing how heavily and disproportionately Asian American women rely on others to influence their self-esteem and view their bodies. Unlike black and, to a certain extent, Latina women, Asian American women do not have a strong sense of culteral identity that might give them a firmer inner sense of their own beauty and a self-respect that goes beyond appearances. Perhaps Asian American responses mimic the responses of white women not because they share a similar sense of body image, but because they have not developed an alternative way to view themselves.

We need to define for ourselves what attractiveness means. Without having given thought to what we each believe to be personally desirable, we have in essence given that privilege to others, allowing others to do the defining for us.

COMPARATIVE THINKING

"People's attitudes [toward me] inevitably fall into one or two categories," wrote one South Asian woman. "I'm either seen as completely asexual, because South Asians don't fit the Western world [notion] of what 'sexiness' is, or I'm viewed as this interesting, exotic woman." Both attitudes are a dismissal of her individuality. In fact, our struggle for individuality seems to be at the heart of the body image question.

Perhaps we have come to have more respect for our body parts that contradict the stereotypes and less for those that conform. Every ethnic group must deal with stereotypes, but the Asian stereotype is an especially physical one. "We're not just tall," writes journalist Joanne Chen, "we're tall *for an Asian*. We're not just full-figured Asian women, we're full figured *for an Asian*. And even as we defy the stereotype of the petite, boyish-figured Asian woman, we silently reinforce its validity by measuring our bodies against it."

We seem to share a subtle horror in being mistaken for another Asian woman, which we may perceive as an affirmation of our interchangeability. Most of us who have had those experiences have realized that in sticking close to the likes of our own, we may suffer the consequence of anonymity. "My professor gets us mixed up, especially when we sit next to each other," Kari from Kentucky says. Indeed, he did it again, in front of me, as he greeted her by her friend Susan's name. Leslie, an attorney at a large New York law firm, reluctantly admits that she feels it is difficult to work too closely with one of her Asian female peers. "The partners already get us mixed up when we are not working together. They confuse me with the secretaries already, and I'm still trying to figure out how I can distinguish myself from them. I don't want to complicate my deals with clients and attorneys having to put in energy to tell us apart."

Feeling that most non-Asians do feel that "all Asians look alike," whether they care to admit it or not, we have our antennae up. Many of us have even admitted that we have learned to anticipate the discomfort of a non-Asian when he or she is called upon to introduce a group of Asians, for instance, at a cocktail party. "I have learned how to diffuse the tension in those situations," Eleanor says. "I figure they'll get it wrong anyway, so I introduce myself for them before things get embarrassing, just to be on the safe side." Very few women surveyed felt that the inability to distinguish one Asian face from another could be considered racist behavior. "You just learn how to cope with it, that's all," says one Japanese American friend.

It is ironic that Asian American women who have such strong feelings about their individuality also admit that they often compare themselves to others. Even as we begin to explore exactly what our sense of individuality means, we often can't help comparing ourselves to visual markers or stereotypes. Questions like "Am I thinner than she is?" "Is *that* what I look like?" are common among many young women caught in the spiral of outer-directed self-concepts. "I find that I'm always using some outside measurement to figure out how I look," Lisa, a Japanese American graduate student told me. In finding our personal styles, many of us fall back on comparisons that fulfill archetypes. "I look like Connie Chung" was all I could think when I dressed in business suits and my hair was bobbed. When I dressed for a night out, I sometimes looked at myself in my little black dress and started to think that I looked a little *too* Suzie Wongish, maybe my lipstick was too red, or my dress was too short. Looking for a way to define our own style, yet driven by comparison, we create our well of archetypes that keep our self-image outer-directed:

—You're so tan, you look like a Chinese farm girl.
—You're dressing like a preppie suburban girl.
—What are you, a homegirl?
—You look like a call girl in that photograph.

YOU ARE SO BEAUTIFUL TO ME

Neowhite is formulated to whiten skin without the known harmful side effects of lesser brands. . . . There are two Neowhite creams—Fairness Protection Cream formulated with effective sunscreen (SPF 15) and moisturizers to keep skin fair and soft and Moisturizing Pearl Cream which is a combination of moisturizer and light tint that provides the skin with moisture and a natural, even skin tone.

—Advertisement for Avon's Neowhite Fairness Cream

Women in Thailand are getting more breast enhancements than ever and in India, where a slight bit of fat over the edge of a sari had once been considered womanly and desirable, thinness is now the accepted standard of beauty. Images of Western beauty now permeate the media globally, with *Baywatch* being one of the biggest money-making TV series worldwide. According to a survey conducted by an Asian-based lingerie company, Beijing women, on average the tallest of those surveyed, wanted to be even taller; Taipei women sought more of an hourglass figure; Hong Kong and Singaporean women wanted to boost their busts; and Bangkok women wanted rounder hips. And with light-skinned models with Eurasian features dominating present-day advertisements—even in Asian countries like Malaysia and Indonesia, where women are generally darker skinned—everyone wants to be lighter.

"My mother tells me that when they brought me home from the hospital when I was born, my grandmother took one look at me and covered my face with the shadow of her scarf. She didn't want me to get darker than I already was. It was important for her to have a fair-skinned granddaughter," thirty-year-old Preeti, who hails from New Delhi, told me. "I was never allowed to stay out in the sun too long," she adds.

Makeup companies in Asia capitalize on deep-seated Light Skin Worship, marketing skin-bleaching products like UV White and Neowhite and, in India, a cream called Vicco Turmeric, which uses the common spice as its softening and bleaching base. These creams, marketed in Asia, use advertising techniques similar to UV White, which shows a Caucasian woman basking in a halo of light, looking upward, saintly and pure. Although sold only in Asia, UV White is also coveted by Asian women in America. A number of Asian American women tell me that they put in standing orders for UV White with friends and relatives whenever one of them makes a trip to the Far East. Whiteness also comes at a price, reiterating the connection between privilege and complexion. An eight-ounce jar of Shiseido's UV White is forty dollars, equal to one month's wages for an average Thai factory worker.

But while European beauty is still the accepted standard, this does not necessarily imply that the Asian aesthetic goes unappreciated. Asian women find themselves in the peculiar position of having "flavor of the month" status, especially in the media and fashion world. Since the late eighties in Hollywood, a recent California magazine reported, an attractive Asian woman is the preferred trophy date when attending a Hollywood premiere. And in metropolitan centers such as Los Angeles and New York, an Asian woman hanging on to a man's arm, referred to as "arm candy" is often considered an accessory to a proper artistic lifestyle, just as a Mercedes indicates wealth or a tattoo indicates alternative rebellion. Deemed "ornamentals," as a play on the word "Orientals," we have seen over the past few years a new appreciation for the Asian woman's aesthetic. Notions of Asian ultrafemininity and exotic beauty in the mainstream mind can carry such easy fringe benefits that many of us have mixed feelings when it comes to discussing them. Not all of us, for instance, agree that the current trend of "Asian fetish" is bad. In fact, for some of us, the new visibility of Asian women, even though stereotyped, can actually be liberating. As Melissa de la Cruz wrote in a 1997 *New York Press* article:

As for the term Asian fetish itself: I find something deliciously wicked and liberating about it. It reeks of peril and psychosexual obsession, conjuring a milieu of graceful, elegant Suzy Wongs in cheongsam dresses (body-hugging, with mandarin collars and thigh-high slits), handguns tucked in garter belts; of sly, exotic counterparts to the Pamela Andersons and Cindy Crawfords of popular fascination. Charlie Chan's Angels. In one breath it banishes the image of the asexual, four-eyed, Asian superbrain forever, replacing it with a certain prurient attractiveness reserved only for femmes fatales.

Asian fetish? Where do I sign on?

BE A MODEL, OR JUST LOOK LIKE ONE

When Andrea left for college, she finally had the space to emerge from an oppressed younger sister into a beautiful woman. In her sophomore year she met with a representative from a modeling agency who saw her five-foot-nine height and unusually chiseled bone structure and offered her a modeling contract. All of a sudden, those gangly legs that used to be the butt of jokes now earned her the reputation of being "leggy for an Asian." For a couple of years, Andrea appeared in local magazines, ads for department stores, and she walked a runway for local fashion shows. "But I found it strange that they liked to dress me up in exotic outfits," she said. Among her tear sheets is a shot of her with chopsticks in her hair, leaning against an elegant staircase, wearing powder white makeup and black liquid eyeliner that pulls her eyes long and narrow to the sides of her head, bedecked in a kimono. At first she didn't mind. It was interesting to see herself in a costume she would never wear in real life. But she tired of it quickly. "It was too hard to explain to the agency why I wasn't happy doing those types of jobs. I actually didn't understand why I was so bothered by it myself, since I never analyzed the situation in any serious way. I just knew that it felt wrong. Obviously they wanted some faraway, exotic image, which was fine if it was only some of the time." A year later, Andrea decided that modeling was not her fare after all. Instead, she earned her spending money the way many of the rest of her colllege friends did, by volunteering at a local lab as a product tester. She'd go home during spring break with patches soaked with shampoo on her arms, one that even gave her a rash that wouldn't go away for months. But for Andrea, it was preferable to posing in geisha garb. "It was better than posing for a camera in outfits that made me feel like a dress-up doll."

Driven by the "Asian look" trend, the prospects for Asian models have skyrocketed since the early nineties. According to a 1993 report released by the New York Department of Consumer Affairs, only two to three percent of the advertisements appearing in major fashion magazines such as *Vogue, Mademoiselle,* and *Seventeen* featured non-Caucasian models. Only ten Asian American women were represented by any of the top New York modeling agencies, such as Ford, Wilhelmina, and Now Model Management. In 1993, there were still no Asian men represented in those agencies. Yet in just a few short years, the situation has changed dramatically, so that Asian Americans can see themselves regularly depicted in real-life situations. Insurance companies now show us as parents concerned about our children's futures. We see ourselves eating pizza at Pizza Hut and as members of rock bands, as doctors, lawyers, and people whose opinions are televised on the local news. Suddenly, there are choices beyond the rarified romantic images of faraway places. In 1996, a woman named Zhi Ling became the first Asian cover model for Revlon. Others, like closely cropped supermodel Jenny Shimizu, the strong-boned Kevin Louie, and exotic Irina Pantaeva have become staples on the

European and American runways, and others like them have become recognizable faces in the ads of Benetton, Calvin Klein, and Tommy Hilfiger.

Some may herald the appearance of Asian faces as a sign that the multiculture has indeed taken a foothold and that, in fact, we are beginning to breach our aesthetic divides. While this may be true, the newly welcomed Asian aesthetic in today's media may have less to do with an acceptance of different standards of beauty or deeper cultural exchange than with changing consumer demographics. Suddenly Asian American consumer dollars count. Demographic reports showing an exploding Asian American consumer audience (it is projected that the Asian American population will reach twenty million by the year 2020) are the ultimate factor in rolling out the red carpet, finally allowing Asian American men and women to finally see themselves in advertising, magazines, and the television news. And when media kits for Asian audiences pitch the dispensable income, education, and status-driven psychographic of this "fastest growing ethnic niche into the year 2000," increasing by 412.5 percent from 1992 to 2050, we understand that what drives Madison Avenue is no less complicated than the bottom line.

It wasn't a trend that was lost on us when we started presenting *A. Magazine* to advertisers, and we became adept at explaining to them the advantages of "microniching," a marketing strategy that divides large consumer markets into more tailored specialty markets. Microniching allows general messages to be delivered more effectively by using specific language, themes, and images that appeal to smaller target groups. In the case of *A. Magazine* we hoped that our Asian American subscribers would respond well to advertisers who appeared in our publication, because it would show that they supported our developing sense of identity.

Microniching, we felt, was a small step in heralding the acceptance of difference, or at least the willingness to treat our spending dollars seriously. We have joined the ranks of the avid American consumer, and our willingness to spend is buying us a place on the billboard of America and at least a temporary legitimacy. Somehow with that newfound visibility, we exist as we have never existed before.

ASIAN WOMEN = SEX

According to psychologist Judy Slater, body image affects the way we behave sexually and the way we interact in our personal relationships. For Asian American women, our unique issues of our body image intersect directly with the complicated ways in which we view our sexuality.

As I walked across a street in Bangkok ten years ago, I realized that I had forgotten my watch. I knew that I would be late, with Bangkok traffic crawling along even more sluggishly than New York City's rush-hour traffic on a Friday afternoon. I needed to know the time. Spotting a fellow business traveler, a Caucasian man dressed in a suit, and thinking that he'd be more apt to speak English than any of the Thai vendors I passed, I approached him, asking him what time it was. As I came nearer, he started to veer away from me.

"Not right now, miss," he said.

I looked at him confused, since I hadn't said anything to him yet. So I tried to ask him again for the time.

"I said no," he said, this time annoyed at my intrusion, as he walked away.

It took a few minutes, but I finally realized that this man had seen me as a Thai prostitute, one of the many that must approach men like him daily. My American accent wouldn't set me apart. He walked away without stopping, feeling hassled by the nuisance. I began to feel uncomfortable, wanting to wipe off my tanned face whatever it was that could have made his reaction possible. It was then that I realized the denominator of face and its implication that I shared with every Asian-looking woman in Bangkok. I began to notice how Asian women there would casually eye each other, scrutinizing for telltale signs of who and what we were. "Is she or isn't she?" we think to ourselves. European couples remained silent in the elevators as my husband and I rode the lift with them, thinking perhaps that they were witnessing a business deal in action.

It happened again in Bombay, where Indian men would say, "Nepali girl! Nepali girl!" slowing their trucks alongside my sister and me in the evenings, thinking that we were two of the thousands of young women that are either abducted or sold across the Nepali border to cater to Indian men. And in Nairobi, vacationing men of all nationalities and ages would approach and proposition, assuming again that a young Asian woman, sitting by herself at a café, must be announcing her sexual services for hire. As I got closer to Europe, men became more aggressive, fascinated more by exoticism. *I've never slept with an Asian woman,* they'd say to me in French and Italian accents, assuming I might be intrigued by the idea of becoming part of their sexual round-the-world checklist.

This is not a new story. Women face these advances regardless of race, whether on the streets of Rome, New Delhi, Los Angeles, or New York. Yet the issue of harassment, presumption, and sexuality for Asian women is unique. While hypersexualized, commodifying images exist for all women, and especially women of color, the image of the Asian woman combines with this the notion of ultrapassivity. Sexuality for an Asian woman is so tightly wound up in issues of power and global economic order that it is virtually impossible to address the specter of an Asian woman's sexuality without examining the subtle roles of governments and enterprise in perpetuating this situation, especially in developing countries.

Following the three wars that have taken place on Asian soil over the last fifty years, a legacy of prostitution that began in the servicing of American and European soldiers has since flourished into a sex tourism industry that has grown into a major source of foreign exchange that rivals the gross national product of many developing nations. According to Marina Budhos in her *Ms. Magazine* article, "Putting the Heat on Sex Tourism," the worldwide sex tourism industry caters to the global client—Japanese, European, Scandinavian, and American men who find their way to Thailand, Korea, and the Philippines and now to India, Sri Lanka, Vietnam, and Cambodia, where the sex industry is rapidly expanding. "Exact numbers on how many girls and women work in the sex industry and the amount of money it generates are hard to pin down, since it remains an underground economy. But in 1993 there were an estimated two million prostitutes in Thailand, one to one and a half million in Korea, and between three hundred thousand and five hundred thousand in the Philippines." One researcher estimates that the sex trade in Thailand earns four to five times more than the agricultural industry does.

Companies such as Big Apple Oriental Tours, Bushwhackers, and Philippine Adventure Tours offer the spectrum of sexual services, from "the intimate company of young and exotic Oriental women" to "blow job specialists." Sex tour packages offer cheap entertainment, selling the notion that Asian women are docile, adoring, and willing to do anything for a green card. One brochure reads, "The ladies working the bars are there for one reason and one reason only, to find a husband, preferably an American. It is their ultimate American dream."

Local economies have also been built on Asian female sexuality, feeding the syndicates that create the prostitution houses, the local officials and police who turn a blind eye to their practices, the brothel and bar owners, and the military. There are also all the ancillary businesses that benefit from sex tourism. Along every sex strip in Patphong, the notorious red-light district in Bangkok that has become a disturbing tourist attraction where even suburban Western tour groups come to gawk, there are now bars and restaurants, tailor shops, video parlors, and electronics stores.

On the domestic front, it is estimated that two to three thousand men each year find wives through mail-order catalogs from companies such as Pacific Romance and Cherry Blossoms. And perhaps because of the situations that feed into the sexual stereotypes, there has grown a great demand for Asian women in the three-billion-dollar-a-year adult video industry that has its epicenter in California's San Fernando Valley. Eight of 1994's twenty most-rented adult videos featured or included Asian actresses.

Even the Internet reminds us that the merging of sexuality and commerce is a key theme for Asian women. Renee, who worked with a New York businesswomen's support group called Asian Women in Business, combed the Internet one day looking for groups similar to hers, which assists Asian women in their entrepreneurial pursuits. She keyed in the words, "Asian," "women," and "business," thinking that her search would produce networking possibilities. Instead her search generated a list of mail-order bride companies.

Asian sexuality has not been limited to the tawdry. The eroticism of Asian women has been elevated to the level of high art as well. Internationally acclaimed fine art photographer Andre Serrano, who is known for his irreverence for icons, nevertheless included in his exhibition entitled "A History of Sex," a geisha-faced Asian woman ravaged and bound in ropes, looking pitifully away from the camera against a backdrop of bamboo. The best-seller *Memoirs of a Geisha* captivated the American public with the same formula of submission. The "cage" district on Bombay's infamous Falkland Road, where women are kept behind iron bars until they pay off their indenture through prostitution, is a source of many a film documentary and doctoral dissertation. It seems that the image of an Asian woman's subservience remains firmly embedded, even within the progressive, artistic, and intellectual mind.

"Why is it necessary for me to know this?" asks Diane, who feels that the experiences of Asian women involved in the sex industry have nothing to do with her existence as a college student at Wellesley. "I grew up in America, was raised in Illinois, and all I want to do is graduate and become a medical researcher in a few years. I might visit the Far East a couple of times in my life, and I certainly feel badly for the unfortunate women there, but their situation is not mine."

Regardless of whether Diane chooses to explore those links, they will affect her life, the perception of her as a woman, and as a worker. If she is seen as having little or no power or influence in America, it is in part because those women across the ocean have no power or influence. If she finds herself valued or judged by a degrading comment about her sexuality, it is in part because "those unfortunate women there" are seen as sex-for-hire around the world. If Diane finds that she is undervalued or treated differently on the job from her professional peers, it may be partly due to a widespread notion that Asian female labor "over there" is about high-grade work for low-grade wages, and that her services are easily exploitable. Unless Diane sees the global links and begins to process their impact on her personal experience, she will continue to have to struggle with the burden of proving that she is "not like those other women." To work on our identity as Asian American women, we must search deeply and broadly for an understanding of why it is that we are perceived in certain ways. The stereotyped perception of us does not stop at national borders. The way we are perceived has its roots in history that came long before us, and its themes about power have no boundaries.

Without this historical perspective, it is easier to call these stereotypes ridiculous. It is easier to call those who harbor them "ignorant." We divorce ourselves from the image of the prostitute overseas, using class and education and other social walls to separate us from them. Hiroko is aghast and insulted if people ask her whether she met her American husband during World War II. "I am *not* one of those war brides. I was a famous radio personality in Japan. Not like one of *those* women." Others of us might sidestep the issue, asserting that "each of us is an individual," without thinking about the greater connections we may share with women on the other side of the world, with whom we are interchangeable in the eyes of many, regardless of how well we may speak English or how long our families have been in this country.

Sociologist George Kelly once wrote that we can be witness to a tremendous parade of episodes in our lives and yet, if we fail to keep making something out of them, we gain little in the way of experience from having been around when they happened. According to Kelly, it is not what happens around us that makes us "experienced," it is the successive construing and reconstruing of what happens, as it happens, that enriches and informs our lives. It would have been easy for Andrea, for instance, to shrug off her modeling experience as something that proved to be just plain uninteresting. But real experience occurred when she realized a sense of discomfort and explored and articulated it instead of tucking it away. Analysis beyond the event itself allows us to fit everyday instances into patterns that explain larger truths.

"THE TOUCH AND TASTE"

When responding to an *A. Magazine* survey about Asian Americans and sexuality, one Asian American woman contributed this beautifully worded passage:

> When I think of Asian American sexuality, I wish for a body of music, movies, and accessible reading that I can see myself in and be inspired by. Ntozake Shange, in the introduction to the book *Black Erotica*, asks the question I want the answer to about our peoples too: "What are the names—the touch and taste of our bodies? Where do our tongues linger on each other? What is the nature of the language we speak?" We need works to celebrate our love and sexual selves.

Celebrating the sexual and aesthetic self without leaning on preconceived, Westernized notions of what is "beautiful" or "desirable" was difficult, even at *A. Magazine,* a publication that sought to create a pride and self-awareness among young Asian Americans. There, as fashion spreads were designed and models were chosen for its pages, we found ourselves struggling with how to show a beauty and sensuality that was as inclusive as possible without devolving into stereotypes. Should the photographer use models that mimicked what Madison Avenue thought was attractive among Asians? Was it really a good idea if the women models assumed poses that made them look vulnerable, seductive, and passive, as many mainstream models did? If the fashion editor wanted a steamy fashion section, should we adhere to standard formulas of male/female seduction, with all the power politics that it implies? Given the concern that so many of our male readers voiced about being seen as effeminate, should we depict our Asian men in the homoerotic poses that were made popular at the time by Calvin Klein and other fashion giants? How would our decision make our gay readership feel? Positioning a publication that was a maverick voice for Asian Americans carried with it a large responsibility. If we were framing a discussion, the depictions of our community had to match our message of social empowerment, for men as well as women. Representing beauty and sexuality became doubly difficult because we used professional models, who for the most part had the Westernized Asian characteristics, the chiseled cheekbones and high noses, that their advertising and fashion clients were looking for. When we used regular Asian Americans as models, young people who had character if not classic beauty, we would get calls from subscribers complaining that our use of "unattractive"people was insulting to Asian Americans.

How do we find ways to celebrate a beauty and sexuality without falling into confusion or hypocrisy? Healthy attraction begins with a process of reclamation.

RECLAMATION

Can We Talk?

When we are enraged by the images of submissive erotic Asian women, we are angered by the *subjugation* and not by our *sexuality*. One of the ways we can counter the use of our sexuality by others is to demystify it by giving it a voice.

Being able to talk about body image and sensuality more freely among those we can trust is the first step toward reclaiming our sexual power.

Some of the most enlightening discussions among young Asian American women on these subjects have taken place on chat lines and message boards on the Internet, where young women have created Web chats to take back the conversation about their own bodies. They discuss media portrayals that perpetuate stereotypes. They describe their own experiences, as well as their constructive reactions to statements that have made them feel sexually ashamed or disempowered. These women are creating an inspiring international dialogue that has left some people feeling very angry or threatened. Often I've observed that as Asian women begin to congregate around a healthy discussion, a participant will enter the chat room hoping to disrupt the dialogue with racist and sexist epithets, statements about his love for sexy Asian women, and descriptions of his sexual exploits while serving in the army. Powerful discussion will inevitably attract anger and envy. It is a testament to the women who are participating in these Web site discussions that they are often able to chase those voices of hate away.

What Does It Mean to Be Sensual?

Paula, a thirty-two-year-old Thai American woman who has been married for five years describes a view of her own sensuality: "I began to be very uncomfortable with my body. When I began to think about all the issues of being an Asian woman—how we are perceived, for example—I started to get really uncomfortable sexually in my own relationship. Like there was no way to be a sexual Asian woman without feeling like it was somehow bad. I come from a very Catholic family where my mother used to take us to church practically every day, and so I guess I still have the idea that 'sex is bad' in the back of my mind. But now I'm an adult and my marriage is suffering because of my confusion."

It is difficult for many of us to actualize a sexuality and a body comfort that is celebratory and reverential without devolving into stereotype. We often cannot distinguish what is erotic and sensual from what is demeaning and stereotypical. When conversations about healthy sexuality are stifled, we are left thinking about ourselves as either vestal virgins or fallen prostitutes. And yet, Asian history is rife with life-giving and sacred sexuality. A journey across Asia reveals the enormous number of temples and cere-monies dedicated to the celebration of sensual pleasure and fertility by both women and men, from the lingams that surround the Shinto temples from Nara, Japan, to Mandalay in Myanmar (Burma), to the erotic sculptures of Khajraho in central India. In agrarian Japan, sexuality was a primary subject for more than a thousand-year span of its literature and art, and sex represented neither romantic love nor a phallic rite—it was simply a joyful union of two opposing natural forces. Japanese Buddhist artisans and holy men appreciated the eighteenth-century Japanese erotic *shunga* paintings of the artist Utamaro. For Jains, members of an ancient religion that is widely followed in what is now India, sexuality is a celebration that incorpo-rates the concept of spiritual and earthly balance, of the cerebral with the corporeal. In Indian Ayurvedic traditions, a woman's second chakra, or energy point, located near her womb, is an important and grounding energy center, chan-neling sexual, life-giving energy to the entire body.

Intimate relationships based on a sensuality that has its roots in respect and equality require us to ask ourselves some intimate questions. Can you envision a sensuality that is open, respectful, and free of traditional power roles of the aggressor and the subjugated? How do the themes of power and control play out in your physical relationships? Do you ever use physical relationships as a way to establish control or perhaps even to *avoid* intimacy? What do we do to be attractive in the eyes of our partners?

What Is the Core of Your Sensual Attraction?

A few years ago, I witnessed a workshop where a male participant was asked to enter a circle of people. His task was to do whatever he could to get others to join him in dancing in the circle. There was only one rule: he wasn't allowed to talk. On his first attempt, he grabbed a very attractive woman from the circle and started to dance with her. Nobody else budged. Using a pretty woman as "bait" didn't work, although it might have at other points in his life. On the second try, he danced by himself in a constricted, inhibited way. That didn't work either. On his third attempt, he danced by himself again, exasperated at not having succeeded the first two times. His desperation was painful to watch, and again, it didn't work. The workshop leader told him to sit down. She told him that if he hadn't yet figured out his inner sense of attraction, how would anyone else find him attractive? His proximity to a beautiful woman didn't do it. Neither did an insincere dance. Until he could find the honest, confident part of him that was trusting of his own place and worth, the relationships he entered into with women as well as men would continue to have hidden issues and miscommunication.

Do you know how you are attractive when that attractiveness is not linked to seduction or sexuality? What kinds of bait have you used? Can you envision a sensuality that is not sexual? What is it about you that gives energy to others?

Lesson Six

SHE KNOWS *WHY* SHE LOVES

Each of the special people in our lives—partners, lovers, and friends—represents an active choice we have made. And in choosing, we have also forgone alternatives. What makes us "go for" certain relationships at the cost of other, equally viable ones?

Enduring love, meaningful love, is less about the knock between the eyes that romance novels describe, and more about the way we see ourselves placed in our world. Figuring out why we love whom we love—whom we find attractive, whom we spend our lives with—becomes an act of self-discovery, giving us a deeper knowledge of ourselves and, therefore, giving us power.

Whom do you love and why?

When I moved out of my tiny apartment in the Little Italy section of lower Manhattan, I did it in resignation over a failed relationship. It wasn't easy to admit that it was over. I had always been the one to leave a relationship, always the one who dictated its moods and its madnesses. For five years I had lived with Fabrizio, in an old Italian enclave where the shopkeepers still sold fresh cannelloni and prosciutto. Our Sullivan Street block boasted one of the lowest petty crime rates of any in New York City. We all knew we lived in a Cosa Nostra "safe zone." Each summer, the noisy Italian American feast in honor of Saint Anthony—full of its cheesy calzones, fattening zeppoles, and carnival arcades—would leave drunken weekenders collapsed on our front stoop, so that Fabrizio and I would have to step over them to get to our front door.

We usually spent Sunday evenings on Sullivan Street with our seventy-year-old Sicilian landlord, Mrs. Gianni, who would prepare a sumptuous dinner for her four favorite Sicilian tenants and me. At Mrs. Gianni's table, it was an accepted rule that Sicilian dialect, not classic Italian, would be spoken. Those evenings, I now realize, were reserved for familiarity and leisure, where Sicilians could just be Sicilians, without having to either conjugate in English, or act like fast-paced Americans. It was up to me to try to understand, through a combination of their gestures and tones, or zone out of the conversation.

In a roomful of loud Sicilians at the dinner table, it is easy to just sit like a cat, watch and hear without listening. When my energy was high, I would try to catch a phrase here or there, laugh when everybody else laughed, look serious when I sensed that politics was being discussed. But for the most part I kept quiet while eating my pasta. It was second nature to me not to understand. I had lived a lifetime of it. Whether it was Sicilian Italian or my relatives' Cantonese, it didn't make a difference. I had already spent more than twenty years surrendering to the comfort of not knowing or caring what was being said around me.

Mmmm, yes, I agree. Anything you say . . . can you pass the pasta, please?

Most weekday nights Fabrizio and I would spend a few hours at Paolo and Elizabetta's place down the hall, where we'd go through the same routine. Paolo would sit in his La-z-Boy lounger watching *Star Trek* while Elizabetta yelled at him for being such a vegetable as she polished her nails. We were like the Kramdens and the Nortons, the Ricardos and the Mertzes. On evenings when no one wanted to cook dinner, we would always go to the same table at the same restaurant across the street, where the waiters were also Sicilian, making us feel like we were at our own dining room table. We were creatures of habit, not much changed in our routines day to day.

I recount this to a friend, who asks me, "It sounded pretty strange; why did you stay so long? You couldn't even understand them half the time."

"They were all my friends," I tell her. "We were a unit, *la famiglia*. They had rules and history and loyalty, and I was part of them. Fabrizio and I, we were part of *il gruppo.*"

"You mean Fabrizio was part of the group, not you."

"No, I was part of their group, too."

"Even though they didn't speak in a language you could understand? You were Fabrizio's girlfriend; that's why they accepted you. From their actions, it didn't seem to matter whether you were there or not. From the outside it looks to me like you were alone for five years, Phoebe, just kind of hanging on."

I'm wincing at her remark, but she goes on. "Face it, you picked an *old world* crowd. A tight-knit, closed-off group that didn't even allow you to enter their conversations. The real question is, if you truly wanted to belong to a group, why did you pick such an extreme situation?"

Girlfriends are there to tell you the truth, but her remarks still hurt. I was not proud of my behavior during those past five years. Each day I had given so much ground, let so much audacious behavior pass unchecked, that in the end I had only a tiny piece of myself left. Loudmouth, in-your-face, feminist-leaning me had to admit there was something that kept me transfixed by my own erosion, fading to a shadow, losing twenty pounds without even trying. It was hard to admit that my friend was right. Epiphanies that reveal a growing process are usually painful when first perceived.

Having thought about my friend's words, I now know how important it was for me to hear them. They made me understand that I have always looked for a sense of family, always longed for a membership in a group, and always in some ways fallen short of achieving it. The Sicilians for me represented an ideal of affiliation, iron solidity, a team to root for, a center for support and a table reserved, a home base. But that Sicilian group was extreme in its rigidity and exclusivity. The price of membership was forfeiture of all else in my life, my free time, my self-value, and my "frustrated American feminist friends," as Fabrizio liked to call them. Predictable, solid, and narrow, it was a fossil from a fast-dying way of life that centered around the village clan. And I loved it.

When we float, when we have only vague notions of who we are or from where we have come, we search constantly, and at times unreasonably, for things to believe in and to cherish. My grief when Fabrizio and I parted came from something deeper than I had realized. In calling it quits with Fabrizio, and therefore the Sicilians, I was giving up a sense, however false, of home. From then on, I would have no tribe.

I wish I could have talked honestly then about why that relationship didn't work—about the incompatibilities of our values and hopes that were glaringly obvious from the day we met. My optimism and belief in people were never enough to counter his suspicious nature. Fabrizio always preferred to dwell in the past, while my own sights were directed toward the future. I wish I had the courage to admit that cultural differences, while they might have played a part, were not what ultimately sunk us. Instead I leaned on lofty theories about gender inequalities and deeply embedded stereotypes that I accused Fabrizio of harboring, without looking at my own. Only recently did I realize that the lessons of this relationship were less about Fabrizio and me, and more about *why* I loved *whom* I loved. Yet, those lessons would become apparent to me only many years later.

In relationships, interracial or not, nothing is guaranteed. But there are certain constants that can guide us through every *right* relationship we enter into. A sanctified relationship is one in which neither party silences or sacrifices, and each is responsible for expressing his or her strength and vulnerability. Real closeness, I now know, cannot be pursued or demanded. Love is the passion of two people clarifying their beliefs and values through each other.

THEMES IN OUR RELATIONSHIPS

The people to whom we are attracted often reveal larger life themes. If we feel power and self-determination, it is echoed at work, in relationships, and with family. We can confidently say that we are happy in our jobs, satisfied with our accomplishments, and excited with our partners when they bring out our strengths as opposed to prey on our weaknesses. We can feel whole and content even at times when we find ourselves without an intimate partner in our lives. The type and quality of relationships we choose do not substitute for our own lack or provide for our unmet needs. Each relationship we enter—with lovers, friends, business partners, and work—strengthens our sense of self-respect and buttresses our value system. When we feel powerful, we are also able to say no and have the strength to avoid those who are destructive or limiting to us.

If, on the other hand, we feel powerless, the relationships we pursue often end up echoing our own powerlessness. Our choices may require us to change our demeanor, our tone, and our politics at each shift in the wind. When we feel powerless, we choose our partners and our friends, not because they strengthen us, but because they represent the power and confidence that we crave but do not possess ourselves. Our choices become defined by outer expectations and signify, not what we have determined to be of worth but what other people approve of or accept. In those instances, we may gravitate to status, to dollar figures, to impressive titles, to men and women who have superficial symbols of worth and accomplishment. Themes of power, or lack of it, provide the drumbeat for every aspect in our lives.

If our relationships mirror the themes we live by, then what our partners symbolize to us takes on great importance. If we see them as our caretakers, we might ask ourselves if or why we chose to relinquish responsibility for ourselves. If we do not receive enough attention from them, perhaps we might examine our need for the attention in the first place. If we see our partners as helpless, we might explore how our acts of rescue have given us control. How can we begin to understand that the strengths and weaknesses we see in our partners are a mirror of our own strengths and weaknesses? These are questions for long and deep introspection, and their answers are never quickly apparent. Getting to the point where we can ask them is a process in itself, but first we might have to examine a few more patent issues about the interplay of family expectation, race, and class status. For, while ultimate love might lie in what's *beneath* the surface, what's *on* the surface can sometimes count for even more.

ONE OF YOUR OWN KIND, STICK TO YOUR OWN KIND

All my grandmother wants to hear is that I will marry a Korean man. So when I called her in Los Angeles to tell her I was getting married, all she asked me was: "Is he Korean?" Thank God he was, so I said yes. "That's good," she said, and that was that. No questions about his family background, his age, or even the wedding date. For my grandmother, the simple fact that my future husband would be Korean was all she needed to know.

—Julie, survey respondent

We know the secret wishes of our parents about whom we ought to be with, though they might ultimately grow to accept any choice we make. *"Stick with your own kind,"* they tell us. *"Better for the kids. Better for your sanity. You'll eat better food, and we will be able to spend time with his parents."* Even adopted Asian daughters whose parents are non-Asian often tell me that their mothers encourage them to date Asian men. Several women who prefer relationships with men of their own ethnicity say that such advice is sound. "You know what you're dealing with, same deck of cards, less confusion," as one friend put it.

This is what might have happened. Had I married a nice Chinese boy, like the dentist my mother tried to set me up with when I was twenty-two, she would first have checked out his parents to see if they were savory sorts. If they passed the test, and if we got along, our wedding banquet would have been a ten-course meal in Chinatown. We would have driven away in a car that had a Barbie and Ken doll stuck to the hood to usher us into a prosperous future. As a souvenir of the event, we would have had a red silk cloth embroidered with dragons and the Chinese character for double happiness, which would hold the good wishes of each person who attended. Life would have continued swimmingly, as we would have been surrounded in the bliss that is supposed to be the right of all pure Chinese couples.

If my Parsi Indian husband, Zubin, had married a Parsi Indian girl, he would have continued a tradition that had never been broken through all the generations of his Bombay-based, Parsi family. He would have been married by a Parsi priest who would have chanted the wedding rites in the ancient language of Avestan, sprinkled rose water on Zubin and his bride, and tied their hands seven times with string to hammer home the symbolism of their eternal bond.

Instead, we married each other—a Chinese American bride and an Indian British groom—and were sent reeling into what had to be the most varied and confusing set of wedding receptions ever to befall, or grace, a couple. We had that ten-course Chinese banquet in New York's Chinatown to show my father's family that I really did find a husband, and a handsome one at that. At our reception in India, one of the Taj's glittery and extravagant events of the wedding season that year, I wore a gold sari and met all the new Bombay friends and relations who were eager to meet the "Chinese wife." In London, Zubin's dad feted us with a champagne reception attended by his Oxford law chums and a host of writers and creative types. The reception we had for ourselves, in the forest on the east end of Long Island, included the Parsi priest, the rites chanted in Avestan, the seven-times hand-tying, Thai food (somewhere in between Chinese and Indian cuisine, we thought), and the Chinese red silk sign-in sheet. And with those mixed-up rites, we dubbed ourselves a Chindian couple.

When a law school friend had introduced me to Zubin seven years ago, I saw a beautiful and quiet man who was "one of my own kind." Zubin understood the cultural ambiguities that I had always faced, because he had faced those same ambiguities. Our parents, though his were Indian and mine were Chinese, could have been mirror images of each other. His father came to England as a young boy as did mine to America. His mother arrived in England in her early twenties, around the same age as my mother when she set foot on American soil. It was uncanny that both our families, on different continents, assimilated in similar ways by drastically letting go of a homeland past in order to establish new roots. And so, while growing up, Zubin and I lived out the conflicts and rewards of assimilation and forgetting. As young adults, we both took journeys, he on an odyssey across India at nineteen, and I on a trek across thousands of miles of China at twenty-two, to reclaim pieces of our family story. Identity issues brought us close very quickly at first, and we spent years exploring, experimenting with, and guiding our lives through them. But identity issues sate only temporarily, and we found in year five that we needed something more soulful than our politics. Now our task is to find a way to deepen our marriage as we leave those cerebral issues behind to start working on what makes our marriage work in terms that speak of forever.

We were lucky. My parents loved Zubin and Zubin's parents accepted me, though not because either side felt that ours was an "Asian" marriage. My Chinese American parents and my British Indian in-laws probably do not feel that they share a common culture, as fond as they might be of each other. Yet Zubin and I feel that we did marry "Asian." The affinity we feel is more about our sense of displacement and our similar ways of resolving it, rather than any definition based in geography or cultural likeness. For us, the word "Asian" is a term of rough cultural proximity, where the stress on family and duty and the smell of incense and orange blossoms still hover.

Some of us who come from more demanding families are having a harder time of it, discovering instead that roping in that "nice Asian boy" is more difficult than anticipated. "When my parents asked me to find one of my own kind, they meant Vietnamese, not any old Asian type," Vera told me, after her family forbade her to marry her Chinese boyfriend. "They actually told me that they'd prefer that I marry a white guy if that was the case." To Vera's parents, white was at least marrying up. An Indian Brahmin woman was told to end her relationship with a man from a lower Hindu caste, despite the fact that they were both highly educated and had similar American upbringings. A Korean mother tells me that her daughter never chooses Korean men from the right kind of families and so she refuses to be cordial to them when they visit. While family advice may often be well intentioned and ought to be heard in that way, it can also become a cloak for a much deeper bid for control, a preservation of hierarchies, and a living out of aspirations through our lives that makes our own choices secondary. In these cases, listening to our own hearts becomes that much more difficult, our choices that much more confusing.

What would it have been like if I had grown up around Asian men all my life, took for granted their variety and humanity, without the stereotypes of their supposed lack of power and sexuality that my American upbringing has taught me? What if while growing up I had read books such as *On a Bed of Rice,* a recently published collection of Asian American erotica that breathed the language of sex into Asian America? What if I had come of age in Los Angeles or New York in the present, when those cities explode with all-Asian nightclub scenes where the dance floor is almost exclusively Asian American? Asian men would have been on my radar screen as I went through my dating years, and my ideas about relationships might have been less tied up with themes of power and identity.

But that is not what I had while growing up. What I had were Fu Manchu, James Bond's Dr. No, skinny, sexless computer nerds and Yakuza hoods on television, and through them I learned that Asian men were inscrutable, evil, asexual, and unattractive. And while martial arts heroes Bruce Lee and Jackie Chan have done their best to replace those images with those of power, the image of the kung fu fighter is still the stuff of cartoon and caricature. Asian American manhood has yet to find its real-life depiction in the American mind. And in the meantime, I have had to relearn attraction.

Manufactured images have repercussions. In small group discussions with young women around the country, I continuously hear comments like Lydia's:

> Personally, I would choose a white guy over an Asian guy any day. The reason being is that Asian males don't take risks— they're so shy! White guys are more aggressive and confident. Those are qualities that many of my Asian female friends look for in a guy, and we just don't see that in Asian males.

Why are Lydia's feelings so widely shared? Lydia's portrayal does not reflect the experiences of many Asian American women with close ties to their Asian communities. In my own interactions with Asian and Asian American men, so many have actually been the opposite of that stereotype, macho and self-possessed, perhaps the result of a solid, son-worshiping, Confucian upbringing.

But we may reject our Asian men for other reasons, as well. Yin, for instance, feared that if she chose to be with an Asian man, she would relive what she felt was the terrible oppression of her mother by her father. America offered her a chance at escaping that pattern, and other American men, non-Asian men, provided a freedom she believed she would otherwise never have:

> Talking to a Vietnamese man meant that you had to marry him. With American boyfriends it doesn't mean as much, and so with them I can feel freer, with options. My future isn't set in stone just because I happened to have had coffee with him.
>
> I remember a Vietnamese guy who kept wanting to ask me out. When he finally had the courage to speak to me, his hands were trembling. I told him I didn't feel comfortable with him, and I started to walk home. He followed me and started yelling and pounding on my door, shouting that I had disrespected him. I can understand now that whatever I did to him though my actions—refuted his manhood and his right to be respected—was probably a constant theme in his American experience.

She shared her experiences on discovering that a marriage had been arranged for her when she was a teenager. Although she refused to go through with it, the feelings she still has about Vietnamese men have been shaped by that traumatic circumstance. She contemplated what would have happened had she gone through with her arranged marriage:

> Asian sons have Asian mothers, and who wants to be the daughter-in-law of an Asian mother? It would be a life full of the obligations. I'd have to take care of two families instead of just my own.

For many of us in young relationships, the choice of a non-Asian partner can be an act of independence at a time when the need for self-definition and distance from family is most pronounced. Love of people and things non-Asian can mean a giant step away from one's home base, a public statement of forward movement and a declaration that we have bonded with an American core. Family schisms can often be the consequence.

Yet after veering away from our traditional or constricting families, we may realize that we should have discussed more seriously the cultural differences with our partners at the outset of our relationships. As Evelyn Lee, a psychologist who specializes in Asian American populations describes, "In our haste to escape and in our conviction to making things work with our partners, we might miss some very obvious personality or cultural conflicts. I see many interracial couples coming in for guidance, asking me why their relationships are so stressful. Many times it is because the interracial couple, in their need to establish a strong relationship in the beginning, sacrificed contact and support of their respective family networks. Without the extended family structure that often supports a couples' survival, interracial couples often find themselves with no one, not even their partners, to turn to."

TALL, FAIR, AND HANDSOME

Cinderella themes are alive and well, even in Asian America. In romantic relationships, even the most strong-willed of us may yearn for a partner to protect and provide. In *The Second Sex,* Simone de Beauvoir wrote that at a certain point in their young adult lives, women realize that power is not distributed equally, and that men have most of it. From that point on, de Beauvoir claims, a young woman understands that any power she obtains will be based on her abilities to retain a man's attention and love. De Beauvoir's statements, though no longer as relevant for the urban, American woman, still ring true in Asian cultures, with many examples of how women are shamed when they fail to obtain the commitment of a man. In many South Asian communities, for example, where arranged marriages still take place, the shame associated with being an "old maid" runs deep. In Korean families, it is not uncommon to hear a young Korean woman referred to as "rotten fruit" if she doesn't marry by age thirty. In the Philippines, divorce is unheard of, and under the law, rape is considered not a violation of a woman's body but a crime against chastity. Asian American women might agree with de Beauvoir's statement about men and their power. At a young age we learn, as does every American girl, not only that men have power, but that white men have most of it.

It is impossible to write about our relationships with white men without causing a considerable amount of anger, defensiveness, or incredulity. "Race and culture never mattered to me. I love my partner for who he/she is; that's the end of the story," is the quick response to loaded questions about this particular type of interracial coupledom. It is understandably uncomfortable, even sacrilegious, to look at our relationships and cast them as something besides true, pure love. After all, whom we end up with ideally does transcend race. Whom we choose as our partner will be the result of whom we are exposed to, whom we grew up with, and who has lived in our own communities, no matter what their color. Yet even in the healthiest and most loving of relationships, issues of race and class ought to be examined before they are buried as inconsequential. Only then can our relationships grow into something deeper.

In the same way that we've learned to reject Asian men, the white male ideal is infused in our public and artistic discourse.

From stories of the heroic white soldier of Madame Butterfly, to film footage of strong American troops rescuing little Asian peoples, come our aesthetic coupling of desire with power. White is a handsome Jesus sitting in the clouds. Blond is the color of many a Prince Charming's hair. Blue is the color of a mischievous hero's eyes. Tall, chiseled, and brawny are the qualities of a real man. These are the collective themes that create the common American folklore, reiterating and reinforcing our love of the fair male. Asian American women "marry out" more frequently than other race groups and most of those interracial marriages are to Caucasian spouses. Fifty-five percent of Asian women between the ages of twenty-five and thirty-four, and sixty-six percent of those under twenty-five, are married to non-Asians.

For women of color who have had the opportunity to see the different ways that one can be greeted, treated, and served based on those with whom we keep company, white can also become an insurance policy for our own equitable treatment. As Gail, a *yonsei* (a fourth-generation Japanese American) from Evanston, Illinois, puts it:

When walking down the street with a white man, whether it was a boyfriend or coworker, I was treated well, asked whether I needed help from sales assistants, addressed with more courtesy by waiters and cashiers. Now that I walk down the street with my husband, who is a Malaysian Chinese born in Illinois, I do not receive the same unconditional welcoming. We are looked at as if we are foreigners. Often they speak loudly like they think we don't understand English. It made me sad at first to know that I would have to get used to this. I began to think about how easy it was before when a white man was my *carte blanche*. I liked being treated on equal footing.

Cross-cultural relationships have come with a barrage of discussions among young people who are finding themselves caught between following their heart and becoming a symbol of their entire race, as they try to situate themselves in the puzzle of political sensitivity and awareness. One ethnic studies professor in southern California recalls her Asian students asking questions such as, "If I date a white person, does that mean I'm selling out?"

"Maybe," wrote Janet, echoing our mothers' warnings, "he's not thinking of me as a person, but as something that he doesn't have to take seriously." "I seem to attract guys who were already into karate and B movies," wrote Christina, an adopted Korean American student at a large, midwestern university. Some even interrogate their partners on past romances, as Melissa de la Cruz wrote in a *New York Press* article wryly called "Gook Fetish":

> Boyfriend number three was a writer with a wry smile and a wit almost as quick as mine. I gave him the rudimentary shakedown: who did you use to date and why? He explained that he had been involved with a half-Korean woman for ten years, and that his type was "dark-haired and petite," which meant he was attracted to Asian women because most of them just happened to fall into that category.

Others, such as Leslie, express a frustration with their partners, saying that they are not facing up to underlying truths. As Leslie looked back on her two relationships with Caucasian boyfriends, she understood that there were almost imperceptible assumptions of submissiveness tied to her being an Asian woman, "which is why I didn't like to clean the house or cook too often," she tells me.

I was always making sure that everything was visibly equal. I was tremendously sensitive when it came to the way my boyfriends spoke to me in public and among friends. I think I tolerated less from them and was always concerned about not being taken for granted.

But it just seemed strange that we never talked about being an interracial couple, except to joke about it, like it was a little too intense. It's difficult when a boyfriend doesn't understand his privilege or, worse, if he gets angry if you bring it up. When I tried to bring up issues of how we were treated so differently, he did not want to discuss it. "It's your issue," he'd say to me. "You've got to think better about yourself." Then he'd ask, "Why aren't you happy? What have I done?" In the end, he realized that I would shut up as soon as he called me a raving radical Asian activist, because I certainly wasn't one of those. My goal was not to make him feel guilty or angry. I just wanted to talk about the issues.

When each of those relationships ended, I was terrified that his next girlfriend would turn out to be Asian. In fact, I hoped she would be a tall blue-eyed blonde.

OFF THE BEATEN TRACK

When Ming-Na Wen was seen on the big screen as the wife of Wesley Snipes in a film called *One Night Stand*, and when Sarita Choudhury kissed Denzel Washington in Mira Nair's groundbreaking film, *Mississippi Masala*, American audiences saw a variation of interracial couple that they had seldom before witnessed—Asian American women with men of color. And in stories like "Jeannie" by Mina Kumar, we are learning of another permutation on love—Asian women with other women. When our choice of partner veers off the beaten track, no one knows quite what to make of it. Yet these relationships are happening more frequently and more visibly, unsurprisingly in the nation's most cosmopolitan centers on both coasts but elsewhere too, a natural consequence of a world of dissolving racial and gender boundaries.

As with any unconventional choice, family pressures are heightened, especially in same-sex partnerships. Take for example Heidi's experience in coming out to her parents: "When I told my parents that I was a lesbian, they wanted to know what they had done wrong. I think they are still ashamed. My mother told me that she didn't feel she knew who I was anymore, because I was not the daughter they expected. I was supposed to marry a man. Now they didn't know how to think of my future or theirs. They still aren't comfortable with my girlfriend." Homosexuality is often kept more tightly under wraps in Asian communities, a kind of love that remains private and shamed despite having a long history in Asian homelands. In her 1994 *Amerasia Journal* article, "Stories From the Homefront," Alice Hom reported that there were only two Asian American parents who were members of the San Francisco group Parents and Friends of Lesbians and Gays. As the Asian American contact for the group, one of the parents received fewer than ten calls from other Asian American parents over a two-year period, even though the Asian American gay community is active and vocal in that region of the country.

Family expectations were also strained when June introduced her family to her Cuban husband. "They had their own prejudices at first. My father couldn't even look my husband in the eye for a long time. I think they were more afraid than anything else." But June, who had always been involved with either Asian or white men, knew when she met her husband for the first time that he was the one. "It's a question of comfort," she says. "Race was only one factor that put my husband and me on the same page. Growing up in the suburbs when we were young, we both felt placed in the margins. Being together as adults, we realize every day that experiences are shared which are not specific to Asian American or Latino American experience." For June, as for many Asian American women who are with a partner other than the predictable Asian or Caucasian man, her choice of partner was as much a political decision as an emotional one. For others, such as Yuriko, a relationship with an African American man *taught* her another perspective on life: "I was just exposed to situations I may not [otherwise] have come across. Growing up in an all-white neighborhood, race wasn't an issue . . . but for African Americans, race is an issue every day."

New ethnic neighborhoods are becoming defined more in terms of class than race, providing contact between newly arrived Asian communities and other communities of color. Affinities among them are expanding the breadth of the Asian American experience. Young Cambodian and Vietnamese girls in the Tenderloin district of San Francisco, for example, understand readily that they have more in common with their black and Chicano neighbors than they do with the wealthier Chinese and Japanese in Marin County across the Golden Gate Bridge. It is not uncommon to see these young women with black and Latino partners. Their mannerisms and dress are noticeably hip-hop. Their English is southeast Asian and barrio all rolled into one. "If I had to decide where I share my experience, then I am more black than white, even if I do get beaten up sometimes by the black and Chicano girls in school," one of them said. "I just don't know much about white culture."

Sun Hee, who grew up on army bases through her child-hood, remembers going to schools that were "very integrated." With classmates who were for the most part black, white, and Latino, Sun Hee saw no difference in whether she chose to date white men or black men. Yet one day she was taken aside by her black friends, who warned her that there would be consequences if she decided to date a black friend:

It was when I started to date my current boyfriend, who is black, that I began to realize anything about race dynamics. All of a sudden my black friends would warn me that if I continued to date him, people would begin to look at me differently. They were concerned for me because as black Americans they knew that it would not be a pleasant experience to deal with other people's prejudices. Even though I was a Korean woman adopted into an American family and living in the Midwest, my friends didn't think that I had faced as much prejudice as I was about to experience. They were right.

Sun Hee talked about leaving home to go to college in the south and described the constant affirmative choices she had to make as she considered her position as an Asian American woman within a black American social circle. As she entered the lecture hall on the first day of college classes, she saw that "the class was literally divided by color. On one side were all the black students. On the other were all the white students. So where was I supposed to go?" she asked. "I went where I felt most comfortable, to the black students' side, since that was my community growing up. The black students were surprised."

In a world that loves dichotomy, Asian Americans are given the choice of aligning "white" or "black." "Either you are 'one of us' or you are 'one of them' is always implied," writes Kim. "And by choosing sides, I am treated accordingly. I'm either a homegirl or a good little assimilationist."

But the black/white paradigm is becoming less and less relevant as we begin to recognize that race issues have always been more complex and that as interaction among Asian, black, Latino, white, and biracial people increases, so does the potential for us to realize our common conditions across simple cut and dried lines. "We can no longer see the world in black and white, where those who don't fit the color scheme become shadows," as *Ms. Magazine* contributing editor Helen Zia wrote in a letter to the editor in a recent *New York Times*.

Helen's statements are those of vision. Yet the current reality is that havoc is wreaked on Asian American women, as well as their partners, who are trying hard to make their interracial relationships survive. There are just so many pressures by families and institutions that seem to chip away at their legitimacy.

Kim had been married for seven years to her African American husband, with whom she had a wonderful relationship. They shared political views as well as a sense that they both wanted to serve their communities. Then the riots in Los Angeles erupted in 1992, and Kim and her husband, along with the rest of America, saw repeated televised images of Korean store owners poised on top of their storefront roofs with machine guns pointed at black and Latino rioters. "It shocked us both and ended up ruining my marriage," says Kim. "My husband began to see me as the enemy, as a member of a group that also oppressed black people. 'See?' he'd say to me. 'Even your people are putting our communities down!' I didn't know where to put his comments, but I knew that whatever it was that he was feeling must have been from somewhere very deep inside. I just couldn't understand how he could see me in that way."

What would help Kim heal the gash inflicted on her marriage by media news formulas that thrive on conflict? She needed to know that what news cameras failed to capture was the protest by Asian, black, Latino, and white men and women against the injustice of the Rodney King verdict, in one of the largest showings of coalition-based action that Los Angeles had seen in its history. She needed to explain to her husband the history and context of Korean-black interaction, so that he could understand that *both* communities experienced great psychic losses during the uprising—for example, that many Korean store owners suffered debilitating post-traumatic stress disorders after having lost their entire life savings. She needed to know how the precarious function of Korean store owners, as middlemen between their disempowered clientele and the corporate suppliers of the goods they sell, makes them easy scapegoats for racial hate by the very community that they served. Kim needed to know how "divide and conquer" themes within black and Korean communities shaped the events in her own life and marriage.

Away from all the cameras, as the ashes of the Los Angeles uprising smoldered, groups of hopeful African American and Korean American leaders began to hold community meetings to discuss a healing process. Around them lay the ruins of a city in trauma. More than two thousand seven hundred Korean businesses had been destroyed, resulting in hundreds of millions of dollars in damage. Many blacks and Latinos had been arrested, and the downtown district had been cordoned off, surrounded by hundreds of Los Angeles police clad in assault gear. Hope for the very untraditional relationship between Asian Americans and other communities of color will come slowly, as borders begin to dissipate. In the meantime, what it takes for an interracial couple who love each other to survive in a race-baited world is nothing less than the support and faith of us all.

When can two people leave issues of race behind in order to get on with the business of building a life together? After all, there eventually comes a time when we either accept or reject those whom we have chosen, deal with the consequences of that choice, and begin to build on love. At that point, how love survives will have little to do with the racial pressures of the outside world and more to do with how we validate and listen to each other and how we take responsibility for ourselves. Strong love, in the end, is about our confidence—our power to be authentic, giving, and nonjudgmental.

TESTIMONIAL

A language of the heart is taking shape. After many years of experimenting with the language of courtship, Asian American writers are telling strong stories of respect and compassion for each other. Shawn Wong, for instance, in his breakthrough novel *American Knees,* puts on paper a seldom-heard sweetness that takes place between an Asian American man, Raymond, and the biracial Asian American woman he grows to love, Aurora. In doing so, he shows us that we can appreciate each other in ways that are real and complicated and, best of all, erotic:

Aurora turned around to face Raymond. She didn't speak.
He took a step toward her, but she put up her hand as if

she wanted him to stop. He waited. Her hand stayed where it was, raised at shoulder height, as if she were waiting to ask a question in class. She placed her open palm behind her ear, against her neck.

He began to say something, but her look told him not to speak. He walked across the room and stood before her with his hands at his sides. Slowly Aurora raised both arms and pulled Raymond to her, held him to her, and buried her face against his neck.

Raymond fought the urge to make admissions, explanations, excuses. He returned the pressure of Aurora's arms exactly. As if she had read his mind and wanted to silence his thoughts, Aurora kissed him softly, then even more softly, then brushed her lips against his closed eyelids, then even more softly, then touched her lips to his ears, then kissed him even more softly until her breath was all he felt.

What we need to hear are love stories like these, of equal strength and power. What we need to create are the themes about how the love we offer as Asian American women means so much more than being the exotic, beautiful object of a lover's fantasy. What we need to appreciate is the masculinity and profundity of our Asian men. What we are not taught, what may exist but is not shown, we cannot know. And so we must acknowledge our loves when they exist, to give them an embodiment, and in doing so, a home.

Why I Love You, Zubin

Because we are kind to each other when we have every chance to be cruel.

Because through the hard times, your heart is still guided by "forever."

Because you do the *nampapalao* dance when no one is
  looking.

Because we keep each other's secrets.

Because through our trials you preserve my hopes, and
  in you I see the world.

Perhaps in learning to love each other, we might also
learn to love ourselves.

SHE BRIDGES DISTANCE

For those who are walled up, everything is a wall . . . even an open door.

—Rene Char

I'll never forget the day Julie Rhee came into my high school science class. She was pretty. She started to make friends with my friends. And she had a heavy Korean accent. She spent a lot of time with her younger brother and, in so doing, violated the laws of high school cooldom. I stayed as far away from Julie as I possibly could, even when I had so many questions I wanted to ask her.

Recently, at a restaurant, I and my Indian friend say hello to a neighbor who is also dining there. He introduces us to his guest, an older, stately Indian woman. She glances quickly up and down at my Indian friend and turns away, apparently more interested in the pictures on the walls. At sixteen or sixty, we know how to keep our distances.

Why do we create those distances?

And how can bridging distance help us to grow?

It might happen like this. You arrive at the party and glance around the room. And by doing so, you see that this is the kind of gathering that you are used to. The same cast of characters, the same way of dressing, familiar. You settle in, pour yourself a glass of wine, and start up what will be a string of conversations with friends. But then another one, just like you, walks in. You catch a glimpse of this new woman, that split-second kind of glimpse that you cast when no one is watching, checking out her manner, looking for signs of attitude. You might see that this woman is as confident as you are. And what you know but cannot see is that this woman is casting glimpses at you as well. Throughout the evening you both move about the room, finely tuning your positions imperceptibly and perhaps even unintentionally, avoiding contact, like same magnetic poles. So alike that you repel each other.

Women of privilege do this to one another. Beautiful women do it. Ask those who have made a lifetime of fitting in, whatever color or class they might be. They do it, too. I ask my friends who are leaders in all sorts of communities, women, African Americans, you name it, and they will nod in recognition. Distance, they tell me, is the learned behavior of anxiety.

THE DANCE OF DISTANCING

When I think about the harshness that exists so often within the least encounter between Black women, the judgment and the sizing up, that cruel refusal to connect. I now sometimes feel like it is worth my life to disagree with another Black woman, better to ignore her, withdraw from her, go around her, just don't deal with her. Not just because she irritates me, but because she might destroy me with the cruel force of her response to what must feel like an affront, namely me. Or I might destroy her with the force of mine, for the very same reason. The fears are equal.

—Audre Lorde,
Eye to Eye

With distancing, our interaction with one another becomes more of the symbolic kind, rife with nuance and subtle messages. It is in the way we eye each other, then look away. The way we stand back and watch, rather than approach, sometimes furtively as through a rearview mirror. We may be more cautious with one another than we would otherwise be. More quick to criticize. More suspicious of each other's motives, less willing to trust, more destructive in our anger. The dance of distance is not necessarily born of a fear that we have for one another or a hatred that we have for ourselves. In most cases it is not even intentional. Instead, it seems to be the most efficient way of avoiding a deeper inquiry. For many of us it might be too difficult to gravitate toward others that remind us of some unidentifiable alienation of our replaceability. Offhand and sometimes humorous, we've developed a language of differentiation:

Some Terms of Distance

Kuppie, Chuppie: Korean yuppie, Chinese yuppie

Banana: Asian on the outside, white on the inside

Coconut: brown on the outside, white on the inside

Popcorn: always acting dark or ethnic until it gets too hot, then we turn white

Wonder Bread: brown crust on the outside, soft and white on the inside, and lots of air in between

Asian Feminist

Suburban Girl

Asian Dyke

Asian American Sell-out

Traitor

Ivy League Snob

Immigrant

"I am different from you," is what these terms imply. "You are not part of my experience." "I do what I want, and you do what you want." These thought processes are voluntary acts of banishing—of ourselves from the common experiences that we might share with each other but never discover, or of others who don't share our ideologies on the "real way to be Asian American."

To the extent that we have not carved out a clear and whole sense of self, we will always feel in some danger of being swallowed up in the anonymity that togetherness implies. The distance among us does not necessarily stem from an indifference to each other. It comes instead from the possibility of too much closeness. When we see each other, we may see too much of ourselves, our flaws, our shortcomings.

Distancing isn't so much *premeditated* as it is *instinctive,* especially if one happens to live in an area outside of an Asian American metropolis, where a congregation of three Asian faces is enough to attract some notice. We know the price of coming together. It is in the extra efforts we have to make, the noted glances of others, our overcompensation and compulsion to explain our gathering. Irene, who has been a champion in her office of mentoring her younger Asian American associates, admits, "I have to try triply hard to convince people that we are not in cahoots when I am working with Asian coworkers." And Lisa, a sociology professor, tells me, "In classes, I have to be sure not to be too generous with my Asian American students, and doing so, I might be coming down harder on them instead, to prove that we don't cut each other slack." With these acts of distance, we are able to preserve the notion of our individuality, our harmlessness, and our assimilation.

Nancy was on her way back from a weekend on the east end of Long Island when she found herself in a train car with two other Asian American women. Both of them were tall, like her, both of them dressed in the standard weekend wear of professional, well-put-together Manhattan women—black leather jackets, black T-shirts, and jeans. Nancy is sure that both were also most likely returning from weekends in the Hamptons, just as she was:

Had they been young students, or older women, immigrants perhaps, I would not have been as uncomfortable. But we really did all look so much alike—with our shoulder-length hair, our black jackets and black T-shirts, same kind of makeup with eyeliner and lipstick—that my first reaction was to put on my glasses and bury my head in the newspaper just to set me apart from the other two. It was absurd! I am an individual, and I don't want to be reminded that we all look alike.

Nancy has internalized a stereotype of her sameness to the extent that her natural reaction is to be aghast at her similarities with the other two women. Hers is a constant and relentless vigilance that allows her to preserve a sense of unique self in a world that she knows would rather perceive her for her sameness. That sort of distancing requires mental energy and micromaneuvering that can often be exhausting.

Through it all, we never stop to ask why we feel the need to compartmentalize ourselves in the first place. Has the American ideal of the grand individual been so deeply ingrained that it has actually prevented us from exploring our potential as a community? How fragile and tenuous our sense of individuality must be, if two or three of us coming together can actually threaten that sense of self-determination.

In our symbolic distance, we are ever vigilant not to behave stereotypically, sometimes taking this to extremes. As one woman admits, "I refuse to be the one who carries the camera on vacation," she says. "I don't want to look like a Japanese tourist." We may convince ourselves that by not carrying a camera we can somehow distinguish ourselves from "that other kind of Asian." In another statement of distance, a young Cambodian girl tells her teacher, "Some students call me chingchong Chinese, but they've got it all wrong. Can't they see that I'm

Cambodian?" Sometimes differentiation becomes an attempt at self-preservation. To avoid persecution, Asian shopkeepers posted signs during the Los Angeles riots indicating that they weren't Korean. Chinese and Koreans wore buttons proclaiming that they were "not Japanese" during World War II.

Distance can also preserve hierarchies, as Bonnie's story demonstrates. She remembers bringing her friend, a UN ambassador who happened also to be an Asian woman, to a Korean restaurant, where they were greeted and seated by their Korean hostess. As she remembers, the restaurant was empty and had many tables. Nevertheless, Bonnie and her friend were brought to the worst table, behind a pillar and near the kitchen. When they requested to be seated at another table, the best table in the house, the hostess tried to argue but reluctantly obliged. As Bonnie described it:

> The whole situation really got my friend mad. For the rest of the evening we'd watch where this hostess sat people. She inevitably put the Asian businessmen at the best tables, and put the single women at the same bad table she tried to give to us. When finally the place became packed, only the bad table was left. Another businessman walked in for dinner. The hostess showed him the only table left and apologized for its location, telling him that he could have another when one was available.
>
> When I shared this with another friend, she told me that she was also brought to that bad table when she dined there, that she felt insulted but didn't want to make a fuss, so she sat there. She probably didn't want to admit to herself that another Asian woman might be discriminating against her. It's too painful to admit sometimes.

Amoeba Girl

Dances of distance also allow us to perform what one survey respondent referred to as "a disappearing act," achieving, as Monica Sone put it in her book *Nisei Daughter,* "amoebic bliss." We can slip so easily from one environment to the next, becoming excellent "blenders," by taking on the accepted mores of our surroundings, like a mood ring that changes with the temperature. We can fit in as well (or perhaps just as uncomfortably) with a group of white professionals as we can at a black friend's book party or a political banquet in Koreatown. In essence, we become expert chameleons, changing our tones and mannerisms of speech, clothing, and demeanor, to become part of whatever the common folkway is at the moment.

We can sit at the intersection of many worlds, and by virtue of our small presence, we often have access and conditional acceptance, as long as we dress the part, speak with the proper intonation, and take on the attitudes of our environments. Law professor Sharon Hom writes of how her role and her power levels shift in her many different environments:

> As a Chinese/American female law professor, I often also experience what I call an "Alice in Wonderland" effect of sudden shifts of significance, of authoritativeness, as I "land" in different "rooms," mediated by the ideological operation of gender and race, performing my multiple roles for shifting audiences. As a visiting professor standing in front of a class of predominantly white students, as a Chinese/American Fulbright scholar teaching in China, as a professor in my home institution, a diverse and public interest community, I grow and shrink in perceived size, power, and authority, sometimes within seconds.

Yet the chameleon role has its limits. Some of us have learned to play the part so well that we have never stopped to think about where our identities and our cultures are truly grounded. Like Method actors who have gone too far in perfecting their roles, we got too involved in our characters. To act genuinely would imply a paradigm shift. We'd have to compromise our chameleon instincts. For many of us, playing the chameleon is much easier than defining who we are, what makes us proud, and what larger ideas we stand for.

MOTHER LOSS

Distancing comes from other places as well. The barnacle-like hold of mothers on their Asian American daughters, for instance, can also encourage a daughter's general tendency to distance. Mothers can often cling to their daughters as their strong alter egos, often leaving daughters feeling suffocated, overprotected, used as an anchor for their mother's life.

According to Hope Edelman, author of *Motherless Daughters,* if we have heavy family responsibilities from the time we are very young, or if we have been left to fend for ourselves, we will have learned to survive by approaching our close relationships, particularly with other women, cautiously. Lack of what Edelman called the Motherline, a passing of factual and emotional information by mother to daughter through generations, contributes to a daughter's tendency to distance from other women. If the communication lines between mother and daughter have been tenuous, if language and cultural differences have set them apart, a daughter's reaction may be to feel loss, anger, or emotional abandonment by the mother figure she never had. In those cases, we may choose to avoid potentially intense relationships with other women that might prove just as confusing or emotionally taxing as the mother-daughter relationships that we remember. We may convince ourselves that even the most casual of friendships will spiral into a web of obligation. Some of us might react by bringing self-sufficiency to an extreme, refusing to ask for assistance or seek advice, or lean on a shoulder when we are tired or overwhelmed.

Women who have had to assume great responsibility at home tend to separate cleanly, if not abruptly, from friends and lovers. If things aren't working in our relationships, we may tend to end things quickly. "I have so much responsibility taking care of everybody and myself that I have to cut off the relationships that will take up too much of my time or effort. It's like I need to cut out the weakness in my life before it drags me down," one Asian American girlfriend tells me. This seems to have been the motto for many Asian American women, having learned to be so self-reliant and emotionally self-contained that they no longer have room to let anyone in.

Distancing can also be a way to manage the intensity in other key family relationships. Creating emotional space can be an essential first move to ensure our well-being and even our survival. It can take us away from an explosive situation and allow us to calm down enough to choose a more constructive behavior. Often, however, we rely on distance to exit permanently from significant relationships.

Anna, a nisei woman from Chicago, speaks very little to her parents about her husband and family as a way to keep them from "meddling" in the upbringing of her children and her marriage. Debbie, a South Asian student from Austin, Texas, uses distance to avoid her brothers, who she has always felt "got everything, while the girls did all the work." While distance preserves Anna's and Debbie's peace of mind in the short term, it can also prevent them from addressing important issues in themselves. Can Anna find a way, either herself or through an intermediary, to confront her parents and draw her boundaries so that a new family dynamic is created? Can Debbie find it within herself to breach the distance with her brothers and parents by letting them know how hurt she has been all these years?

WHEN TIMES GET TOUGH, DISTANCE LESSENS

Lorraine is a thirty-eight-year-old Korean American who grew up in Chicago. She had never thought about issues such as distancing from other Asian American women until she worked for twelve years at the same Big Eight accounting firm, was passed up for a promotion to vice president twice, and was required to train her new boss each time she was bypassed. In college she remembers, "the students that were into Asian American activism were too intense for me, and their concerns were too political. I was just a business school type, wanted the A's and a good job, and thought the rest of it was a waste of time." Lorraine could not understand why she was never given the opportunity to advance past lower middle management. "They seemed happy with my work, so I didn't understand what happened." This confusion prompted Lorraine to follow up with an Asian American professional group, and conversations with other members taught her that her pattern was a common one. "Before I had the guts to share that experience with them, I kept blaming myself for some kind of inadequacy on the job. I kept harping on the mistakes I might have made at work, or the stupid things that I must have said, or the possibility that I just didn't try hard enough." Alone, Lorraine's analysis of her situation was completely inner-directed. Without being able to acknowledge that others like her had endured similar situations, she remained focused on herself and what she must have done wrong.

Madhu is a housewife in New Jersey who was once married to a man who drank too much and physically abused her. She never felt the need to find her South Asian community, keeping herself busy by raising three children at home, until her relationship grew life-threatening and she reached a point of desperation. Her first move toward embracing a community of South Asian women was to call the hot line of Manavi, a community organization made up of South Asian women and fellow survivors of domestic violence.

Distance from one another is easy enough to maintain when there are only low-level issues. It is when times get tough that the doors open for reconsideration of alliances with those whom we might have resisted before. Lorraine and Madhu came to bridge their distance from their respective communities because of dire circumstances, proving that the stakes have to be high, the need immediate, and the results tangible for many of us to seek out the group associations that once made us feel uncomfortable.

Our distance lessens when we realize that no other framework of analysis seems to get at our visceral truths. Perhaps this is the reason that identity politics are often associated with complaint or insecurity. Some see it as a crutch—an excuse for not succeeding by the traditional rules of competition and merit. If something unfortunate befalls us, we must have deserved it.

Critical race theorists agree that the current discussion of identity politics is based in part in the recognition that discrimination has taken place against a patently definable group of people. Identity politics for the Asian American community, as is the case for many communities of color, became an exercise in fighting back and coming to the aid of those who had been wronged. Case in point: the Asian American community experienced a renaissance, according to Chinese American journalist Helen Zia, when we became the target of a wave of racially motivated attacks in the 1980s. All of a sudden we were being targeted as opposed to ignored. And in the wake of the Los Angeles uprising of 1992, Asian Americans again understood the *disadvantages* of distance, and we attempted to come together in response to the siege of our communities.

But bridging distance can also mean so much more. Consider our potential for learning if instead of coming together only in times of strife, we were able to bridge distance when there were no fires to put out, if we could unlearn the various ways we distance ourselves from one another and learn how to stay focused on what we have in common. Lorraine might have been able to get her promotion by letting the office know that her links to the Asian American community were a resource and that she could bring those viewpoints to the management table. Madhu might have been able to use her ties to other South Asian women to educate others that they need not have to endure violence in their homes. Bridging distance becomes an act of tremendous potential power.

DISTANCE FROM THE "POLITICAL"

About ten minutes through my presentations to college audiences about what I feel is an emerging sense of Asian America, I might use the word "political." With the mere utterance of the word, I begin to see slight signs of discomfort. Asian American students glance around the room, trying to assess whether professors and other non-Asian students are bothered about what I am saying. My lecture entitled "Emerging Asian America" can mean so many things, and each audience member has come with his or her own expectations.

Some have come to hear a soft presentation, folktales my grandmother told me. Some thought I would talk about the rise of Pacific Rim economies and about who's moving Asian markets. I have even been asked once about what one should order on a Chinese menu. Not all of us are comfortable with the phrase "political" or the concept of viewing Asian American identity as a vehicle to social and political change.

If we are reluctant to participate in political life, there are several understandable reasons. Recent immigrants can point to the horrifying consequences of past political activity. In Korea, there were massacres of students who dared to demand that their government change. In China, one could face life imprisonment for daring to question the government party line. In Taiwan, riots and fistfights go hand in hand with political life. In Indonesia, being "political" can cost you your life. In India, politics means digging deep into your pockets. The word "political" leaves a bad taste in the mouth, especially among Asian immigrants who remember vividly.

As the children of immigrants, we are taught that American success has much less to do with a political life and more to do with bootstrapping. *Study! Compete! Advance!* With teaching like this, there is often little motivation to get involved in anything that won't advance a grade point average and a résumé. We convince ourselves that if we make enough money and get the right jobs, we will be protected from the behavior that others complain of. Only later, as every Asian American eventually finds, our money is not always seen as equal, our hard work does not guarantee that we will be let in at higher levels, and as women, we will continue to face presumptions of our submissiveness, even when vying for that CEO job.

The stories of bridged distance are creating an Asian American community. Connection is creating power in the following ways:

We Are Working on Capitol Hill

When Congress opened hearings on campaign finance reform in 1997, Asian Americans saw a more ruthless side of American politics. Because of the reported improprieties of "Asian Connection" donations, Asian American political contributors around the country found themselves selectively scrutinized and identified from campaign donor lists by their Asian surnames. The media had a field day. With an easy news hook, headlines foretold of an "Asian invasion" of corrupt foreign moneys from dubious Asian givers, which sidetracked the real issue of special-interest campaign giving by much larger, more powerful donors. Finally, Asian Americans realized that access to the democratic process and the freedom to contribute to campaigns as a means of political expression, supposedly the right of every American, were going to have to be fought for. In the fall of 1997 Asian American advocacy groups filed a petition with the U.S. Commission on Civil Rights, which lead to a Commission hearing. Jesse Jackson, the ACLU, and others voiced their support. New groups such as the National Asian Pacific American Legal Consortium and the Asian Pacific American Institute for Congressional Studies are working on Capitol Hill to ensure that Asian American rights are not further eroded.

We're Using Media Power

A new generation of Asian American communicators is bringing our communities together by way of the Internet. That new generation includes Irene Shen, a self-proclaimed computer wizard, who developed a Web site called AsiangURLs, the "First Virtual Clubhouse on the Net for Female CyberAsians." After searching for months for a cyber-site where Asian American women could share ideas, she realized there were very few. Since she launched AsiangURLs in

1996, Irene has welcomed thousands of net visitors, with a comprehensive site that contains serious news, chat rooms, and hyperlinks into other Web sites related to the Asian-gURLs mission.

We're creating a voice of influence through new technology, as E-mail messages detailing incidents of anti-Asian discrimination flash across the country and around the world, along with phone numbers and E-mail addresses to lodge complaints. Internet strategies worked in triggering several management investigations of employees who have made discriminatory comments to Asian clientele. The Internet community links, especially in California's Bay Area, were so effective that some Bay Area Asian Americans received several copies of some of those action alerts.

We're a Spiritual Force

There are now roughly two thousand Korean, six hundred fifty Chinese, and two hundred Japanese Christian organizations in the United States, and hundreds of Buddhist, Hindu, and Asian Muslim places of worship dotting the country, concentrated especially on the West Coast. This translates into a vast, established network that is changing the face and practice of religion in America.

We're Talking in the Workplace

A young woman is told at her office that her boss likes Filipina women. If she spends time with him in the evenings, she is told that her chances of advancement will be better. She says no. She reports her boss to higher management. She gets fired. She finds her community of Asian American women and discovers that this is a common barrier many of them face in their professional lives. With the help of a community working in coalition, she is able to file a complaint with the Equal

Employment Opportunity Commission. Her case brings to light what is known as "racialized harassment," a specific kind of harassment that occurs as a result of both gender-and race-based assumptions. Coincidentally at the time of this incident, a survey was commissioned that gauged the issues of Asian American women in the workplace. That survey found that one-third of those surveyed had been targets of sexual harassment on the job. Two-thirds knew another Asian American friend who had experienced workplace harassment. Over sixty percent of Asian American women in that same survey acknowledged that they faced glass-ceiling issues in the workplace and an absence of mentors to guide them.

We Have Created Precedents

Faced with backbreaking work conditions, hundreds of Filipina maids in San Francisco helped to change their own conditions by becoming part of a new union leadership. It was necessary. For all the dues they paid, the union had failed to protect them. When maids wanted to report a violation, their confidentiality was not protected, and they were terrorized and threatened. The nearly impossible work quota meant that they could not eat lunch or take breaks. In the 1980s, when the Filipina maids finally organized together, they realized a new strength in their numbers and were able to strike successfully for more humane conditions. Their deal with hotel management became a model that every hotel union in San Francisco fought for and eventually got. Since then, powerhouse unions such as the AFL-CIO have recognized that the input of Asian American labor leadership is key to the union's survival into the next century. Over the past decade, they have contributed substantial financial and technical assistance to set up the Asian Pacific American Labor Alliance, one of the most effective labor groups in the country.

IDENTITY IS A PROCESS, NOT A DESTINATION

Being part and not-part at once is home. Home is the privilege and loneliness, power and vertigo, of multiple and dynamic positioning.

—Margaret Chon
Being Between

A young Taiwan-born student with a strong Chinese accent comes up to me after a lecture and tells me, "There is no Asian American identity." It is not the first time I've heard it, and yet I have to refrain from feeling sad or angry that he has said it. It has never been easy to convince a first-generation arrival that a Pan-Asian identity is possible. I try to flesh out what he is trying to say. "What drew you to my lecture tonight?" I ask him. "You saw an Asian face. Something compelled you to be here. Isn't the very act of our discussion a symbol of an identity in formation? And even if we may have had very different experiences, you and I, do you feel even a small vestige of a cultural affinity?" I can't help but think that the student before me is asking me to give him an easy answer. He wants me to clarify his own thoughts or to give him a reason to feel that he is right, so that he can go home. He responds by saying, "Tell me what an Asian American is, and then I'll tell you if I am one."

I ask him to think about the issues of his own life, and whatever they might be, I tell him that I consider them to be Asian American experiences. I am sure that he went away dissatisfied with my answer. I chose not to give him the absolute definition he sought. And in not finding the easy answer, he too easily discarded the possibilities of a thoughtful exploration.

Asian American identity, like American identity, is a fluid one. It will change as we change. Perhaps at its core, it is the identity of the marginal that is trying hard to become part of the center. At the very least, it can be defined by a yearning to know more and to find what is common among us so that distance from one another isn't the only sensible solution. If it can't be captured rationally, it can be captured in the heart. As a Japanese American writer from Minnesota, David Mura, wrote:

> Asian America is something that exists, which we are just beginning to define. I know that when I sit with a mixed group of Asian Americans it feels differently from when I am the sole Asian American. I know that when I sit with Japanese Americans it feels differently than if I'm with a mixed group of Asian Americans and whites. And I know that when I'm with a group of people of color it feels differently from being with any of these other groups. And as an artist, I know that when I read my work to an Asian American audience the response is different than from a white audience. There is less bewilderment and more empathetic understanding. From other poets, less jealousy or inattention and more camaraderie and encouragement.

When I was in my twenties, I, like my inquisitor, searched for absolutes. I needed standards and boundaries that could help me define what was "right" and "wrong," so I could determine what was good or bad with the world, and what was "acceptable" or "unacceptable" behavior of friends and family. I felt it necessary to begin with universal templates. But there comes a time when simplicity no longer works, when we realize that to operate effectively we must acknowledge that the ebb and flow of human interaction makes it impossible to see the world as a definitive set of rules. Recognizing that the grace of life exists not in the black-and-white proclamations, but in the shades of gray, is a part of developing a mature politics. That recognition allows us to see what we have in common, as well as what sets us apart.

THE MARKERS OF IDENTITY

Does an Asian American community exist? If we consider the facts below, the answer is indeed yes. An identity called Asian America is finally taking shape.

Asian American Women Want to Come Together, and Are Doing So

Over the last decade, at least six national networks have emerged that join thousands of Asian American women around areas of politics, leadership, and health. One such group, the Denver-based Asian Pacific American Women's Leadership Institute, grew from a base of one hundred "Founding Sisters" who contributed one hundred dollars each to enhance the leadership skills of one hundred Asian Pacific American women—professionals, politicians, and labor organizers alike. Since then, the Institute has graduated its third group of leadership fellows, coordinating its efforts with the Gallup Leadership Institute. Once a year they have a national summit meeting that attracts hundreds of Asian American women, who, by their very gathering, are proof of an Asian American sisterhood in the making. The institute has received a vote of confidence from the Kellogg Foundation, which has pledged over six hundred thousand dollars in support of this group's efforts.

We Are Gathering Information

When groups such as Asian Pacific Islanders in Reproductive Health and the Asian American Health Forum began to disaggregate national statistics, they found that Asian American women have unique health concerns. Southeast Asian and Chinese American women have higher incidences of cervical cancer as compared to the general U.S. population. Chinese and Filipino Americans have higher rates of esophageal cancer, and lung cancer is more prevalent among Chinese American women and Southeast Asian men. With this knowledge, researchers can now investigate the possible reasons for these health disparities. Preliminary findings point to the lack of education about preventative health care such as Pap smears and yearly physicals, absence of translators or English-language abilities during doctor and hospital visits, and the cultural stigmas that might attach to illness. Information borne of identity politics is bringing us the power to live healthier lives.

We Want to Learn About Our History

An Internet search yields at least seven thousand sites that concern themselves with Asian American topics. There are currently hundreds of Asian American professional and collegiate organizations where discussions about identity and reconciliation take place. Asian American book buyers helped to buoy the success of recent best-sellers such as Arundati Roy's *The God of Small Things* and Iris Chang's *The Rape of Nanjing.* Disney's *Mulan,* our favorite woman warrior, brought in over $160 million at the global box office, proving not only that the media giant's hunch was correct that American ticket buyers could now accept looking eastward for their blockbusters, but also that burgeoning numbers of Asian American families would support the movie with their numbers.

We Are a Youthful Population

Roughly thirty-seven percent of the Asian American population is between the ages of fifteen and thirty-five. Within that group there are over one million who are now in college, facing crossroads and choices. Asian America is coming of age, bringing along with it new ways of discussing identity. We are coming to understand that Asian America isn't necessarily a dogma to follow, but a constant articulation of a moving experience. Books such as *Q & A: Queer Asian America,* edited by David Eng and Alice Hom, can find audiences just as well as Eric Liu's contemplation on assimilation, *The Accidental Asian.* As the Asian experience becomes more permanently situated in America, a new generation is finding that distances are no longer necessary and that there is more than one way to define the state of Asian America.

When we can begin to take pride in ourselves, not just as Asian women in America, *but more important, as confident participants in our world*, we begin the journey to a truer self-determination. It is no longer necessary to hack off histories, hide from similarities, or criticize those who don't play the same tune. Instead we learn to negotiate our position in the world by striving toward what we have in common as opposed to feeling the need to differentiate.

Women with a profound comfort in their identities as Asian American women have had to acknowledge the influence of internalized stereotypes. They know that despite other people's assumptions that we all look and act alike, there is a tremendous diversity among us that has remained unexplored because of our self-imposed distances. That realization gives us back our humanity and allows us to act freely. When we encounter one another for the first time without cloaks of distance, worlds open up as we recognize our sisters for the first time and finally are able to surrender into the company of each other.

Leni, a Filipina American from San Francisco, once said, *"In you I see myself, and as we mirror each other, we also transform and change together."* To see the uniqueness that is us and then, more important, to be able to tie it to the universal—that is the essence of and the reason for exploring identity, no matter who or what we are.

When we speak of our new communities, we will make our road by walking it. Together, one hopes, rather than apart.

Part III

SURVIVAL

SKILLS

SHE BECOMES A WISER FIGHTER

> *Then we are forced to fight for what we find dear, fight to be*
> *serious about what we are about, fight to develop past our*
> *superficial spiritual moves . . . fight to hold on to the deeper*
> *knowledge, fight to finish what we have begun.*
>
> —Clarissa Pinkola-Estes
> *Women Who Run With the Wolves*

For years, my motto of conflict was this: Mountains always result
from molehills.

If I avoided conflict, I'd always be safe. Don't take sides; don't
get involved.

Do you agree?

Do you walk away when inside you know that you should
stand and fight? Does a negative comment have you running for
the hills, hurt your feelings, or make you arch your back in defense?

You are now entering the hallowed halls of warrior school, where
the first lesson is that sometimes we've got to force ourselves into
battle—for beliefs, for our boundaries, and to defend big pictures.

Becoming a wise fighter, after all, is less about shouting and
more about strategy.

It has been said that Chinese history has proved itself to be one of change through cataclysm, and that gradual, democratically based change has never had a place in such a large country. For thousands of years, dynasties with names like Shang and Ming lived and died by the sword, building empires and being annihilated in fell swoops, horrific massacres, and overhauling revolutions. It is said that the Chinese are not a people of subtle change. Conflicts are handled with swift action, and outcomes are immediate. Mao came marching into Tiananman Square and turned the tables right on the heads of the Kuomintang. Genghis Khan swept westward across China, killing everyone in his path to avoid mutiny, and the Empress Dowager was run out of town on her little bound feet after supporting the Boxer Rebellion. When I conjure up my picture of Chinese conflict, what comes to mind is a white-hot flash of light, like the momentary intensity of an atom bomb.

"Whoever said that Asians are averse to confrontation never stepped through the doors of my house," Korean American college student Jean tells me. "Plates would fly, the curses would spew, and believe me, there are some pretty radical things you can say in Korean if you use your imagination. I remember my aunt and uncle fighting one evening and a bread box goes flying across the room, so that we all had to duck. Those two just kept grabbing whatever was near them and flinging them at each other, hiding around corners, like an ambush. The issue was that my aunt wanted to stock her brother's bread in their ice cream store, and my uncle didn't want to. But now that I think about it, I'm sure there must have been some underlying meaning there." While each Asian culture, in fact, *each family,* may act out their hostilities to different degrees, the truth is that behind closed doors, we fight as ruthlessly, as foolishly, and as intensely as any other family next door.

When my aunt Anna married a white guy in the early 1960s in Clifton, New Jersey, my grandfather banished her from the family. Aunt Anna was never allowed to come home again, not even to visit her mother when she lay dying. That day, Anna stood on the sidewalk begging to be let in, as her brothers and sisters watched from the window upstairs. During those painful years, my father was the only one in the family to visit Anna, that is, until the day my grandfather died. Then the others came out of the woodwork, telling Anna how cruel their father was and how much they wanted to say so when he was alive.

When my grandfather died, he left a modest estate to his four sons, naming my father, the number-one artist son, as the executor of his will. "Let's split the inheritance with our four sisters," he suggested. His brothers didn't agree.

And that's when all havoc broke loose. Although I'll never know what actually happened, since no one in the family wants to dredge up bad memories, this is how I, at ten years old, saw the events unfold.

Four brothers fought it out like brothers do. There were evenings when the women and children would huddle around the kitchen table, while those four brothers came to blows out on the porch, grown men resorting to fistfights and the ugliest language I have ever heard. The four sisters just stood back crying, letting their voices be spoken through the lone, just voice of my father. In the end, my father relinquished his executorship and gave his share of his inheritance to his sisters. His younger brother, the business-man, assumed control of the modest estate, as he had wanted to, and proceeded to persuade every single one of his sib-lings, even the four sisters, to invest their inheritance in his new business venture. My father, who walked away in dis-gust, and his siblings, who didn't know what to say, have chosen not to share their lives since then.

This is the Eng family legacy of what it means to fight. And when disagreement means that one can be disowned, when a difference of opinion can set the groundwork for vendettas that last a lifetime, one learns to avoid conflict at all costs and to appease when it becomes inevitable.

So I learned how to be the great conciliator. Wise like Solomon, I always strained to see both sides of every argument. I never took a side, even when a side should have been taken. Conflict in any form was for losers. It was for people who couldn't look past their own subconscious resentments at big-ger pictures. In my world, conflicts *always* escalated, and with drastic results. In my world, even the smallest irritation or the voicing of a different view would inevitably grow and become permanently destructive, unless I intervened.

Many Asian American women tend to be the keepers of the harmony. But the explanations for our reluctance to engage in conflict aren't always so obvious. It doesn't seem, from the responses I hear, that we are frightened of entering a fray. Or that we are trying to respect authority by keeping our mouths shut when we shouldn't. More, it seems that we are just very accustomed to keeping the peace. We keep control of our world by not losing control ourselves.

Inevitably it is the patterns that we want to avoid the most that become our most insistent visitors, assaulting us again and again until we deal with them in healthier ways. These situations ask us to roll up our sleeves and fight to defend our most meaningful boundaries. For many of us the recurrent theme will be one of how to deal with and engage in meaningful battle.

When I gave myself the role of peacekeeper, I learned to take three steps back and observe, because it hurt less that way. Conflict was too painful for me to touch, so instead I learned to judge from a distance. It took time to learn that conflict, if handled well, is often necessary and healing. That conflict is contact, and that contact requires power.

Now after a couple of scrapes and battles, I know that fighting can have many faces, that stifling anger only to have a conniption fit later never leads to productive results. In most cases, neither does passive resistance in the face of an aggression. Neither does retreat or indifference when confronted by ill-motivated accusations. And neither does shadowboxing.

SHADOWBOXING

When we do choose to fight, many of us tend to be "high context" fighters, resorting to subtle gestures instead of a verbal punch in the face. When we shadowbox, our reluctance to do battle with others leads us to choose subversive and backdoor tactics that don't require confrontation.

Stella gives an example of a recent shadowboxing experience: "I was paying my dry-cleaning bill many weeks too late, which, I admit, was very lame of me. The Korean store owner, who is usually very friendly, must have been annoyed by this, because she turned her chair to face the wall and wouldn't look at me as I spoke to her, and even as she accepted my money."

In another example of high-context fighting, I recall an informal dinner meeting that I attended at a Chinese restaurant owned by a friend. One of the attendees, a woman who is known for her generosity, felt that as a gesture of Asian hospitality, our host would offer us some small token gesture of welcome, a cold drink, or a small appetizer. When our host offered menus instead and encouraged us to order some dishes as paying customers, this woman was affronted.

For half an hour it was obvious that this usually gracious woman couldn't concentrate, so disturbed was she at our host's bad form. As a flourish that was supposed to teach our host a lesson, this woman brought out from her bag a box of dumplings she had planned to take home, offering it with false humility to the group so that our host would notice and understand her faux pas. "A good Chinese host *always* offers to her guests," this woman told me later. "Or she could have offered us something, *anything*. What kind of Chinese woman is she? She should know how to treat her guests."

As the dumplings were put on the table and we all dug in with our chopsticks, our host was noticeably horrified and most certainly ashamed. Since then, both women have refused to be in the same room together, refusing to attend our meetings with comments like, "If that other woman is going to be there, I want no part of it."

Sometimes, our symbolic aggression reaches into more graphic terrain. One young woman wrote about a final "kiss off" that she engineered for a former roommate who wanted her out of the apartment with only a few weeks' notice. While her roommate had gone on vacation, she opened up bags of flour and threw them around the carpets and furniture. She also left a dismembered Barbie doll's body parts strewn through the apartment, the head floating in the toilet. Strange but true behavior, proving that hell hath no fury like an Asian woman scorned. The hell may just be a little less audible and a little more symbolic.

Regardless of its subtleties, shadowboxing still allows us, like stealthy assassins, to go for the jugular. We send out anger like mist, like deadly gas from a stove, unnoticeable yet potent. There's only one problem. When aggression is not accompanied with confrontation, the intensity of our feeling often goes unnoticed. The effect may be that only *we* know the value of our artfully crafted symbolic behavior. When conflict is indirect and full of subtle ambiguities, it tends to confuse or, worse, be ignored. Our behavior may even seem strange or "deranged," and our opinions remain unvoiced. In effect, we conduct ourselves like well-seasoned diplomats, only there is no common code of etiquette that puts us all on the same page. Our actions must be deciphered by others, sometimes wrongly. When my Japanese friend won't look at me because she is upset at something I've said, her boss may interpret that same gesture as inattention or weakness. When we give a stony silent treatment to someone who has insulted us, it may be read as geisha-girl silence. High-context conflict only works when two people are operating with a shared list of gestures and meaning. In a world that is converging so quickly, where cultural and generational differences promise to confuse, it becomes increasingly more unlikely that two people will have the well-matched common codes that made this kind of high-context fighting effective and meaningful in old, closed Asian societies.

HOW WE AVOID THE GOOD FIGHT

What is it that prevents us from engaging in direct conflict with one another? And what stops us from making those confrontations healthy and constructive when we do?

At the age of twenty-six, Janice was appointed the executive director of a respected Southeast Asian community group. While the appointment was a coup for Janice, her staff didn't agree. They thought Janice was too young for the position. As older, more traditional Southeast Asian women whose beliefs leaned to the Confucian, the staff could not bring themselves to respect Janice because of her young, single-woman status. Instead, they began to sabotage her efforts as a leader and to silently show her how to respect her elders. They would call in sick. They would open Janice's mail and make copies, hoping to uncover a mistake that could be brought to the attention of the board of directors. They demanded that she drop everything she was doing to attend hastily called meetings without disclosing the agenda to her. They went directly to major funders without telling Janice and initiated a scandal that almost crippled the organization permanently.

All this happened because the staff could not confront Janice with their doubts about her ability to perform. And yet, it would have been so easy for them to do so. They could have made their concerns known in a way that was honest and diplomatic. They could have worked together to set joint goals, and Janice would have had the opportunity to participate in their concerns. Instead, the staff's behavior became typical of how many of us handle our daily instances of conflict, large or small. We go for swift kills and quick exits. We wait for a slipup so that we can pounce, or we wait for backs to be turned. We may use our slight suspicions as ammunition to bring each other down. Silent maneuvers like these are full of high drama, scandal, and secrecy.

As Janice's example shows, the inability to give voice, presence, and closure to situations of conflict often has larger implications. Janice's organization lost valuable time at a critical moment in its growth, as happens in many situations of great collaborative hope. The lack of good fighting and communication skills among us has often become a serious roadblock to the success of projects both noble and promising.

Jennie had been given a less than favorable review from her boss and feels she deserved better. At first, she spent several days feeling down, used, and unhappy at work and unappreciated for the times that she has spent at the office on weekends. What about that campaign she just pitched to a prospective client and won? How about the times she has been there as a sounding board for her boss's personal life? Didn't Jennie stay late many nights to help bail her boss out of a crisis? After so many years, she thought that her boss was her friend.

Jennie knows so much about her boss's life. So, in anger Jennie starts to talk to her coworkers about how horrible it is to work for her and begins to share her private information. Her coworkers are inclined to agree and are eager to hear about the hidden private life of one of the team heads. Jennie starts to divulge small indiscretions of her boss's that no one else would otherwise know. Her boss's troubles at home with her husband, her opinions about other company employees. All are hurtful to her boss's ability to lead, but telling them is a great release for Jennie.

For Jennie, gossip and back-stabbing were the easier ways to deal with anger and disappointment over unfairness. When confrontation was too difficult, she chose to circumvent a communication process (approaching her boss and discussing the issue) that could have helped her to grow. She opted instead for a process that gave her short-term release but no productive outcome, either for her job or her psyche.

So Jennie is now caught between a rock and a hard place. If her boss begins to trace where her bad publicity is coming from, Jennie will be called on to explain. Or she might suffer future unfavorable reviews. She may even be fired. Because she won't be open about her disappointment and confusion, Jennie must decide on her own whether the less-than-favorable review was an invitation for her to resign or a nudge given by her boss to improve her skills so that she can advance to higher positions. Jennie is setting up a structure for her own professional demise, which should never have had to happen.

Perhaps our reluctance to confront is the product of upbringing. In a 1974 study by psychologists William Caudill and Lois Frost, it was found that Euro-American mothers try to stimulate their infants to vocalize so that infants can communicate their needs, whereas Japanese American mothers try harder to anticipate the needs of their infants. From the time we are born, we may be more accustomed to having our needs met through more subtle cues and to perceiving the needs of others more readily. Perhaps we do not realize the necessity to articulate what we feel must be so glaringly obvious. We may feel, for example, that our anger, tacit as it may be, *must be* readily understood. We may find it difficult to believe that our cues are just not being comprehended.

Until we can recognize how we avoid productive conflict, we will be kept in a state of powerlessness. How do
we do this?

We Walk Away

Although she never voiced it, Trisha, a nisei computer tech-
nologist from San Jose, disagreed with her business partners.
The software system she had created was being used and
marketed incorrectly. According to Trisha, her partners
"obviously didn't get it" and didn't have enough technical
experience to realize that. After a few months of stewing
over how stupid her partners were, Trisha decided that she
had had enough and left her partners along with the full
rights to her program, off for greener pastures. She decided
to start from scratch and build her own software company,
without having to work with "difficult people."

When Annie's father starts to yell and scream, Annie does
not dare to walk out of the room, but neither is she listening
to him. "It might be disrespectful to turn my back, but he
cannot see me turn off my ears," she tells me. Annie, believing
herself a more traditional Vietnamese woman, does not see the
use or need of asserting her rights or opinions in arguing with
her father, who is an authority figure in her family.

When we drop out of conflict, when we convince ourselves that being on our own is better than being in the
fight, or when we just plain walk away, we lose the opportunity to practice sparring techniques that are an important
part of any relationship, whether professional or personal. We
remain novices in the skills of fighting.

Trisha walked away from a conflict that may have been
painful, but had she stayed to duke it out, she might have
learned much more. Without voicing her disappointments or
even her opinion, Trisha allowed her partners full rights to

the programs that she had created and denied herself the opportunity to share in the future profit that her product would bring. Instead, her withdrawal sent her back to the drawing board as she found out the hard way that starting a new technology company from scratch was difficult, as was finding reliable talent. She realized that conflict and differences were bound to exist within any team.

When Annie shuts out her father's shouting and chooses not to respond, she is viewing conflict as an either/or proposition. *Either* she engages in an out-and-out battle with him *or* she must retreat into silence. In fact, constructive conflict may be a compromise between the two. What Annie finally realizes is that tuning out may be fine, as long as her father is in a state of uncontrollable ranting rage. "I've learned to sit and wait out the fury, and then tell my father that we will return to the discussion later when both of us has calmed down." Annie walks away in the short-term, with the obligation that she will return to the conflict on her terms, in an environment where discussion and compromise are possible. It allows her to be respectful to her father without being trampled or terrorized by him.

We Grow Accustomed to Powerlessness

During the yellow peril hysteria of World War II, over one hundred thousand Japanese Americans were sent to internment camps across the country as a result of President Roosevelt's Executive Order 9066. Abiding by the executive order, the Japanese American internees withstood abhorrent conditions for many years, moving into abandoned cattle stables and aluminum shacks, often without plumbing or insulation. Many of them were able to survive that assault on their freedom by focusing on thoughts of destiny and acceptance. "*Shikata ga nai*" meaning, "It cannot be helped," was what many of them answered when their children asked them why their homes, land, and property were taken away and why they were being sent from the West Coast to the dusty middle of the country. There was little they could do. Until very recently, few Americans were even aware that the Japanese American internment was part of our country's history.

"'The president thinks we are spies' is what my *obaasan* [grandmother] should have told me," said one sansei [third-generation Japanese American] internee, now sixty-two years old. "She should have told me another side of the story—that some Americans thought we were receiving messages from our Japanese relatives across the ocean, and that the President of the United States didn't trust us to live so close to the Pacific. She should have told me that we were paying for Pearl Harbor. If she had said that, I would have understood how senseless and unjust this whole thing was, and even though I was very young, I would have been angry."

Shikata ga nai is a pact with destiny. Born out of the concept that life is in union with the cosmos, it is a sigh of quiet resignation. To a Japanese American interned at a camp, it also became the hope of a better tomorrow. It is a healing, restorative phrase, meant for high-ground contemplation, not necessarily one that should be used as a response to injustice. *Shikata ga nai* was not meant to justify the mass imprisonment of a people.

There comes a time when we have to shed complacency and find a balance between what is peaceful and what causes friction. Philosophies of acceptance must sometimes be put on the back burner. Contrary to what Buddha may have preached, life need not be suffering. Contrary to the Hindu tradition of *samsara,* where we are taught to rely on our next lives and rebirth to transcend our present conditions, life requires that *we take actions* to push the scales toward fairness and balance. Not even Confucius preached resignation and blind obedience to those in authority. His writings tell us to respect and abide by only the leaders that are just and exemplary. Even stodgy, conservative Confucius leaves some room for conflict and rebellion.

The danger in relinquishing power over too many generations is that we begin to lose the qualities we need to preserve our willingness to spar. Later generations of Japanese Americans realized this and began to counter despair in their actions, taking up the fight to demand redress and reparations for the losses their families suffered as a result of the internment.

We Implode on Ourselves

Conflict is so painful for many of us that we often turn it in on ourselves rather than come out with a dissonant voice. Tranh, a successful Vietnamese American investment banker in New York, strives for perfection, as she was always taught to do. She is a most excellent hostess and mother, and her coworkers and clients love her. But when Tranh sleeps at night, she wears a bite plate so that her tooth grinding does not wear her teeth into short little nubs. She has bitten through several of them. It has always been hard if not impossible for Tranh to express words of disapproval, to put her own interests or opinions first, or to fight an outward, potentially ugly battle.

• Meena, a mother from Gujarat, India, breaks out into nervous rashes because of the tension she keeps to herself from raising her twenty-year-old, "surly" American-born daughter.

- In post–World War II Japan, many survivors suffered long-lasting, stress-induced traumas, such as Hashimoto's thyroiditis, a life-threatening affliction that suppresses and slows the metabolic processes of the body as if to protect it from shock.

- Lynn, a Shanghai-born artist, takes eight hundred milligrams of Tagamet every day to control a peptic ulcer that her friend tells her is induced by her unhappy marriage.

When we refuse to allow ourselves to engage in the difficult activity of dealing with the stress of conflict, our bodies will react for us.

According to psychologist Jennie Yee, resident clinical psychologist at North Beach Asian Mental Health Services in San Francisco, there is substantial research that shows that Asian Americans, particularly those of immigrant generations, tend to "somaticize" their conflicts, which means they manifest their psychological suppressions as physical complaints. As Yee explains, "Many of my clients tend to voice their stresses by describing pains they experience in their bodies. A young woman may be experiencing coping problems with her family, but she will tell me instead about the pain in her chest, her inability to sleep, or a nagging stomachache." Psychologist Laura Uba, a lecturer at California State University, Northridge, feels that somaticizing may be an indirect way of asking for help, since somatic problems do not carry the stigma or negative social consequences that psychological and emotional concerns do. In other cases, it is the way we have learned to internalize that which we are unwilling to release.

In her book *Women's Bodies, Women's Wisdom,* Dr. Christiane Northrup writes that when we have unresolved chronic conflict in our lives, we set ourselves up for physical stresses due to the biochemical effect that those suppressed conflicts have on our immune and endocrine systems. When we hold in distress, our immune systems begin to turn against the body, potentially inviting a host of "autoimmune" diseases—such as rheumatoid arthritis, multiple sclerosis, and certain thyroid diseases—to take hold of us. According to Northrup, stress is also associated with the release of chemicals that prevent white blood cells from protecting the body from cancer and infection. People who perceive their situations as being uncontrollably stressful and who feel hopeless and despairing actually release chemicals that numb the cells of their bodies, rendering them incapable of destroying cancer cells if this condition is prolonged. As Northrup writes, "It is not the *stress itself* that creates immune system problems, it is, rather, the perception that the stress is *inescapable*—that there is nothing a person can do to prevent it."

We Confuse Conflict With Competition

Good fights are those of substance—the battles that stave off affronts to our ideas and integrity. All too often we never get to fight "good fights" because there are too many diversions along the way. If we cannot distinguish between *tangential issues* and *core ideas,* there is no hope for the good fight, and there is no powerful result. *When we confuse conflict with competition, the fights we do choose tend to be the wrong ones.*

Power struggles about *who gets to lead* are the most important examples of derailed conflict and revolve around "who ends up on top" and whether "I got more than you." They are false competitions that divert our time and energy, and drain our power. "Who?" becomes paramount over "Why?" Consumed with what is immediate to us, we forget to look outside at the battles we really want to fight.

As an activist friend once said, "Sometimes it's like being in a firing squad in a circle. Everyone's got their guns pointed at each other as opposed to outside." False competitions have no meaningful resolution or potential to help us grow as individuals.

In traditional conflict, someone always wins and someone always loses. *But learning the good fight means understanding that our successes do not imply the failure of others. We must believe that there is plenty to go around.*

A Missed Opportunity

A Chinatown community was celebrating, but few people realized how high a price was paid for their victory. The court had made a landmark decision in their favor. The community got what it wanted—a luxury high-rise in their neighborhood would not be built until an impact study was completed, which would show the effects the project would have in displacing the surrounding community. Yet, the battle had exacted tremendous losses as well. Over the course of the case, communication between two of Chinatown's leading Asian community groups had deteriorated. One group, composed mostly of grassroots community activists, had opted for protest-style strategies. The other, a lawyers group, felt that the campaign should have been more restrained, played by the rules, "within the system." The two groups began to label each other, setting the stage for the tensions and competition that would ensue. The community group felt that the "uptight" lawyers were "sellouts." The lawyers felt that the grassroots activists were obstructing progress because their methods were "radical," "rabble rousing," and disrespectful of process. What the two groups could not recognize was that each of them played an integral role in the larger success. The lawyers needed those activists to put on pressure and attract public attention to the case. The activists needed the lawyers to fight the battle in court. Without acknowledging the balance they established, each side began to recruit allies, aligning along "philosophical" lines, and community members had to choose. Were we "team players," as the lawyers were seen? Or were we committed to "real change," as the grassroots activists were seen? Being both was not an option. To be in the camp of one meant being less-than-welcomed by the other. Even after many years, the old wounds have turned into personality wars. And memories have not faded. It is the overall Asian American community that has suffered most, having lost the collaboration of two of their most effective organizations.

False competitions involve the wrong sparring partners. They are the equivalent of friendly fire that leads to weakened potential.

How do we know when we are leading ourselves into one of these? How many of our struggles are based on our need to be recognized as right or declared the winner? Do conflicts always have to spin into competition? Does the drive to win or to be seen as the "definitive one and only" prevent you from trying to understand where other persons in the group are coming from? Are you focused on getting your piece of a very small pie? Are you convinced that there is only so much to go around? Are you investing energy in a power struggle instead of taking responsibility for your own issues?

We Protect Our Turf

Turf protection is another form of fighting for little meaningful purpose. A close cousin of false competition, our tendencies to protect turf come from a mind-set of siege. It is behavior that comes from our fear of potential loss.

When we fight to protect turf, we do so because we believe in scarcity and that in order to have a sense of worth, we must be the queens of our own fiefdoms.

Fighting the good fight means recognizing that empowering others can be the same as empowering yourself. A friend, one of the few Asian American women on the collegiate sports circuit, once told me that she was one of the highest scorers on her basketball team, but realized that there was power in making her teammates better. She could enjoy herself just as much if she passed the ball as she did when she scored the points herself. By passing the ball, my friend jeopardizes her recognition as the highest scorer. How many of us are truly willing to do that? My friend, after all, has no idea whether her teammates will deliver the points that she knows she can. Sharing turf can be difficult if your gain means that others have to lose. Fighting the good fight requires a confidence in others and a refusal to act from fear.

The good fighter understands and can trust that leadership is shared over time and that leaders must be willing to be fluid and trusting in another's ability to deliver. By taking the risk of believing in each other and by making ourselves vulnerable to the flaws of others, we give ourselves the opportunity to become empowered by connection.

Classic Turf Protection: Cut Your Nose, Spite Your Face

Bei Yee has always been the strong arm of the family, and she intends to keep it that way. She is the keeper of the purse strings, the engine behind her husband's career, the stern mother for her daughter, and the one and only object of her son's ultimate admiration. Bei Yee has to take care of everything, and she is good at it. Without her resourcefulness, she is convinced that all of them—husband, daughter, and son—would flounder into obscurity.

When Bei Yee's son began to date, Bei Yee insisted on meeting each of his romantic interests, and for fifteen years Bei Yee has nixed every one of them as not good enough for him. A few of them were too American brazen. A few of them weren't from the right neighborhood in Shanghai, where Bei Yee's family has its industrialist roots. Some of them were "country girls" from families with poor backgrounds. Now, however, Bei Yee's son is tiring of his mother's destructive pull on his life. He is living with a woman that, yet again, Bei Yee has a problem with, but this time, he is letting his mother know that his relationships are off limits to her. Bei Yee tries hard to create conflict between her son and his girlfriend. "She's trying to marry up. She's cunning. Can't you see she's trying to trick you?" Bei Yee says to him.

Bei Yee uses conflict as a way to chase away her nervousness. All of a sudden her turf as the ultimate power over her son is being slowly won over by an encroacher. What will she do in the world without her children? After all, America for Bei Yee will be a lonely place once they leave the nest. Instead of approaching her son and his girlfriend and working to establish a balance, Bei Yee begins to thrash. Because of the tension she creates, her son's relationship begins to flounder. His girlfriend leaves, not interested in small family feuds that nibble away at what they were trying to build. Bei Yee has used her ability to battle in the most destructive and stunting of ways.

Turf protection happens in many contexts. It happens in families, it happens at work, it happens in community organizing. We are loath to give up easily what influence we have. We know, after all, that we are competent. And we have convinced ourselves that there is only so much to go around.

SEVEN SPARRING LESSONS

When we can recognize the ways we avoid conflict, we can work to hone our fighting skills by employing a few simple ideas that show us that conflict can be just as important as consensus when we are talking about progress and power.

Lesson One: Conflict Is Necessary

The Buddha may have said that peace is a natural state, but the "harmony" that we may be taught to maintain is not numbness or failing to confront. Instead, it is *dynamic calm*—created through the conflict of two equally opposing and balanced forces. In Buddha's terms, conflict is a *necessary* element of peace.

Ho Puna Puna

In Hawaii, there is a way of resolving conflicts known as *ho puna puna,* meaning "making things right." Puanani, a poet and community mediator from Hawaii, explained *ho puna puna* this way:

> *Ho puna puna* recognizes that "justice" isn't always "fair," and that "fact" isn't always "truth." That there is no right and wrong, only differing ways of seeing things that must be resolved in the most right of ways.
>
> My little brother was once caught stealing a quarter out of my aunt's purse. My aunt was furious at him. She was screaming and yelling, "You no good!" which turned into "Your family no good!" and "Your mother no good!" We needed *ho puna puna* to make things right again. First, we got a third person from the family to hear what my aunt and my brother had to say. It was that person's job to decide whether both of them were ready and willing to take part in a healing process.

If that mediator decided that this was not the case, then *ho puna puna* doesn't go any further. There is no *ho puna puna* unless two people are ready and open. It turns out that my brother stole that quarter because he had been shamed by his friends at the candy store. They had all bought candy and my brother couldn't, and he felt that he had lost face. He didn't want the candy. He wanted to redeem his honor.

Ho puna puna recognizes that life and its conflicts are multi-layered and complicated, and requires us to look past facts to get at truths. As Puanani describes, "In Hawaiian, when we repeat words, it's like smashing them together to express more intensity. *Puna* in Hawaiian means 'right,' so when we say *puna puna,* it means *righteous* right, righter than right. *Ho puna puna* is about larger truth." Puanani's brother was forgiven by his aunt, without requiring him to return the money that he had taken from her. *Ho puna puna* uncovered a larger truth than the taking of that quarter.

Conflict is necessary because difference is inherent in every endeavor. We can work toward ways of resolving our conflicts that conclude as equitably as possible. Leslie is one of the few Asian American producers in Hollywood. She has a reputation of getting things done quickly and keeping her production teams working together. "When I started out as a producer, I'd try to put out all the brushfires before they happened because I didn't want to deal with fighting on the set. I wanted to make sure everyone was happy. But then I realized that without conflict, we'd have a dull film. Filmmaking is about being creative, and that means sparks have to fly. I pick good people who know how to disagree, people who don't have attitudes, who can give in sometimes and win sometimes, and get on with the show. That's why my sets are so civilized."

Leslie stays in the fray, forging compromise out of many creative conflicts. She is aware of the limitations of collaboration, so she uses her position as a leader to intuit the tenor of the group, redirecting tense creative discussions only after conflict proves no longer productive.

Lesson Two: Saying "No" Is Okay and, In Fact, You Must Draw Your Lines

How many times do we catch ourselves accepting behavior that we disapprove of, or saying yes when we really want to say no? Drawing lines is not easy, especially if we have been taught to please, and especially if we really *do* want to do all the wonderful things we are asked to do. But boundaries are necessary. They allow us to know when we are tired, when our mental and emotional energy is tapped out. Saying no requires that we know ourselves and what we ultimately want. Drawing our lines is practice in defining the self. "No" is a word of power. When we can use it, we identify what is truly important to us as opposed to what is *supposed* to be important to us. We begin to establish a core of principles to fight for.

What Is Important?

Mai Yan races back and forth from the hospital to her medical office at least three times a day. She wants to stay connected to her patients, her fellow doctors, all the people who want a little piece of her—her advice, her support, her glowing optimism, and if that means that she has to be a veritable Speedy Gonzales, well, then, she will do it. Several times a week she is asked to join a hospital committee, participate in an interview, or give a fledgling medical student some advice. She finds herself almost always saying yes, which is more often than she wants or can handle. "Someone asked me to promise that I would be peppy in a keynote speech I was to deliver that evening. I told them I'd promise nothing at this point other than to remain standing." After a hectic few years of honoring everyone's wishes, Mai Yan knew that she had to take a step back. "I realized that I don't have to be involved in everything. What I can do is choose what I want to do, and by doing so, others can be informed by my actions and apply it to their own efforts." Mai Yan learned to say no, even though some projects sounded quite interesting to her. She needed the time to rest, to be with her family, and "to eat slowly, sleep deeply, and breathe."

For many of us, life is demanding enough, and projects and assignments often come through the door faster than we can handle them. We "put ourselves through the meat grinder," as one respondent said, "and never complain about being run down," because we believe in what we do or because someone above us is dictating that we get the job done. Being unable to say no in either case is self-destructive. Whether it is pressure from a higher authority or the whip that we use on ourselves, trying to do it all catches up with us in the end. "I began to accept assignments that I knew I couldn't possibly accomplish on time, because I couldn't refuse. I felt it was an honor to be asked to do the work, which is the way that I've been taught. It was a pretty effective form of career self-destruction," Radha wrote. Another respondent tells me: "When I don't want to do something, I just remain silent, because saying no is impolite. I won't say anything, I'll just continue to smile. Sometimes I don't want to spend time with someone; I won't show up even if I've made a plan to do so."

Drawing lines also means saying no to certain relationships, refusing to give of ourselves or take part in situations that do not enforce our life principles as well. It means not accepting the put-downs that a husband or lover or friend may offhandedly fling, setting up patterns of communication that put our bosses on notice that we will not be spoken to disrespectfully, or making it clear to parents or children what behavior we will and won't tolerate. It means listening to our intuition, telling us the *ho puna puna* way.

Lesson Three: "Defense of Honor" Is Often a Deterrent to Good Conflict

Writer Shawn Wong once mused that all Chinese movie plots have at their core the themes of honor, betrayal, and revenge. Conflict seen in this way is larger-than-life, and every dissonance is interpreted as an assault to honor. Be wary of the "honor" strategy that is often used against strident young women to preserve hierarchies that keep us in our places. We waste our energy and we waste our time when we have to defend ourselves against it.

Priscina, a Thai American college student, felt that her Chinese American uncle Ling was not being fair. She saw that her uncle Ling treated his daughter differently from his son and pointed out the disparity. "This is America, Uncle Ling, not China. You should treat your daughter as you treat your son." Ling felt that Priscina was completely disrespectful. According to Ling, it wasn't Priscina's place to criticize an elder on the way he chose to deal with his children. Ling called Priscina's father and told him that Priscina was no good, that she had gone too far and had tried to shame him. Ling tried to use his "honor" as a way to silence the substance of Priscina's statement. By being affronted and putting Priscina on the defensive, forcing an apology, the issue of his unequal treatment of his daughter was left untouched. By refusing to respect Priscina because of her age and position in the family, and because preserving his honor was his more important goal, Ling was able to escape the more meaningful conflict.

Honor has always been used as a way to keep dissent and conflict from becoming a tool for change in ancestral Asian countries. With thousands of years of Confucian teaching to back it up, the "honor" defense is so irrefutable and effective. Knowing our elders have issues of honor, we may want to deliver important messages "the Asian way," through an emissary—the sympathetic, older family member or a respected friend—so that the content of the message is more constructively received. Although this may seem like a "withdrawal" from our righteous belief that women should speak and be heard for themselves, sometimes communication of an important idea takes precedence over who delivers it.

Lesson Four: Conflict Is Not Brutality
In the tale of the woman warrior Fa Mu Lan, she returned home after battle, put on her simple white tunic, and resumed her work at the spinning wheel. She hadn't hardened her heart even after her battles. In the same way, my folklore movie heroine Wing Chun returned to her home village after long, hard fights and was able to embrace what was creative and life-giving. Like Fa Mu Lan, Wing Chun also spared her opponents' lives. She hadn't felt it necessary to annihilate.

But how were they able to do that? I wondered. How could it be that Fa Mu Lan and Wing Chun were more satisfied in sparing life than they would have been in taking it? Weren't Fa Mu Lan and Wing Chun fearful that their opponents would sneak-attack them again?

"It is insecurity that makes people tyrants," one Vietnamese friend responded. Only when we feel unsure that our ideas will be accepted by the group, or when our fight is not consistent with moral principles, do we start to fight by squelching dissent or acting tacitly in order to win. Insecurity never leads to satisfaction, because it allows for diversionary and terrorist tactics that lead us into false competitions.

There is a Japanese word *toronoko*, which literally means "tiger cub." In regular usage though, it means a "paper tiger" and is used to describe someone who appears brash but is actually quite cowardly. *Toronoko* is equivalent to the roar of a cowardly lion. Get behind the facade, and all that is there is a lonely, fearful person.

*Toronoko*s are those who doubt their strength and feel the need to overcompensate. A *toronoko* believes she must trample opponents in order to win, because her inexperience in the good fight tells her that this is so. But as experienced fighters know, they can fight with the purpose and center of the strongest adversaries and still maintain what is kind and giving within them. They can command respect for their ability to be consistent and competent. They teach their opponents through their actions that it is not necessary to destroy in order to win.

Conflict need not be brutality. Fighting need not mean "to the bitter end." Different opinions will always exist. As a matter of fact, it is always more productive to have good opponents available to constantly test one's skills than it is to reign unchallenged.

Lesson Five: Battles Must Be Chosen

Every day we are confronted with situations and people that will challenge us in many ways, small and large. From the coworker who cracks offensive jokes, to the construction worker who whistles when we walk by, to the friend who calls and berates us for not keeping in touch. Not all of those conflicts are worth getting into. Many of them are false competitions. Some of them come from the lack of balance of the person that has initiated the fight. An intuitive person, guided by her specific set of principles, can distinguish between the battle and the war because she understands her objectives. "I used to run at the wall, you know, kamikaze style, whenever I came up against someone or something that I didn't agree with," says Sharon. "*But to fight also means to survive,* which meant that I had to stop doing this macho thing all the time because it wasn't helping me. Running at the wall really runs you down, and it isn't always the most effective means of fighting, either."

Which are the fights that can create change in your life? Each of us will have a different barometer to make these choices. For some it is valuable to deliver a quick word to the slimy guy that just told you to "go back to Korea where you belong." Your doing so might make him think twice about doing it again if he knows that the next Asian woman he insults like that might embarrass him as you just did. For others who have to deal with intense conflict every day, such as a tenants' attorney who dukes it out eight hours a day in court, or a clerk with an argumentative boss, or an unhappy wife who listens to her husband's rantings as soon as she comes home, it might be just too much to fight that street battle with the ignorant passerby as well.

Emily, an activist for over thirty years who lives in San Francisco, has a hard-and-fast line that helps her to distinguish which personal battles she will fight. Emily is an easygoing woman who doesn't feel it's necessary to wear a hard exterior to show that she can be tough. Her ability to focus her fight is driven by this bright line rule:

I try to be nice to everyone. Everyone's got their own hang-ups, so I try to understand where they're coming from. But if anyone ever takes my respect for granted, if someone tries to be tricky or dishonest or manipulative, thinking that my manner means I'm a pushover, I will take the offensive. No one deserves to be treated like that. I don't like it when people take my good nature for granted, because it's not a signal that they can walk all over me. If that happens, I get into a mode that's more like, "Don't mess with me because you have no idea how tough I can be."

Lesson Six: Successful Fighters Respect Difference

Operations were up and running at our fledgling magazine office. We were so busy with the day-to-day tasks of keeping a business going that a year went by without us even blinking an eye. But after a few successes and as we grew used to one another, something began to change in the way we communicated. As our staff grew, so did our need for space, which lead to the editorial staff being separated by two walls and a hallway from the publishing staff. With that physical separation came an emotional separation, along with the "brick wall" that traditionally exists between editors and publishers that says that the "creative team" should stay clear of the "business team" to preserve journalistic purity. While the "brick wall" concept might be necessary in a corporate publishing venture, it had little use in our project, which envisioned a new kind of empowerment for an otherwise invisible and unempowered group. After all, we had no money, and we just wanted to create the strongest publication possible. What we were creating was an activist mode of publishing that required a finely tuned ebb and flow between those who created and those who had to convey to others what we were trying to do.

Arguments ensued. The classic publisher-versus-editor struggle began. Wanting creative freedom, the editor sometimes felt limited by my business concerns. Wanting the most successful magazine possible, I would constantly question whether it was as coherent as it needed to be for our readers and advertisers to understand. All of a sudden, our choices became naively two-sided, a simplistic choice between "numbers chasing" and "journalistic freedom." Opinions between us became so polarized that eventually every discussion devolved into an argument. Each of us needed to win, and because winning was often the goal, we weren't able to negotiate a basic understanding of conflict as a banter of ideas, rather than all-out war.

Striking a balance between conflict and creativity was so crucial to us, as it is to all good creative teams. But, because of the intensity of deadlines and the fact that our bank accounts were bleeding cash, we sometimes found it difficult to listen and understand that *differences of perspective are needed to create and fulfill large visions.* What makes these differences negotiable is our ability to respect and communicate without ego, without pretext, and without underlying motive.

Good conflicts do not involve manipulating or convincing others to follow blindly. Creative fighting demands so much more than that. It requires patience and energy to convince our adversaries to broaden their thinking. *Good conflicts also require active listening, allowing our own biases and expectations of our opponents to fall away.* When we actively listen, we gain information that helps us become more effective, *less reactive,* fighters. When someone insults or calls us to task with accusatory words, it becomes more important to pay attention to our own reaction or accusation than it is to blame the other party for delivering it. Which one of our buttons is being pushed and why? What might be motivating the aggression from the other person? Because conflict is so integral in an open communication system, it is important to say what we really mean and listen with heart.

But open listening does not always come naturally. Sometimes we need practice that can only be had with training. To get the most out of conflict, we may need to appoint a mediator, a third-party witness that is able to hear and translate for us so that we can begin to hear each other accurately. For example, in some well-run meetings, a witness will be appointed from the group whose role it is to listen carefully for the nuances, to perceive body language and the flow of the group discussion. It is up to the mediator to point out to the group a potential trouble spot and to try to work out and translate the conflicts before people start to dig in their heels.

Lesson Seven: Conflict Opens Doors

The groups and people that lead the most graced existences—whether they be lovers, spouses, friends, or corporations—are those that have learned how to use conflict as a way to grow and understand themselves more deeply. For such people, dissonance provides opportunity for growth, because that is how the best ideas develop—through give and take, with alternating intensity and backing off of parties that respect one another even through differences.

KaYing used conflict as an opportunity that brought her Hmong community closer to healing from the ravages of the Vietnam war. By befriending a Vietnamese woman and being seen with her in her community, KaYing was initially labeled a betrayer and a black sheep because of the history of war only one generation ago between her own Hmong people and Vietnamese villages across the borders: "My community took it badly and thought that I was acting disloyal. They thought my behavior in having a Vietnamese friend was too Americanized. Because I had to learn English to translate for everyone else, they thought I was even more American. But I had to show them that there must be a time for healing."

KaYing made choices that cast her in a questionable light and ruffled some feathers, but her opting to do so has certainly allowed younger Hmong Americans to make their choices more easily. The fruits of these conflicts are always slow to come, but long-lasting. While KaYing's community will never forget the ravages of their past interethnic conflicts at the North Vietnamese border, the future begins to present itself as a time of communication, healing, and hope. Conflict means taking chances and trusting in our vulnerability. It is only then that we can grow.

Handling conflict well can also serve as an initiation rite. Marlene, for example, remembers a big rift in her Filipino community. By the early eighties, a newer, wealthier, professional group of Filipino immigrants began to arrive in numbers, changing the makeup of the Filipino immigrant community. At one point, a group of these new wealthy immigrants wanted to buy a community center that had long been run by a group of older, poorer immigrants from the agricultural community. As Marlene recalls, "It was a bitter fight where both sides had lawyers. The older generation who had been here for years, the poorer farmworkers, thought that we should hit the wealthy newcomers where it would hurt them most. The best thing they could do, they felt, was to report the newer wealthy immigrants for illegal immigration practices. 'They own companies that employ undocumented people; we should turn them in,' they'd say."

Marlene's mother asked Marlene to help. "When the fighting got very bad, I told them that we couldn't do this to one another. That we were all immigrants at one point and that there were other ways to work through our problems without destroying each other. It diffused the group, and they were open enough to understand that I was right. That's when things changed for me and my position in the group. All of a sudden here I was, this young woman, telling my aunts and uncles that they couldn't do something. It showed my parents that I was an adult. It showed me that I had changed."

BECOMING A WARRIOR

Often when we make a bid for ourselves, we will be perceived as too bold, too forward, out of line, or inappropriate. For those who believe that power is limited, power gained means that someone else has lost power. Even the *I Ching* tells us that the price of increasing power is increasing opposition and reminds us that resistance, by its very nature, will always involve elements of conflict that may not be easy. And yet accepting power means that we will have to force ourselves to enter into these frays, guided, one hopes, by correct reasons and with a sense of perspective.

In an ancient book about an old idyllic city called Shambala, the birth of a warrior's strength is likened to the first growth of a reindeer's horns. "At first," says the book, "those horns emerge from the reindeer's head soft and rubbery, unable to be used by the reindeer who is eager to use them to fight. Slowly they harden. Stronger points begin to sprout." As the Shambala book teaches us, fearlessness is like those rubbery horns. At first, they may seem ready, but it takes time and patience to put strength into them. At first, the reindeer feels they are awkward and unwieldy. But then a reindeer instinctively realizes that he should have horns. They are part of his birthright. In the same way, says the book of Shambala, we first give birth to the tender heart of warriorship. Fighting skills take time and practice. But as the reindeer knows its birthright, we know that we have the power of the fight within us, and an innate sense of truth that tells us when fighting is necessary.

Think back to times when you encountered difficulties and examine how you dealt with them. Was it with more unfocused rage than was really needed? Did you walk away? Did you stand your ground only to be shocked or embarrassed later at your loss of control? Becoming a warrior will require that you know your own power and focus it in ways that affirm your connection to yourself and your most cherished beliefs. With the recognition of those beliefs, may you fight the good fight.

SHE FINDS HER TEACHERS

I taught her what makes the world a living place: sunrise and sunset, heat and cold, dust and heat, dust and wind, dust and rain.

I taught her what is worth listening to in this world: wind, thunder, horses galloping in the dust, pebbles falling in the water.

I taught her what is frightening to hear: fast footsteps at night, soft cloth slowly ripping, dogs barking, the silence of crickets.

—Amy Tan
The Hundred Secret Senses

Every warrior needs her training and a guide. How are we to know which block to use, which way to lean, when to refrain, and when to advance? In Chinese, we call that guide the sifu, a master, usually older, usually gray and wizened. The question is, how on earth do we find her?

Teenage boredom in Long Island on a Saturday afternoon. Up in my attic room, with sloping painted wood panel walls, I'd lie on the bed and stare at the ceiling for hours, thinking about how bored I was. Once in a while, I would descend from my coop to rummage around in the refrigerator for something to eat.

"I'm bored," I'd say to my mother. In front of me on the refrigerator shelf was what looked like a mad scientist's experiments: the half full jar of dried black beans, Maxwell House coffee jar full of dried mushrooms, weird Chinese pickle stuff in a Tupperware container, a tiny jar of dried up shrimp. I reached past all of them to grab for two Kraft American cheese singles, my favorites.

"If you're so bored, then do something," my mother would answer, as she rushed around, dusting the furniture, vacuuming, wiping down the kitchen, unpacking the groceries, and folding the laundry before she went in for the swing shift at the hospital at three in the afternoon.

I'd look up to the ceiling and shake my head, thinking that she couldn't relate to my angst. And then I'd retreat, bringing my Kraft singles, along with a pitcher of iced tea and bag of Oreos back upstairs with me, leaving her with all of the housework while I resumed my contemplation of boredom.

Sometimes I would stare at the mirror, waiting for signs. I had nothing else to do. My eyes would rest on the eyes in the mirror, and then something strange would begin to happen.

I'd get a ringing in my ears as it fell eerily silent all around me. Staring so hard, I would begin to see my image in the mirror blur and then fade into a series of moving dots. The face in front of me would begin to transform in shape, my hair becoming just a black borderless mass, the eyes getting smaller, the mouth turning down, morphing into a barely distinguishable blur, and there in front of me would be the face of my *po-po,* my father's mother, sitting across from me in my same pose, staring silently. There are the telltale Eng smile lines, a crevice on each side, from nose to mouth. There are the full lips and the intense gaze. It is my father's face, it is her face, emerging from mine. On afternoons when I dared that experiment, I could summon my grandmother's spirit to me, swept up in my fascination at the time in stories of little girl witches, magic spells, and sorcery. I would look at her, trying to make contact, knowing that if I moved too suddenly I would break that fragile vision. *I've got you here now, Grandma, don't go.*

It scared me at first, this strange sort of imagination game. I never dared to tell anyone about it. "Spooky girl," they'd probably have said. It might have worried my parents, who would have laughed and pretended to be entertained, all the while being absolutely petrified.

My grandmother died at the age of sixty, when I was six years old, of a cerebral aneurysm, and took my grandfather with her one year afterward. At six, I didn't understand whom I had lost. Her funeral, though, is completely clear in my memory—the open casket at the True Light Lutheran Church with the red double doors facing catty-corner on Mulberry Street in Chinatown. The smell of incense sticks, stinky, smoky orange, makes me choke. Near her is a box of takeout chicken and rice with a pair of chopsticks stuck in, just in case her spirit got hungry on her journey into forever. I see clearly my older aunts, who don't speak English, falling to the ground, screaming, wailing, prostrating themselves, half out of fright, half out of grief. Over and over they walk up the aisle to view the casket as if they are daring themselves to do something dangerous. And then they collapse into screams that scare the living daylights out of me. Next to the casket, *po-po's* picture hangs in the middle of a wreath, a black-and-white old-fashioned Chinese photograph, maybe even a blown-up passport picture, which meant that she was not smiling. My father brought me to the open casket and told me to bow three times. *Po-po* looked so alive, lying there. She could have gotten up right in front of us and it wouldn't have surprised me.

Twenty-eight years later, I learned about the ritual of Ching Ming, the day in early spring when all dutiful relatives clear the graves of dead ancestors and pay their respects. My dad always goes to his parents grave alone, braving the gusting spring wind that blows off their burial hill in the Bushwick area of Brooklyn, where hundreds of plots are reserved by Chinatown funeral homes. There my grandparents rest in peace together, in the comfort of other Chinese-speaking souls. On those trips, my father doesn't ask us to accompany him, saying it is too much trouble for everyone else to make the trip. I figure he wants to be alone, so I never push too hard. I wonder if he bows three times at the double gravestone that marks his parents' grave, with their no-smiling black-and-white pictures mounted on it, to show his reverence despite a generation's worth of misunderstanding.

Years later I would open up the photograph book to a picture where my *po-po* is helping me celebrate my first birthday. Disheveled, wispy-haired, with a Cro-Magnon–like huge bulbous forehead (*meaning you had brains,* my mother says), I am standing as Grandma holds me balanced on her lap, her hands gripping me tight under my layers of sweaters. I have my finger to my mouth, telling everyone to *shhhh!* so I can blow out my one candle. Behind us there is a wire from the wall clock that hangs above us. My *po-po* has a perm.

My grandmother pushes two *hong baos,* little red envelopes with money, through the little crack in our Chrysler Valiant window so that the air-conditioning does not leak through. Her white socks and Chinese embroidery slippers, her light cotton dress in a blue-and-white flower pattern, are so clear to me now.

Oh, yea! I got money! was all I could register whenever I saw the red-and-gold *hong bao. Is it one dollar? Is it five maybe? Maybe even . . . ten?*

That was the extent of our visits—quick, drive-by glimpses, over in a matter of minutes, through a backseat car window. Grandma never exchanged a comprehensible word with me, except that she would say my name, which came out sounding more like "Huay Bee," showing that she was trying, and I would say, "Thank you, Grandma," because I was told to. I feared my grandma, like some alien being. Because she couldn't speak English, she seemed so strange to me. As a five-year-old staring at one who was sixty, she looked *so old.*

When Grandma died, so did my chance of getting the

real family story. She was the only one who really knew my father and thus was my key to understanding what really made him tick. At least I've found a way to bring her back, though only through a spine-tingling, silent apparition that appears to me, at whim, in the mirror. I will have to be satisfied with fleeting contact as I look into her eyes.

If I had understood Cantonese, what would *po-po* have told me? What is it that she would have said to a six-year-old girl, or a granddaughter on her fifteenth birthday? At twenty-seven? How about at thirty-five?

Are there grandma substitutes? Who are the elders that make it possible to know who we are? So many of us agree—it is usually not our mothers, as they are too close to us, too wrapped up in what we symbolize in their lives. Where can we uncover the important themes of our recent pasts? Who has the real stories of who we are, what we have come from, who we can be? Is there anyone who is up to the task?

How are we going to pass down the fire?

HEROINES

In finding workable wisdom and in making sense of our places here and now, many of us are left without ties to our family past. My search and the search of many other Asian women for ultimate heroes, those that embody grace coupled with power, continues. From a young age, through my teenage years, and even through college and my professional life, I have looked for that direction. Where is the confident and compassionate Asian American woman who shares my face and my history? Where are the teachers among us?

It may be true that Asian women in America can look to

many sources for guides. There are, for instance, women leaders of the traditional American women's movement like Gloria Steinem, or the strong contemporary literary voices of African American women like Maya Angelou or Alice Walker, or the many public figures who appear on television and in newspapers, whether men or women. We are not bound by race and gender when looking for mentors. Many of us even turn to the strong men in our lives, as Wen did when she began college:

> When I started college, I attended a remedial English writing class for minorities, and I had a young professor who was born in Mexico. He walked into the room with torn jeans, skateboard, Walkman. I had never seen anything like that. After a few weeks, he didn't come to class and I read in the papers that he had been arrested because he was protesting the opening of a nuclear power plant nearby. Up till then, this professor was as close to my experience as I had come by, kind of an outcast, and he was fighting for things he believed in. He showed me that I wasn't alone and that it was possible to participate in bigger things. I wanted to be just like him.

We are often at a loss, however, in identifying women who can inform our notions of power while also sharing our common experiences as Asian American women, an experience that has its peculiar issues, responses, and complexities. Given our shared knowledge and traditions, Asian American women need one another to draw up the past and link it to *practical* notions of the future. We can show each other how we have learned to balance our ambitions as professional women with the deep obligations to stay close to our families. We can offer one another suggestions for more effective ways of speaking up in family gatherings so that we can work effectively within the parameters of an Asian family's power dynamics.

I have thought long and hard about why it has been so difficult to find such women, and why it has been like pulling teeth to get them to impart advice. *I now realize that we have created so few environments of trust where the instructive spirit of our mentors is encouraged, sustained, and deemed important.*

Mentorship begins with the development of links that extend the web of teaching past the family bond. When I speak at college campuses, I often ask Asian American women in my audiences to identify the person who has been their most significant role model. More often than not, they answer categorically, saying there are no Asian American role models out there for them, or that there have never been women who served in the role of life teacher for them. For those who have identified their role models, their choices tend to be removed and inaccessible, national figures like Connie Chung or Hillary Clinton—women who may have qualities that these women want to emulate and whose success they desire, but who play no role in actually mentoring their daily practice of power. Many women also describe a defaulted sense of self-sufficiency with an answer like Miya's, a Japanese American woman adopted by Caucasian parents, who recently moved from the Midwest to Tokyo to explore her Japanese ancestry and culture: "I am my own mentor," she says. "I learned early on that I couldn't depend on the experiences of others to shape my life." I came to know Miya in her state of exploration through transpacific Internet conversations about her job, her relationship with her boyfriend, and her family life in America. Underlying her words was the voice of a self-imposed loner. Miya had grown accustomed to not expecting assistance, understanding, or instruction at work or in her personal life. "I can do it myself" is the motto for so many of us. Having grown so self-sufficient, we often forget to look up. Had we done so, we would have watched our potential mentors pass us by.

THE LEGACY OF THE MENTOR

When the student is ready, the teacher will appear. They pop up when we need them most, in symbols and in people we meet. Whether or not we apply their teaching is up to us. In Japan, the concept of student and teacher is *seito* and *sensei,* and it is necessary to be both *seito* and *sensei* together at various points in life, so that one never grows too old or too important to learn. Teach and learn, be one who is mentored and one who mentors, so that collective wisdom spirals upward.

At eighteen I went searching for the closest form of mentorship that I could and found its embodiment in Sharon, only a few years older than me, my informal teacher of life and living who eventually became a peer and an inspiration, not just to me but to dozens of young Asian American women as well.

Sharon was a product of the fifties and sixties, the only daughter of Chinese immigrants who settled in the colorful cauldron of Flushing, Queens, which has since become one of the most culturally diverse communities in the country. I met Sharon during an interview I was conducting as an intern for a small paper in San Francisco. One of my assignments brought me up to a rickety New York dance studio in the Chinatown part of the Bowery where Sharon was choreographing a performance piece with an Asian American dance company. Sharon, like my warrior-fighter Wing Chun, was a multitasker. Somehow, in between her responsibilities at the dance studio, she also worked full time as a law professor and was a single mother.

When I watched Sharon dance, I felt her power. She allowed herself to move freely, with her own expression, out of the confines of a rigid classical training that might have hemmed her in with form and correctness. Sharon was completely uninhibited, almost embarrassing me with her openness. I learned from friends that Sharon had been active in student government at Sarah Lawrence. She admitted that she had dated eccentric guys when she was young. It was then that I saw Sharon's human side. She was real, and because of that I knew that I could trust her.

It must have been a spirit of defiance that I found so seductive in Sharon. She had that same fearlessness I remember in my big cousin, "take-no-shit" Sandra, who used to tease her hair high and wear pasted-on, two-inch-long fake eyelashes and the highest platform shoes I ever saw. Sandra had mesmerized me. Because she cannot tell me her story now, I piece my bits of information together and imagine that she would have said this:

I was born in Hong Kong and came here when I was about fifteen or sixteen. Once I had a boyfriend who was a white policeman from the Fifth Precinct in Chinatown, which was a little tricky, because my father ran illegal mah-jong tables in the cellar of our candy store only three blocks away. While I was growing up, my father felt it was his fault that I spent time with the tough boys because they used to hang around his gambling house. But these were my choices. I did whatever I wanted.

It was Sandra who first showed me that I could do anything I wanted to do, too. If I wanted to wear lipstick, she'd let me try hers and then give me two of her own to take home. If I wanted to clomp around in Sandra's bright red clogs, which my mother told me would ruin my feet, Sandra would grab my arm, take me to the shoe store near the Staten Island Ferry, and buy me a pair of my own. She gave me great costume jewelry, which I treated like royal jewels. Sandra was wild, my parents used to tell me; she had the mark of trouble on her head. But I was drawn to her, like the proverbial moth to the flame. As I got older and we moved into the suburbs, far from the reaches of Chinatown, I would hear about Sandra's fiascos. Her husband, a bartender, spent too much time away from home. Sometimes Sandra would drag her husband out of his Long Island bar into the street and give him a good talking down. In 1968, Sandra was a maverick Fiercegirl.

On the day of my wedding, I had not seen Sandra for many years and looked forward to seeing her especially. It was on that day that I learned from family that Sandra had been missing for many months. One evening, she went downstairs to buy milk for dinner and never came back. Maybe "bad elements" were involved, or maybe Sandra knew something she shouldn't have known, and so she wound up missing. Maybe Sandra got mixed up with the wrong man and found herself in major trouble. I now think of Sandra constantly, trying to make sense of her strange disappearance and trying to understand how such a powerful, seductive woman could have vanished into thin air. It's been over four years now, and still I think that one day Sandra will walk through the door and tell us her incredible story.

It is the power of Sandra that I remember most. She understood in her own way that power was not for others to give to us. It was Sandra's legacy to have a beautiful daughter,

Erica, who, when she was younger, led the Chinese New Year's lion dance in Chinatown. Erica held that lion's head, traditionally a boy's job, and shook it high above her own while she performed the intricate steps that took the lion through the streets and up to each of the Chinatown storefronts. Although she wouldn't say it quite this way, I know that Sandra must have taught Erica, as she once taught me through example, that *any power that comes from approval for our good behavior, blind obedience, or a refusal to think deeply is false power, because it is for others to give at their pleasure.*

Sandra and Sharon were two women whose lives fell so far from each other's in terms of background, language, community support, and opportunity, and yet they shared the same spark and fire. Sandra expressed power by defying convention, made within her more circumscribed world of Chinatown. She fought for herself as best she could. Sharon crafted her defiance in a different way. Brainy and recognized for it ever since she was young, Sharon could have played by the rules if she wanted, settled down in a nice comfortable lawyer's job and marriage, but she didn't opt for those roads. Instead she felt it necessary to push the rules around, choosing her own view of life, which was one of artistry and humanity.

She'd set up challenges in most places she went. When she was asked not to talk about her divorce and single motherhood while accepting an award from an Asian American community group, Sharon decided that it was the best time to openly air it. If they were rewarding her for being an Asian American role model, they would honor her for what she was *in her entirety.* At the 1995 UN World Women's Conference in Beijing, Sharon questioned China's record on human rights abuses in front of the global press, even though she knew that by doing so she would jeopardize her ability to return to China. And while this might have been a small price to pay for many of the American women who joined her there, Sharon, who is known as a China expert, was risking her livelihood. Instead of being intimidated by the possibility of such a reprimand, she relied on her instincts, counting on the morality of a world community to ensure that she and other women who spoke out against injustice would be allowed to return.

Twenty years after we met, it is gratifying to see Sharon at some of the same gatherings that I attend, and we greet each other as peers, as adults, and as distinct individuals with complementary strengths. It was sheer chance that put us in the same room together in that dance studio many years ago. Since then, we have relied on our past, as teacher and student, to build a new relationship that is mutually instructive and even more rewarding.

I may have wisdom that I can share with her now, as well. When I called Sharon to arrange an interview for this book, I caught her in between breaths as she dashed from one city to the next, writing scholarly law-journal articles, teaching law classes, and being a mother to her seventeen-year-old son. She was swamped. Yet, as overwhelmed as she was, she told me about a dream she'd had the night before: "I dreamt that someone was hugging me and said, 'You know, I really used to like you,' as if that person didn't like me anymore. And then I realized it was *me* that was hugging *me*. I am afraid that I'm turning into a grumpy old woman who's rushing around all the time, and I don't want that to happen." Even with all of her commitments, she took several hours to talk to me for this book.

"You need more joy," I told her. "Maybe you need some time off, or to cut out a few projects right now so that you can take it easy. What is it that you *really* want to do?" I asked her.

She told me she wanted to work on a project with her son. It would be his last year home before he went away to college.

"Then go for it, Sharon; you've only got one life, and one son. Do what makes you happy, and I'll help you get there any way I can."

And then I told her what an impact she'd had on my life, on my choice to go to law school and to always pursue whatever I wanted, regardless of what anyone else demanded or expected from me. For a few seconds, Sharon was silent. I don't think she'd ever known this. In being so honest and thankful, I felt that I had somehow given her back some of the goodness that she had once given me. *Sensei* and *seito*, teach and be taught. Students one day become teachers.

Our Would-be Mentors Are Not Born, They Are Made

Our mentors have to be coaxed and questioned to impart the stories and the lessons that have informed their lives. But the teachers among us are those who have succeeded against some tremendous odds. Closed communication channels over many generations—between mothers and daughters, women and other women—have convinced us that we have nothing to impart to others and nothing valuable to learn from them. "What can I possibly tell some young woman?" a forty-year-old Chinese American seamstress once asked me. "My life is a worker's life. I'm not successful. I never went to college. I'm just a regular person with no interesting stories to tell. And no good advice." Professors, housewives, and young professionals echo this feeling as I asked them to tell me whether they have the ability to be mentors.

More often than not, they shared the feeling that their words were "not important enough," that they were "not worthy" of giving advice to others. They were not celebrities. For some respondents, giving advice was deemed presumptuous and self-important, proving again how deeply rooted the self-silencer is in so many of us. Many respondents felt awkward when I asked about their capacity to serve as a role model for young women. "Just tell them to work hard, be happy. That's all," one respondent wrote. Could this be false humility? Could it be that I would never get to the core of some of these women, that they would never reveal their real prides and conceits to a prying writer? Or was this really a case of how we see ourselves, with no valuable messages to give, no resonant themes to receive?

To many of the women I spoke with, mentoring was equated with scholarly instruction, more in line with the feudal function of the scholar in ancient China, Japan, or Korea, an individual who had a highly-esteemed position in society, anointed with all the badges and honors that proved his knowledge. The passing on of advice in a practical, everyday sense was a strange and sometimes needless function to many of them, who felt that everyday survival could be handled by every woman on her own.

"Why talk about how we have to teach each other? Why not just *do*?" older women often ask. "Put your nose to the grindstone and just get on with living and putting food on the table." With little sense of connection, we become task-oriented worker bees, less interested in the all-important process of developing leadership than in simply "getting things done."

We forget that a sewing woman is well-equipped to teach us what persistence means, or that a career woman, having survived ten years of corporate office politics, can tell us about endurance, or that a wife and mother running the corner greengrocer knows better than most about daily financial survival. We look past those who could be fine instructors in the everyday, forgetting that we are all the daughters of survivors.

Ours are generations that are often born of resilience in the face of struggle and great change. And yet, our mothers' generations often choose to forget those rich experiences, or they forget to pass those stories on to us. So the search for our mentors goes on, and we continue to rely on far-removed icons. We look for superwomen on TV. We look for Connie Chung. We look for Hillary Clinton.

THE MENTOR QUEST

Beginning the Search

Think about what guidance you need most to make self-determining moments more frequent in your life. Identify those who have encouraged you and those who have held you back. Become active in the choice of the company you keep. Are there destructive relationships that are limiting your ability to see yourself as valuable? Are you able to let them go? Are there friendships and people with philosophies that affirm what you feel the world ought to be? How can you develop them and build them into your long-term vision?

Put yourself in venues where your own values and interests are explored and seek those who share them. Put yourself on mailing lists of organizations that speak to your newly defined interests. Pass out your business cards by the bushel. Put your hand out and introduce yourself to people who you feel would never give you the time of day. Efforts such as these are time-consuming and they take chutzpah. They will require a commitment of energy and sometimes forgoing a leisurely evening at home or at the movies with friends. But the effort, in and of itself, becomes an act of long-term empowerment. If you've heard someone interesting in a radio interview, or if you've read of the person in an article, or learned of someone through your informal grapevine, make it a point to track that person down by writing, calling, or E-mailing to establish a contact. This is how you will build a circle of mentors. Make it a weekly routine to actively forge the links of mentor and student in your life. And as a student, figure out how you can give back or contribute to your mentors' efforts. Teaching is always a two-way giving process.

Become a Teacher

Can you name three people that have advanced in some way through your efforts? No matter how old or young we are, whether we are college sophomores or CEOs, we have the capacity to pass down knowledge to those who are one step behind us. The question becomes whether we are secure enough in our sense of self to share our knowledge, friends, and professional contacts and whether we are sincerely willing to dedicate quality time to a mentoring effort. What often happens with potential mentors, even among activists, is that we become consumed with a "treadmill mentality," so that we feel we have no time to train or pass on knowledge that might make organizing our projects easier. We're convinced that we're just too busy to be showing anyone the ropes.

Group power only happens when we create "ladders" of experience, ones where we can look to those ahead of us as well as behind us to create a strong leadership chain. If we lack a process for passing on knowledge, we aren't working within the basic structure of a group empowerment model.

In his book *Principle-Centered Leadership,* Steven Covey writes that there is always a time to be a student as well as a teacher. Leadership is the ability to understand when to assume which role at any given time. Covey has these suggestions in determining how and when to assume the role of teacher:

It's Time to Teach

- When people are not threatened. (As Covey writes, efforts to teach when people feel threatened will only increase their resentment, so wait for or create a new situation in which the person feels more secure and receptive.)

- When you're not angry or frustrated.

- When you have feelings of affection, respect, and inward security.

- When the other person needs help and support. (To rush in with success formulas when someone is emotionally low or fatigued or under a lot of pressure is comparable to trying to teach a drowning man to swim.)

There are always right projects for right moments, and for me, writing this book has been one of them. This book was itself a mentor. As I wrote about power, I was changing as my ideas changed. Only by going through the process of talking to hundreds of amazing women did I begin to understand that power, more than anything else, was about connection. Not respect, not recognition, not notions of "excellence."

For the longest time, writer's block gripped me every time I picked up my pen, which I hear is typical of most writers with their first books. How would I ever be able to write an entire book? What if I just wasn't up to it? What if no one liked what I had to say?

At around that time, I had a dream that I still recall vividly. In the dream, I had a baby. It had appeared out of nowhere one day without my noticing. The baby was tiny, I mean *very tiny,* smaller than my pinky nail. It looked more like a little worm than a baby. I picked it up and looked at it carefully on the pad of my finger. I thought, "How would I be able to take care of this small, squirming thing?" It was so minuscule and fragile. I could have crushed it like an insect. But in my dream I never thought the baby would die. It just needed extra-special care and it would survive, but I had no idea how.

That was over a year ago. Only recently, I had another strange dream. Again, I had a baby. Only this one was huge, about the size of a toddler, much bigger than the newborn it was supposed to be, with a full head of hair and round saucer eyes. It just stood there on my stomach as I lay down, staring as if it knew something that I didn't, smiling, with arms crossed. The strangest thing was that this baby had two fins on its back, covered in pink baby skin. Maybe they were wings. The smiling baby said, "Wait for two years, and you'll see."

Until I began to read books about dream analysis, I didn't know that these two dreams are archetypal dreams that many women have when they are going through rites of spiritual passage. A dream about a tiny baby translates into a tiny, needy spirit, one that is beginning, yet needs instruction and nourishment. The large baby of the second dream, bedecked with wings, tells me that my spirit has indeed grown. It is now something confident, sure, and centered.

The prediction of that second dream leaves me wondering. I don't know what will happen in two years' time. What I know is that I am still an apprentice, and I am still learning.

May we always continue to learn.

Part IV

THROUGH

THE FIRE

SHE TAKES RISKS

Will we be able to recognize the moments when doors begin to open? Our calls to adventure will not necessarily come in the form of earth-shattering events. They may instead be instances that temporarily disrupt our lives, shaking loose our roles and our sense of how the world works, like a blast that knocks a hole in the way we've seen things up till then.

Are we confident enough to allow that chaos to linger, or will we grab for the nearest anchor and set things back to the orderly ways we are used to?

When the time comes, how will we answer risk's call?

L ast March, I finally escaped the craziness of New York City and used every scrap of savings I had to buy a house far away from its treadmill madness. One hot afternoon, when all three phone lines in my tiny, windowless New York office were ringing nonstop, I finally realized that any truth worth discovering would only be revealed in the silence I'd find when leaving behind all agendas and the breakneck speed of the fastest city in the world. I began to crave a way of moving through time and gauging life's progress through something more than just my résumé. It wasn't easy heading for quieter spaces. I still felt the dread of cold-turkey withdrawal, even as I breathed my first bit of clean country air. New York is for winners, and in leaving, was I no longer one of them? Would my senses go dull? Would I turn into a Stepford Suburbanite? Despite these fears, I am told by those I trust, and feel intuitively, that removal from distraction is one of the most important things a writer can do to begin to write from the heart.

I now have a haven, a modest cedarwood house nestled in a forest of white pine, bamboo grasses, and pepperidge trees, far enough from any sign of city bustle, where the mysteries of life and inspiration are encoded not in meeting agendas, piles of paper, press releases, and a stackful of awards, but in the cycles of the seasons and the fascinating order of nature. My truths now lie in the muddled clarity of an untamed forest and its millions of coincidences that make whatever happens within it happen over and over again.

Protected from the craziness of New York City, I am able to pound out on my laptop the chapters, lectures, plans, and proposals that allow me to live the simple, straightforward life I have chosen. It is where I cocoon myself, in the midst of green and an amazing array of birds and wildlife, as my thoughts burrow inward and simultaneously outward.

In the woods, I am superstitious. Despite my lawyer's education that tells me to "please be rational," I have a healthy respect for the unseen and unproven. I listen to fortune-tellers, half amused but attentive. I read my horoscope, for fun and a little bit of seriousness. And at home, I have given credence to *feng shui*, the Chinese art of divination that prescribes ways of positioning a home and its contents so that good luck is welcomed and chooses to remain. I was lucky. After looking at only three houses with my organically minded, back-to-the-earth real estate agent, Marie, I found the perfect one. Trees on the northwest side protect the house and bring happiness. Two rear doors that are not in line with the front door prevent luck from leaving straight out the back. The lot slopes down from north to south, good for *chi,* or what martial arts masters call cosmic breath. The kitchen faces east in the direction of the sun, as it should, since cooking is emblematic of fire. With every room facing in its proper direction, I am assured that the orders of nature are not upset. My house in the woods is a sanctuary, balanced so finely that *to be still* is the most natural activity there is.

But quiet time in the forest has to be counterbalanced with periods of tremendous brainstorming and inspiration. In those moments, I need the ocean, with its vastness and constant change. When it's time to think about the next door I want to go through, I drive to the ocean to be reminded of the unlimited choices that life offers. The horizon reminds me of a faith that, in traveling toward a horizontal line that never seems to get closer, there lies inevitably the safe haven of land. *It is trusting without being able to see.*

The ocean speaks of risk to me, of the great leaps of faith that we must make to accomplish graced moments of real satisfaction. The ocean reminds me that there is always a time for adventure and chance. It is only by taking risks that we ever challenge ourselves to learn.

In *The Hero With a Thousand Faces*, cultural anthropologist Joseph Campbell talked about the "call to adventure" that every hero must follow in order to start her journey into actualization. To begin adventures, we must travel, either through distance or through the spirit, or most desirably, both. The call to adventure is a universal theme, woven through our folktales. Western culture has Homer's epic *The Odyssey*, with the hero Odysseus who ventures across the ocean to slay monsters. There is Jonah traveling the sea as he enters into the belly of the whale. Asian tales also recount heroes' journeys. Fa Mu Lan ventures far from home to defeat treacherous bandits. And then there is my mother's favorite story of Momotaro, the Peach Boy, of Japan.

THE STORY OF MOMOTARO

Just before falling asleep each night, I'd ask my mother to tell me again the story of Peach Boy. *Japanese story, Ah-Phee, taught to me in school when I was little like you.* My mother, named Mei, was also called Meiko, growing up in Japanese-occupied Taiwan in the 1940s. Now putting me to bed, tired from working an eight-hour nursing shift, she'd put a shiny red-foil-wrapped chocolate umbrella on my pillow as I lay on my stomach. She'd pat my back as if she were patting on a very soft drum. *Pi Pi So, Pi Pi So,* she'd tap in 4/4 time, with silence on the fourth beat. That's how I got ready for the Peach Boy story, night after night. She'd tell it to me in whisper voice as I closed my eyes and conjured up the pictures from her words.

Momotaro was a Peach Boy. They called him a Peach Boy because he sprang from the pit of a giant peach. One day, he just broke out, surprising a woodcutter and his wife, who were of course very happy to have a new baby boy. "No wonder that peach was so much bigger than the rest of them!" they thought. Peach Boy grew and grew, and he became stronger, but he always looked just like a little boy, plump round face and fat oompah-loompah body. One day, Peach Boy somehow knew that it was time for him to venture away from home. Peach Boy heard of the *oni* monsters who lived on an island near Hokkaido and who ate wayward travelers and stole their jewels and money. Thanking the woodcutter and his wife for all they had done, Momotaro began his journey. He was off to slay the evil *oni* monsters. Before he left, the woodcutter's wife gave him four delicious *gyoza* "power" dumplings and four *onigiri* rice balls wrapped in seaweed with a little pink spot of pickled plum right in the middle. The woodcutter gave Momotaro his *tonfa* fighting stick for protection.

As Momotaro made his way across Japan, he met up with a surly dog, a petulant monkey, and an arrogant pheasant, all of whom became his friends as soon as Peach Boy offered them one of his delicious dumplings. By eating the dumplings, each of them became as strong as one hundred men.

Needless to say, Peach Boy reached the *oni* island and with the help of his faithful animal friends, slays only enough *oni* monsters as was necessary to make the other *oni*s surrender. Peach Boy returns home with his three friends, with the recognition and appreciation of the emperor of Japan, who was able to tell his people that they no longer had to live in fear.

Like Dorothy in *The Wizard of Oz,* Momotaro manages to convince three creatures of the forest to join him in a journey to conquer a threatening demon. Momotaro, like Superman, Odysseus, Fa Mu Lan, and other mythic heroes, embarks on a journey into the unknown to meet intimidating forces that test his skills. The call to adventure is an allegory for a rite of passage. Each of the stories shows us that triumph comes only after the willingness to risk something important.

As hero myths demonstrate, risk requires a brave refusal to accept what is normal or expected and to venture into the soul. And to do this is to face tension or chaos without needing to suppress it. It requires us to understand the possibility of danger, but also that whatever happens will put us in a better place. We may fall, but we will end up with our feet on the ground. And it will inevitably be new ground.

Taking risks will upset family comfort zones. Trinh took her risk by rebelling against her role as the oldest daughter in her Vietnamese family, one that dictated that she remain at home taking care of her younger brothers and sisters until they went off to college. Trinh remembers telling her parents that she had chosen to attend a college two hours away, which meant she wouldn't be coming home every day to fulfill the responsibilities of the eldest daughter. It took Trinh months to tell her family. Because she was upsetting the family balance, there were arguments. Her mother pulled out the family photo album and tried to make Trinh feel guilty for her selfish choice. And yet Trinh was convinced that leaving home was the only way she could grow and pursue her own interests, without the protection or judgment of the family. Trinh finally convinced them of the wisdom of her choice by saying that a college experience away from home was for the good of her education, making it difficult for her parents to refuse. Trinh understood that her parents needed her near home because they counted on her help at their grocery store. So that her parents weren't left without help, she made sure that her brothers and sisters would take turns working at the store during the time that she was away.

The call to adventure comes in so many ways. We may have lost a loved one or been let go from a job or ended a relationship. How many of us have had the rug pulled out from under us in some way and read it as a gigantic failure of our character or abilities? At times like this, how many of us can face these adversities and recast them as calls to adventure? How many of us will seek out the lesson that is contained within the crisis?

SHOCK WAVES

Rama has been in the work world for a good seven years when the world comes crashing down around her. She has been on track, receiving the promotions for which she worked so hard. Rama looks at her life at thirty-one and finds that an impressive job title and a car service that takes her home at night are not as satisfying as they used to be. Her friends are not as available as they once were—now married or involved in relationships that keep them at home with their partners. Rama goes home each night and wonders what exactly happened in the past seven years without her noticing. It's not that she wants to find someone special, although her parents are worried that their Indian daughter's marriage prospects diminish with each day she remains single. Rama is happy enough as she is. It's just that she feels that her life has no spark. She considers a change, a quality-of-life shift, but looks at her comfortable salary and her ironclad position as a vice president in the company and decides not to think about it anymore. After all, she has achieved everything a successful Indian parent could want. When Rama's company is acquired by a competitor, however, she loses her job in the transition. Caught by surprise with little saved for this unforeseen disaster, Rama is faced with choices that pose an opportunity for risk taking.

When Mariel married Emil, it was a nearly perfect white wedding in the Philippines. Mariel still looks at the pictures seventeen years later and can't understand where it all went wrong. It's not as if Emil isn't a good husband. It's just that she feels that she has done enough for everyone, putting Emil through graduate school, raising their children, running the household. Now she wants to do something for herself. It was only when she started a small jewelry business that the friction with her husband began. Mariel began to make money, which shifted her very traditional role as a good wife and mother into one of "earner" as well. Her business took time away from her household chores, and Emil did not appreciate it. Mariel began to do very well in her business at a time when Emil was having problems at work. And when Emil was let go, Mariel became the sole wage earner. As Emil sank into depression, Mariel began to look back and wonder what had happened. Being the sole caretaker of the family was exhausting, and so Mariel considered using the three months of vacation time she had never taken to go back to the Philippines so that she could think about her own life for once. But to do so when everyone is counting on her would make her feel guilty. It might cause shame in her family. She might lose her business and bare the brunt of her husband's unpredictable reaction. Can she risk that?

With risk there must be either a deep, heartfelt yearning or an abrupt deviation from the normal patterns of our daily lives. Describing the call to adventure, Campbell talks of the "blunder, a mere chance occurrence that reveals to us an unsuspected world, full of circumstances that are not rightly understood." These blunders are not necessarily born out of haphazard chance; instead they are often the result of suppressed desires and conflicts. They are ripples on the surface of life, produced by unsuspected rumblings that may be very deep, as deep as the soul itself. The blunder may result in the opening of a destiny, placing us in strange circumstances where we know intuitively that we have little choice but to heed adventure's call.

The Chinese word for "crisis" is composed of two characters. One is the symbol for danger. The other is the symbol for opportunity. Often it is crisis that forces risk, and therefore change. Are the instances like the ones Rama and Mariel experienced the "blunders" that Campbell talks about? Instead of looking at them as confirmations that our lives have gone awry, can we begin to think that rejections, endings, or tragedies can also be invitations to grow in different ways? Can they provide an opportunity to think about whether we were happy in the first place? Can we look past our hurt or anger to see a message that might clarify our own life principles?

What are the voices inside that convince us to remain in stasis? What are the fears that tell us to stay put and compromise our limitless possibility? What are the voices that kill the instinctive call to risk? When we learn to banish those voices, when we begin to listen to who we are, we can begin to take the chances that allow us to become the powerful women that we know we are inside.

Lora took a risk for the first time when she was sixteen. She remembers riding home on her school bus when she saw a picket line of Chinese immigrant women in their thirties, forties, and fifties. They were unionizing a fashion designer's sweatshop, marching around with signs:

> I looked at that picket line, and I had this exhilarating feeling about Asian women standing up for themselves. I got so excited. The next day, I went into the high school cafeteria and gave my first political speech, convincing people to come out and support those women on the picket line. In my mind a union was a safe haven, a safe haven for oppressed immigrant women.

Lora heeded her calling, and for the past thirty years she has been living up to the commitment of that risk she first took at sixteen. She is one of the country's most effective grassroots labor attorneys working with immigrant communities.

Sharon found her calling in an incident foisted upon her when she was young. Like Lora, she was a teenager, when INS officials raided her family's Chinese take-out restaurant. The uniformed men terrorized and humiliated them in a crowded store of customers. They demanded to see her family's papers and demanded to know if they spoke English. Even though she was only a high school student at the time, Sharon grew very furious and shouted at them, as she recalls years later:

"You can't treat us this way; we're people." As they threatened my father to tell me to shut up, as they walked away in the parking lot ignoring my screaming at their backs, "I want your badge numbers," I think the revelation of the law as an instrument of power (and disempowerment) began to emerge in inchoate ways. No, I did not dream of becoming a lawyer. Growing up, loving to read books, I wanted to be a writer because I was convinced this was the way one could change the world, create visions of a better world, better yet, create those worlds on the written page.

For many years, Sharon resisted her calling to write—she had always felt it was self-indulgent, a moral luxury. It is only now, in her late forties, that she has begun to write the stories from the heart that have been buried behind the academic and scholarly texts of her amazingly prolific legal career.

TURNING PLANS INTO ACTION

"You're Going to Do *What?*"

Nobody thought it would work. It had been tried at least half a dozen times by some very able people in the past twenty years. A national magazine that somehow addressed the experience of Asians in America? It couldn't be done. "It requires too much upfront investment, millions of dollars," our banker friends told us. "Too risky for us. You'll have to hemorrhage millions before expecting to see even a dollar of profit." Friends who worked on Madison Avenue told us that advertisers, the lifeblood of the magazine business, would not be interested in us, at least in the short term.

"Asians are assimilated aren't they? Aren't they just like white people who happen to look different?" seemed to be the typical response to our presentations. "If Asians read *The*

Wall Street Journal and the *Los Angeles Times* and *Mademoiselle*, then," as advertisers would say, "we've already got them. We don't need your editorial 'environment' to reach them."

As if advertisers' skepticism weren't enough, we had other strikes against us as well. With no historical information or demographic studies, we didn't know whether Asian Americans would even go near a magazine with an Asian face on the cover. All we had was our gut instinct, and the hundreds of letters, E-mails, and words of support from friends. And always at the back of my mind was *the only sure fact we did know:* Every publishing project that had started within the Asian American community, despite all the good intentions and sometimes even a big pocketful of cash, inevitably ended up with spats and power struggles and, utimately, bankruptcy.

Only fools try to do what has already proven impossible.

What to do with the aching feeling that it had to be attempted again? With no concrete reasons, except that we knew that *we* would be interested in seeing such a thing available, a few dozen brave Asian American souls decided to take a kamikaze leap. If it were done correctly—if we went into the project with our eyes open, willing to learn—it seemed to be the right time to try again, despite the probability of failure that everyone reminded us of daily.

And that's how *A. Magazine* was launched, at first, a hobbling, kind of, sort of quarterly publication. With all our savings and with the sometimes foolhardy but always visionary energy that empassioned risk involves, we took a plunge into the shark-infested waters of entrepreneurialism. With my Rolodex, bar association membership, the human-interest "hook" of a corporate lawyer gone gonzo entrepreneur, and the sharp, quick wit of our Harvard grad founding editor, Jeff Yang, *A. Magazine* caused a stir in the early nineties for being an in-your-face, hip Asian American magazine with a political bite. By the time our first issue came out, I had maxed out one MasterCard and was quickly eating away at the limit of the Visa.

UNLEARNING FEAR

What makes people do crazy things? To explain, I have to take a step back.

Right before taking the leap out of my day job, I remembered what my friend Martha had told me many years before. At the time I met Martha, she was in her early forties, a real "earth mother" and practicing Buddhist who lived in Marin County with her partner, Tam, a man at least fifteen years her junior. Martha was my first boss and a real social changer, who taught me how to get the big media to listen to small, but positive messages. Martha's training has been the backbone of every successful project on which I have embarked, not just the ones involving social change or media attention. Martha was an instructor in many other aspects of life, and her advice continues to have a profound impact on the way I live in general. Martha taught me for instance, that *I had to unlearn fear,* and that I would have to identify what terrified me in order to take necessary risks. Martha showed me that, *in order to experience fearlessness, it is necessary first to experience fear.*

In ancient cultures, holy people learned that naming your fears was a practical way to begin to take power over them. In *A Path With Heart,* Jack Kornfield explains that every spiritual path includes a language for the common difficulties we encounter: "The Sufis call them Nafs, the Desert Christians who practiced nearly two thousand years ago in the deserts of Egypt called them demons. Buddhist meditators call them Mara, meaning Darkness." By naming our deepest concerns, we own them, and can render them powerless against us.

With Martha's warm voice in mind, I began to analyze what kept me from leaving my job at the law firm and joining a maverick group of would-be journalists to do something potentially monumental with *A. Magazine*. Needing to get it out on paper, one day I scrawled the following:

Why I Don't Want to Take the Big Leap

I don't ever want to be a street person. Don't want to be in poorhouse. Will exhaust savings of family and friends, will be evicted from apartment, will have to live off the spare change of passersby at the Grand Central Station, reading excerpts of *A. Magazine* articles that never got published because the magazine will have folded.

My résumé will have gaping holes, which will spell "reject" to corporate America. Law firm partners will think, "momentary lapse of sanity." Won't be asked back for a second round of interviews.

No more friends. Abandoned because failure will make me a pariah. Nobody will take my calls.

I would never be taken seriously again. Self-explanatory.

My family would be shamed. "Your daughter did what? She's not a lawyer anymore? What went *wrong?*" Eccentric choice would knock the Engs down a few rungs in eyes of competitive Chinese American community.

Just writing down what petrified me clarified it all. I understood then that underlying all my trepidations was the fear of failure. And if that fear wasn't enough of a deterrent, there was something even worse. For some reason, it seemed even more devastating to consider the possibility of achieving only a mediocre result.

Risk takers often understand that true fearlessness is not the elimination of fear but the transcendence of fear, the movement *through* it and not *against* it. This means knowing that there are huge obstacles in front of us, that they are worthy of our concern, but that we can get ourselves to move through them. When we are fearless, we can choose the alternative that challenges us the most, regardless of the trepidation it may cause within us.

The powerful inner critic fears failure even more than death and often stops us in our tracks when we are presented with an open door. It was easy to envision all the horrible things that could happen if I were to fail. That inner critic works to keep us in limbo, and we remain frozen in our tracks.

Yoko is the daughter of two Japanese artists who came to America from Japan when she was five years old. They have always lived the life of fine artists, never giving in to the seduction of "going commercial." The three of them have always been quite happy in their lives, despite the many times when they had to stretch their money. Yoko remembers her childhood as one that was free and creative. She used to draw wonderful pictures, imitating her father's abstract paintings. She remembers, though, that her mother dissuaded her at an early age from developing her artistic side, in an effort to protect her from the hardship that accompanied that lifestyle, even though the three of them enjoyed their lives tremendously.

"Now they tell me that they feel that I am holding myself back somehow. That I am not realizing my potential to know myself. That if I did, I would be very powerful." Because Yoko's parents led a life that transcended convention, they are not referring to Yoko's résumé or her rise up the job ladder or her economic achievement. In all of these areas, Yoko has excelled. Instead, they see her obstruction as artists would, as a block of her creative, transformative energy.

Yoko is probably more attuned to the journey she must take than most of us. Though she can't yet point to the question in her life that needs to be answered, she knows that it must lie in her unexplored urge to create. Above all, taking risks is exactly that—a practice of creativity that requires giving voice to the as-of-yet unexpressed. If untapped creativity is at the heart of every risk, it is no wonder then that Yoko's parents, both artists, are the most perceptive of her reluctance to meet her challenges.

Taking risks is never easy. Yet risk taking plays a part in our development from our first year of life. According to psychologists, at about nine months, we begin to seek distance from safety by crawling away from mother and then quickly returning to her when we feel we have reached a precarious limit. Our call to adventure increases steadily, and by the time we have reached our terrible twos and are no longer encumbered by the short distances afforded by crawling, we are exhilarated from our newfound freedom in locomotion. The seed to adventure is planted.

So what happens from that point on? It seems that as we grow older, our tendency to take risks lessens drastically. With the few thousand tumbles that we take from then on, we become motivated more to minimize the pain of potential failures, than to strive for the exhilaration of a potential success. With a stable lifestyle on the line, mortgage payments, partners who count on our consistency, and children who depend on us, our sense of risk can virtually disappear. Yet living life to its full potential, exploring the many talents that we have been given, requires us to hold tension like a white-hot light, until we can bear it no longer.

ACCEPTING POSSIBLE FAILURES

"It's okay to be wrong," as Tony-award-winning playwright David Henry Hwang said in a lecture to MIT students a few years ago. He was talking about his growth as an artist within the Asian American community. In that hour, Hwang talked candidly about his projects, including those that weren't received as well as he had anticipated. Having reached a level of comfort with his audience, Hwang explained to them why, in retrospect, his cutting-edge play, *Face Values*, was not understood in the ways he had intended. He was able to contemplate his approach to playwriting in a critical way, without the need to put on a good face, in the spirit of discussion with his students.

In fact, we can learn so much through what seems like failure, as Diane, another lawyer-turned-creative, wrote, describing her first attempt at playwriting:

> Prior to the play, my writing had been more journalistic, more nonfiction essays and articles. Going into fiction was a big leap because I was no longer constrained by facts; my only limit was my sense of reality. The characters and their words had emanated from within me. Hearing them speak

aloud to an audience made me feel so vulnerable, like I had opened up my soul to let everyone see what was inside. Very scary, but worth it. Though audiences enjoyed the play and the theater company extended the run, critics were not kind. Yet from that, I learned that not only could I take their criticism, but I could learn from that experience. Having faced "failure" and survived it enabled me truly to understand how liberating it is, not always having to succeed: winning truly isn't everything. It gave me such a sense of freedom to try new things, because I now knew failing wouldn't kill me.

Perceived failures, if addressed with clarity, give us the lessons we need to ultimately succeed, if only because we muster up the courage not to retreat. Congressional representative Patsy Mink, for instance, the first Asian American woman to gain office in Congress, lost her first election for national office, as she described in *The Conversation Begins:*

> When I first ran for national office in 1959 I lost by 8 percent. Losing felt awful. It's terrible enough to be rejected by just one person, but to be rejected by thousands you thought were in love with you is devastating. That's why most people don't run for office. You can run again only if you believe strongly that you have something to contribute. After losing I said, "Never again," but soon I re-entered local politics and was elected to the Hawaii state senate in 1962.

In 1964, when a seat opened in the U.S. House of Representatives, Patsy ran and won. She used her position to push for equity in education, gender equality in federal funding programs, and, perhaps her greatest victory, to co-draft Title IX, which is the federal law prohibiting discrimination based on gender. Others like Patsy, in attempting to gain political office, share her refusal to say "die." Sharon, who was unsuccessful in her first primary bid for a state legislature position, knew that she would give herself another shot at running for office in the next election. She had learned through experience what it meant to run a good campaign and knew what she had to do next time to win. Sharon believed in the possibility, even more, the *probability* that she would get elected if she was relentless in her attempts. In 1998, she ran again, and won.

When we identify the fear of failure, we no longer are victim to it. We can cast it aside and begin to listen to our kinder selves.

COMPETENCY AND REALISM

"When I think about risk, I think about someone jumping out of an airplane, or doing something drastic," says Judy. "I think of something very daring and heroic," said another respondent.

Anybody who thinks that risk is only for daredevils should think again. Risks that allow us to grow are not necessarily the adrenaline-rush risks, the dice-roll risks. They are, instead, the ones that come from minute, often more planned movements, the ones that remind us every day that we are living in the present and for ourselves. When we relegate our risktaking to the most fringe areas of our lives, out of the realm of the practical, and take only the kind that gives us a temporary rush, we avoid the risks that open the possibility of higher understanding of ourselves and greater power.

Risk that encourages transformation requires competency and a reality assessment. What are our capabilities? And what are we willing to sacrifice in order to get a greater return? Do we fully understand and accept what the risk entails?

These questions remind me of a risk that I took along with a number of fellow law students. In my third year, I helped to organize a student-based protest for better minority faculty representation and stronger admissions policies for disadvantaged students. It was suggested along the way that we stage a sit-in at the dean's office as a sign that we were serious. Not yet fully committed to the effort, I felt I had to know the level of commitment in the room before I tossed in my labor and my support. I put out a question to test the waters: "How much do we all believe in this?" I wanted to know. "Who here is willing to be arrested for this cause? Because that *is* one of the possible outcomes of what is being proposed." It was a reasonable question. After all, I was in a roomful of very smart people who must have assessed this possibility before I posed it before them. People fidgeted and looked around, and no one raised their hands.

Perhaps after thinking about the possible repercussions, no one was willing to sacrifice a hard-earned law degree, have a criminal record that would obstruct bar admission, or cause any difficulty to the bright legal future that each of them held. At least everyone was being honest. At least going forward, we were all aware that things would fall apart for us at the first sign of handcuffs. When taking risks, it's important to know the Chicken Factor.

Knowing what we were and were not willing to risk allowed us to create a plan. We would organize the event and all the contingencies to avoid going the "police action" route, and hope for the best. The effort, one of the first in a long string of student protests around the country that continue today, received front-page coverage in the Metro Section of the *New York Times*, as well as major coverage from other national and local newspapers. It lead to meaningful changes in the law school curriculum and a commitment to diversity that the law school continues to try to live up to today. Despite the sweet victory, I know that the careful planning behind it, by a number of able students who went on to become respected leaders in the years that followed, was what put the odds in our favor. I know that if we had ever been threatened with police action, our team very likely would have fallen apart. But knowing that made us stronger, not weaker.

Warren Bennis, an adviser to some of the largest companies and most effective leaders, wrote that the secret to any success is finding the right balance between one's *willingness* and the *reality of the goal*. He used his own life as an example: "I used to think I wanted to be a university president. And for seven godforsaken years I did just that. The problem was that I wanted to *be* a university president but I didn't want to *do* a university president. In retrospect, I realized, there was an unbridgeable chasm between my aspirations and what actually gave me satisfaction and happiness."

Bennis proposed four questions to point the way for anyone seeking success. They are the same considerations that can give us direction in our risk taking:

Do you know the difference between what you want and what you're good at?

Do you know what drives you and what gives you satisfaction?

Do you know what your values and priorities are, and can you identify the differences between the two?

Having measured the differences between what you want and what you're able to do, between what drives you and what satisfies you, and between your values and those of your environments, are you able to overcome those differences?

The idea of following a calling may seem daunting because of the catastrophes we envision, but risks do not have to be leaps off cliffs. When we can break our risks down into small, manageable pieces, the leap doesn't look so dangerous. We can minimize risk by obtaining information and troubleshooting. Risks can be well planned and well prepared for. They can be mapped out.

For me to even begin to take the leap, leave a comfortable living, and become yet another impoverished publisher with a great idea, I needed to psyche myself up. Leaving a six-figure salary voluntarily and saying good-bye to the status of being a lawyer, especially in the middle of the early nineties recession, was not easy. So I needed a game plan.

To Begin With, Make a List

First, I had to convince myself that I had at least the slightest chance of succeeding. I needed to know that other people had made similar moves and had achieved their goals. I combed magazines and books and made a list of all the people who left boring office jobs and went on to live the creative life they always wanted: Tenor Placido Domingo was trained as a lawyer. So were actor Ruben Blades and playwright David Henry Hwang. Award-winning author Amy Tan once worked at an office job. Acclaimed novelist Chang Rae Lee worked in an investment bank. For the year leading up to my final exit, I carried around a copy of *Ebony* publisher John Johnson's book, *Succeeding Against the Odds*. It was Johnson's blueprint of how he had created for black Americans what we wanted to create for Asian Americans through *A. Magazine*. For months it was my bible. He had done it. So could we.

Start Sewing That Safety Net

Then there were the more practical aspects of hedging risk. Before leaving the cushy job, I would need a good six months to a year to start doing the necessary saving. I needed the industry research; I needed a solid business plan. I needed to do the emotional work required to make what I saw as a monumental and, hopefully, permanent life change.

At the end of that year, I had a clear path toward a goal, chopped up into enough increments—tiny month-by-month steps and a list full of self-imposed deadlines—so that even a project as large as launching a national magazine began to seem plausible. There was no need to jump into an abyss. After doing my research, I began to realize that people who acted without some well-thought-through plans usually failed, or if they didn't, they were tremendously lucky or their parents were tremendously rich. Carefully taken risks usually end up successful in one way or another. As one friend put it, "When you define risk that way, with all those specific steps for action, it doesn't seem like a risk at all. Doesn't it just become following what is the most natural way to live?"

Then You Must Have Information

Getting information is always key to a risk well taken. To get what I needed, I persuaded as many publishing experts as possible to sit down with me, so that I could learn the magazine business backward and forward. If I wanted to be a start-up publisher, common sense told me, I would need to know how magazines were run as a business, understand them as more than just glossy books with pretty pictures that we pick up at the newstand. So I asked around and got a number of businesspeople to sit down with me. I put together lists of people that could help, whether I knew them or not. Friends recommended their own contacts, and I followed up with all of them. They included people like *Mad* Magazine's former publisher Joel Cohen, *New York* magazine backer Alan Patricof, Vaughn Benjamin of the Magazine Publishers Association, and Marlene Kahan of the

American Society of Magazine Editors, who became great rooters for the project. I had no shame and a lot of nerve, getting up the courage to either cold call or write to a couple of well-known publishers on the off-chance that they would respond. I attended magazine conferences, sat in the front row of all the panel discussions, and asked lots of questions. That's how I met some influential people who were intrigued with our idea, including Ed Lewis of *Essence* magazine, Rochelle Udell at Condé Nast, and Jackie Leo, who started *Child* magazine with the support of the New York Times Company. At the suggestion of friends, I sent Spike Lee a business plan. I sent Quincy Jones a business plan. Who cared if they received dozens of them every day? Maybe mine would catch their attention. When you're driven by something higher, practically nothing gets in the way.

While I was out pounding pavement, we were able to enlist the solid support of our own community. Asian American journalists from around the country began to call in, offering their support and mentioning us in their newsrooms. They were excited by the prospect of being able to contribute to a publishing effort that was well written and just as good as any major magazine out on the newsstands. NBC correspondent Ti Hua Chang and Columbia Pictures executive Chris Lee were both early supporters. Award-winning writers Jessica Hagedorn and *Ms. Magazine*'s contributing editor Helen Zia supported us from the very outset, lending credibility and faith to our efforts. And then we began to get support from Capitol Hill, from Asian American congressmen like Robert Matsui and Norman Mineta, who saw *A. Magazine* as a welcome rallying tool for an Asian American political voice.

CNN called and did a story. So did *The New York Times* and *The Wall Street Journal*.

After two years in business, it looked as if we had been blessed with a minor sort of miracle. By keeping our vision

locked, we were creating a reality. The letters we were beginning to receive from fans in Illinois, California, Texas, even
Mississippi, showed us that our intuition had been right. People
liked the voice and tone we gave them. We were writing in a
voice of power, without self-consciousness, without apology.

The buzz became louder and clearer, and all of a sudden,
finally, Madison Avenue realized that we presented a huge
opportunity. With a tangible product in hand, they now began
to understand what storyboards and flip charts could never
show them. There *was* such a thing as an Asian American
voice. And it was sitting there right before their eyes. It was an
"editorial environment" that they not only wanted, but that
they realized they needed, as they finally understood by the early
1990s that the face of America was changing. After many
years (yes, years!) of hanging on, sticking through all the rejections, and refusing to accept no for an answer, the staff along
with Karen Wang, the advertising director and a real backbone
of *A. Magazine,* finally convinced American Express,
Metropolitan Life, Discover Card, Calvin Klein, and Microsoft
to come on board as advertisers.

Learning the Art of Hanging Loose

My father has a great story of his first and last swimming
lesson while a college student, which I like to tell as a
metaphor for risk taking, although I don't think he would
see it that way. It goes something like this:

He was just paddling around with a Styrofoam floatboard
with his head in the water. Kicking merrily along in the
indoor pool of the local Philadelphia YMCA, he suddenly
found himself in water above his head, in the deep end, near
the diving board. Caught by surprise, he panicked. For some
strange reason, he also let go of the Styrofoam board. And
then he started to sink like a rock, as he likes to tell it. Right

down to the very bottom. No amount of dog-paddling was getting his head back up above the water. As a matter of fact, it was probably taking him deeper down. The lifeguard blew his whistle from his chair. As my dad tells it, the lifeguard didn't seem to want to go into the water, and did so reluctantly, only when he must have finally realized that my dad, no longer moving, was not coming up any time soon without some help.

Sometimes fear can make us lose heart and focus. We become consumed with the fact that we are no longer in a safe zone, and we begin to thrash and grope for anything that can stabilize us again. Yet the only way that we can extract ourselves from that predicament is to relax and trust in our ability to continue along for the ride. Had my father just continued doing what he was doing, despite the fact that he was in the deep end, he would have paddled himself to safety.

There is a concept called *lungta*, which in Tibetan means "riding the horse." In Buddhism, it means harnessing the momentum of a powerful force, listening to your reflexes, and going with the force that is pushing you forward, without using logic. It is the concept of "being in the zone." I think my father could have used a bit of *lungta* in that YMCA pool fifty years ago. It was certainly what I needed as *A. Magazine* turned the corner from vision to regularly publishing reality, as our bank accounts started to look like the Dow-Jones average on a very bad day.

As good as it sounded, we were always in need of wads of cash. Two years into the running of the magazine, after the fanfare of the launch had left us with some impressive press clippings, we still hadn't found the number of backers that would ensure our success for more than a year or so more. There were many times that I would come into the office and be barraged by a pile of phone messages that had to be returned that day. I would have to make sure our printers could be paid on time, so that the magazines would be released, so that we could be paid by our advertisers and keep our subscribers from screaming about our late publication. I had to make sure that subscribers were being billed and paying for their subscriptions. With little office support, I found myself doing the job of secretary, receptionist, cleaning woman, and mother hen, all at the same time as attending luncheons with community leaders, advertisers, and investors, putting my best foot forward as the publisher of Asian America's premier national magazine. And then, as we realized that magazines really did require truckloads of capital, I began to follow up too many investor leads that led to nothing except lecherous octogenarians trying to lure me into their hotel rooms with the promise of future investment in the magazine. When times got tough and I got scared, I called my headhunter, asking her to set up interviews that would get me back into the law firm that only a little while ago felt like an intolerable prison.

I started to act out of fear. I went on those interviews, thinking that it was better to get a paycheck and be unhappy than it was not to have a paycheck and be just as unhappy. My fear caused me to lose focus and confidence. With fear, my vision, my reason for having put so much on the line in the first place, grew dimmer. What I didn't realize then was that risk requires commitment and that commitments require time and patience.

I was finding it difficult not to lose the momentum. Everything was happening so spontaneously and so naturally that I kept thinking, "If we stop, like my dad did in the middle of his first and only swimming lesson, we're going to sink."

I needed to remember that we had to let things happen and go with the moment, no matter how compulsively neurotic my lawyer tendencies made me. *Find the* lungta, *find the balance, and ride it through.*

To stay buoyant, both financially and emotionally, I had to stay focused on the positive side of every catastrophe. When the file of our subscriber list crashed, I faced the reality that our lists had outgrown our simple computer program and that to keep our subscribers happy, we would need to upgrade our systems. When an advertiser decided not to come on board, I learned to listen to what they were looking for instead of why we weren't right for them. I had to learn not to use our limited resources as an excuse for inaction. Instead, I had to be resourceful, creating barter situations or synergies between parties to accomplish mutual goals. Instead of figuring out how to *trim* small items from our budget, I had to think expansively like a publisher, I had to figure out how to *add* new staff who had the proven expertise we needed for phase two of our growth. To do that, I had to find fellow mavericks who were willing to take equivalent risks with their own careers. Although it now sounds like a fairy tale, we did find them. While it may have been great fortune or good timing, I still believe that *when we want something that is motivated out of a positive change that is greater than ourselves, the power of that conviction is resonant and unbeatable.*

In his book, *A Path With Heart*, Jack Kornfield tells a great story about a poster he remembers well. In it was a famous Hindu guru with gray hair and a long, flowing beard, standing balanced on one foot in the yoga posture known as the "tree pose," while on a surfboard, coasting down a huge wave. At the bottom of the poster it said in large letters, "You can't stop the waves, but you can learn to surf." So surf we did. And we got pummeled and clobbered by a few humongous waves. *A. Magazine* survived through the pain. It continues to be published to this day, driven by the same kind of vision, pride, and tenacity that all of us felt when we first opened our doors many years ago.

CONTAGIOUS BEHAVIOR

According to the philosopher Schopenhauer, all truths go through three steps. First they are ridiculed. Then they are violently opposed. Finally, they are accepted as self-evident. When risk taking becomes habitual, it loses the characteristic of fear and skepticism and becomes the only way we know how to be. "I don't think I've ever taken risks," says Milyoung, who admits that she has always lived an "alternative" lifestyle. The way Milyoung tells it, it sounds as if she has become so accustomed to risk that she doesn't even realize that it is now a natural state for her, as it is for any of us who choose to live a life of our own definition. Milyoung took a risk when she chose to live outside of a corporate life that her parents would have wished for her. She took a risk when she became an activist while studying at Brown University. She risked when she was put on probation for her protesting—not once, but twice. She took a risk when she chose to major in an obscure branch of social science called "development studies" and had to deal with the quizzical looks of her family. She several times took a risk when she took jobs without the promise of a stable salary at fledgling community organizations and built their programs, visibility, and fund-raising potential up within a matter of a few years. Now, ten years after graduating from college, Milyoung has been asked to be a keynote speaker at the same university that placed her on probation while she was a student. Schopenhauer was right, not only in Milyoung's case, but in many of the risk stories that I've heard since then.

Risk itself is a process of constant unfolding. And taking risks is the process of peeling back the layers of what you are and who you want to be. Practice makes perfect, which is why it is necessary to take symbolic risks every day. We take a risk when we speak our mind at a time when we would otherwise keep quiet. We take a risk when we move closer toward something that we have always wished for. When we sign up for a course in something outlandish. When we start up a conversation with a stranger. When we leave something old that gave us comfort but held us back.

One of the successful results of change and risk is that it can alter the larger future. Through the nerve and tenacity of its members, *A. Magazine,* along with other small but visionary ventures, became part of a niche-publishing movement that began to legitimate itself in the early nineties. Over the years and under the new leadership of many talented and committed individuals, through the dedication and drive of Jeff Yang, Angelo Ragaza, Karen Wang, Rod Gonzalo, and a host of others, *A. Magazine* has been the inspiration of at least half a dozen equally visionary Asian American publications. It substantiated the mission statements of a number of fantastic new projects that take note of our varied experiences. Its information wells have spilled over into a Web site, an educational publisher, and a video series. The risk of a few created a reality for many.

There is transformation in risk. It starts from within and then touches the people and community around us. The hope and promise of good risks taken are contagious. With each chance we take, the world changes with us.

SHE MOURNS HER LOSSES

The day comes when remaining the same becomes more painful than the risk to grow. And when that happens there are many good-byes. We leave old patterns, old friends and lovers, old ideas, and some cherished beliefs. Loss and growth are so often one and the same.

Are there ways of mourning our losses so that we come out stronger? And as Asian American women, what are the losses that we face that are like no other?

Sook gives birth and is hit with a wave of postpartum depression that consumes her with despair and fatigue. She has given birth to a thick-haired baby girl, Unjoo. Fat-cheeked and red all over, Unjoo represents promise and hope. And shock. As Sook's hormones adjust, she is left feeling empty and sad. Her body is telling her that a significant period of her life has passed, and she mourns her carefree youth that has in many ways come to an end. She will begin to adjust her vision to the new lens through which she will look at life not as a daughter, but as a mother.

Sook goes through the door.

Every year Michi goes to Japan to visit her parents and her closest friends. For the three weeks that she is there, she is taken care of completely. There, Michi reconnects to a past, her childhood—full of genuine love and uncomplicated days—when she didn't have to think about survival in hectic New York City, the criminals she must defend every day at her job, and the inequities that she sees around her. Every time she gets on the plane and returns to America, Michi's links to Japan grow fainter, as family and friends continue their lives without her and she continues without them. Michi finds herself grieving for several days after she says good-bye to them, again.

Michi reluctantly goes through the door.

After sending a son and a daughter to college, Annanya looked at her life and realized that she needed to try something new. When she went back to school full-time, her husband didn't approve, telling her that she should stay at home as a woman of her station should. After she realized that he was unwilling to compromise, Annanya decided to leave her husband. So now she is alone, self-sufficient, but without a strong circle of friends. There is not a chance she'll go back to India, knowing the stigma that attaches to divorced women of her age. No, she will make her way, somehow, in America. Annanya finds herself going through bouts of tremendous sadness.

Annanya opens the door in front of her and closes the one behind.

"When we think of loss, we think of the losses of the people and things that we love," wrote Judith Viorst in her book, *Necessary Losses*. "But loss is a far more encompassing theme in life. We lose not only through death, but also by leaving or being left, by changing and letting go." When looking at our losses in this way, they will include not only our separations from those we once loved, but also our conscious and unconscious abandonment of romantic ideas, dreams, expectations, and illusions of safety.

Life is full of renunciations, and sometimes we grow by allowing past beliefs to fall away. In growing, we give up deep attachments to patterns and beliefs that might have once given us security. When we no longer focus on pleasing others, when we are no longer motivated by praise, we will grieve the loss of easy formulas for success. When we let go of traditional rules and values, we begin to make life-altering decisions of our own choosing. As a result, we will mourn the loss of our younger, simpler selves. Our own voices and our own wills become clearer and more defined, and the closure helps us to grow. The way we close the book, make the break, will determine whether there will be a continuing story. Constructive losses are the kind that allow us to resolve and grow through grieving.

Loss can be experienced in so many variations. We can experience it in the form of catastrophe, sudden termination, or betrayal of trust in those we counted on. It can take the form of banishment from family for having made "shameful" or "disgraceful" choices. In these instances, we lose something once deemed utterly important to us, whether it be one of our values or our way of making sense of our surroundings.

A STRONG WOMAN'S LOSSES

A strong, resilient woman experiences specific kinds of losses—the most primary being the loss of her emotional armor, the very same protective gear that allowed her to be seen as strong in the first place. How difficult it can be when we have grown accustomed to the mannerisms and behavioral patterns that enabled us to protect what is dear to us. At some point, however, that armor begins to become heavy. It starts to weigh us down and constrict our growth. And when this happens, our swords and shields will have to fall away, making us uncomfortably vulnerable.

Lora, a lawyer in her mid-forties, works round the clock to improve working conditions for women, spearheading landmark legal cases and drafting successful labor laws. She never gives up, and that's why she wins. Yet when reflecting on her own bulldog determination, she realized that her success has come at too high a price. After years of rolling up her sleeves to fight the good fight, Lora understood that she'd lost the ability to feel and to love. As she explained in an essay, "Jade and Armor," "I've lost my sense of femininity. The ability to empathize with pain, cry, understand other people's pain."

Lora feels her desire to fight was a reaction to the power-lessness she had always sensed while growing up. Seeing her mother and other women in her Chinatown community as helpless in many ways, Lora vowed to herself that she would never be in that position. By being the strong one in the family, sticking up for her mother against her father's tirades and maintaining peace under their roof, Lora found her validity. Fighting became a way of rationalizing her world that Lora continued to use well into her adulthood and certainly in her career.

From the time she was very young, she would fight with the boys in the school yard, but "didn't do very well." As she said, "I'd be ferocious but I was small, so I couldn't back it up." Lora shared that toughness with her sisters—hers was a family of Fiercegirls. She remembers at one point how her sisters "accosted a guy once because he sold a lemon of a car to one of them. My older sister brought her numchucks and they threatened to beat him up. Since he didn't have the money to pay them back, they took all his record albums instead. The poor guy started crying," Lora says, half laughing, half apologetically. But all that fighting in Lora's family was bound to take a toll one day.

Lora had cast herself some very narrow margins. Because she understood that her ability to control had worked well for her, Lora continued to walk that road while ignoring other roads that were equally important. Her success had been limited to a logical, attack-oriented approach to life, which left her feeling tired and unsatisfied as she grew older. In recognizing her loss, Lora began to change. She took time off to rest and treat herself well. She spent more time with her husband. She allowed herself to feel again.

Diane, now in her mid-forties, grew up in Seattle's Chinatown and now lives in San Francisco. She recognized her losses, of sacred ideas and of people, as she looked back at the difficult choices she made over the past twenty years.

> The first divorce happened in 1978. I was the first in my extended family, my church, and my contemporaries to get a divorce. The man was smart and good looking, but we were not happy. The precipitating factor was his decision that I should be at home raising a child, even though we had earlier agreed that if we adopted a child, we would work fifty-fifty to raise that child. The second divorce happened in 1994 after over fourteen years of marriage. The man was smart, admired, and good looking, but we had become very unhappy. Ironically the precipitating factor this time was that I had wanted to adopt a child and he had not been committed to the adoption. The process of trying and being rejected by birth mothers finally put too much pressure on the relationship. Our friends and family had seen us as the "perfect couple" and couldn't understand the divorce, but I knew I could not stay with him as things were. Changes could come only out of taking major, risky action. Despite feeling a few loneliness pangs every once in a long while, I find life very fulfilling, happy, and wonderful. Strange.

In letting go of the notions of what she was expected to do and what her parents, church, and community dictated as correct behavior, Diane was able to embark on her own path. The losses of her partners were a necessary part of that journey. Difficult as those choices were, and as lonely as she sometimes feels, Diane lives the life she wants, on her own terms, with a support system of friends and community that affirm her for what she is, rather than what she represents in their lives.

Losses can also be outside of our control. Times of crisis and conflict open up new worlds that give us the opportunity to make great developmental and spiritual leaps, forcing us to face the world with very different eyes.

On a snowy night in February, Priya's car careened off a small ice-slicked country road and cast Priya, along with her husband and her two children, into a ditch, roofside up. It took ten hours to get Priya out of the wreckage and into an ambulance. Luckily, her children and her husband came away with only a few cuts and bruises. Priya, however, had fractured her spinal column and was told two days later in the intensive care unit that she would never walk again.

While it is enough that Priya had to suffer the loss of her mobility, she also had to come to terms with how her disability would be seen within her traditional Indian community. As Priya knew, disabled people, and women especially, become wards of their families, placed behind closed doors in quiet, lonely rooms, wheeled out only to accept the sorrow of friends and family on important occasions. Just as daunting as the challenge of caring for her two young children with her impaired mobility was the prospect that relatives and friends would look at her differently from then on, treating her as someone less than whole.

Priya had always been a self-reliant, healthy, and athletic woman who excelled in sports. She skied with her husband in the winter and swam in the summer. She would lift heavy packages with little effort because, as she says, she was "strong as an ox." Priya had also known what it meant to fend for herself, growing up with a father who had been brutal and controlling, and a mother who relied heavily on Priya to answer to her needs.

Priya understood the realities of loss from a very young age, having lost her younger brother, who drowned when she was nineteen. Days after her own accident, Priya's father died unexpectedly after a massive coronary. And now, as a consequence of her injury, Priya had to accept the loss of her self-reliance and independence that had always carried her through in the past. Always so capable and in control, she now had to depend on the help of strangers and friends, to open doors, carry bags, and help her with her children.

I have decided that I am not going to play the weak, frail, ill woman in order to fit into my Indian community's needs. They will have to learn how to deal with me on different terms—my terms.

I view this accident as some kind of omen, because I do believe that these things happen because there are lessons to learn. Maybe this major event has allowed me to finally lean on others and ask for what I need. I have never been able to do that before. I'm learning that reaching out is not weakness. It can tie me to the world and allow me to accept myself as an entire being—with my weaknesses and frailties. It took an accident to get me to understand this.

HUSHING

To grow through our losses, we need quiet time. The trauma of recognizing uncomfortable truths for the first time allows us to create a veil that obliterates life outside and opens inner reality. It is akin to an idea that writer and pyschotherapist Eric Meisel called "hushing"—that quiet time that is the bedrock of any creative journey, when we calm our minds to catch the ideas that are wanting to surface. According to Meisel, there is no creative life without this ability to hush.

Processing loss requires looking at what and who we are in ways that will make us feel uncomfortable. Loss, as in these cases, becomes an entry point of change.

- By giving selflessly, an immigrant mother has created a pattern of dependency in her family that has given her silent power and a sense of worth. For her, growing through loss will mean letting go of the caretaker role that has given her so much validity and comfort. Only then will she understand that she is valuable, not because she gives, but because she is worthy of love, no matter who she is.

- A woman born of Korean immigrant parents wants to be an artist. To do that she must forfeit old ways of viewing her worth in the family. Loss of approval will sting at first.

- A young Cambodian American girl who aspires to be a leader in her community must say good-bye to the assumption that there are clear-cut, proven paths for her to follow. When she understands this, she loses a sense of security about her future, however false it may have been. She can begin to accept that it is *her journey* that will inform those who follow her.

Weathering loss can open wounds, but it also allows us the psychological space that we need in order to transform. Emotional growth may require that we subject ourselves to accusations of being audacious, disrespectful, shameful, and heretic. It will force us to question what has gone unquestioned. Letting go of core beliefs and patterns that we hold sacred will be painful. When Asian American women lose for the sake of growing, we change in the following ways.

WE LOSE "SAFE LOVE"

American-born daughters of Asian parents often have large yokes to bear. We are told that the road to success is paved for us, as the beneficiaries of the American women's movements that have given us opportunities to strike out and advance in ways unavailable to previous generations. Achievement becomes even more important for us, especially if we are the daughters of immigrants, because it is linked with family honor, status, and pride. Success ends up being measured in the most irrefutable of ways—how many honors we earn, how much we make, how many degrees follow our names. At home, achievement may be measured in how well we marry, how expensive our houses are, how well we keep the peace, or how many children we bear. We have often learned that to be valued, we must constantly achieve and perform.

Achievement has become the learned method of earning love for many Asian American daughters, and the price we have had to pay is high. Along the way, we may have lost our sense of inherent worth, of being valued unconditionally for who we are without the trappings of outward honors and recognition.

Kim is a twenty-eight-year-old Korean American who came to America with her parents at the age of seven. She has been graced with the assets that most of us wish for, a beautiful face, amazing intellect, disarmingly down-to-earth personality. She breezed through an MBA at Stanford University, glided right into a position at one of the most prestigious investment banks, and married a Korean American man whom her parents adore.

Kim knows she is her Korean parents' dream. She's done it all the right way and has taken every step that was meant for her. Why then does Kim go home in the evenings wondering why she is not happy? Is she being ridiculous and spoiled for questioning her privilege? Why can't she share her misgivings with the family she loves and the friends who shower her with compliments? Kim doesn't feel comfortable voicing these nagging feelings. She does not show weakness, and never has, to those who are closest to her. Not to her husband, who counts on her to be happy and stable. Not to her parents, who have banked their dreams on her. Not to friends and coworkers, who cannot stop giving her comments of envy and admiration. Kim can never be weak. To be weak may mean that she has to forfeit love.

We labor under American Dreams—living out our hard-working parents' wishes for our financial stability, the perfect family, the trophies and promotions—never allowing ourselves the time and space to question the underpinnings of those dreams. But living up to these demands can be exhausting. Like Kim, so many of my respondents feel as if they are on a treadmill, living up to unrealistic and unmeaningful expectations, conforming to wishes that are not their own.

When the pressures to perform become too great, our psyches may suffer. Psychological studies show us that the patterns found in many Asian American families trying to assimilate into American culture can create a breeding ground for depression among Asian American daughters. Psychologists have found that depression can result when we grow up in socially isolated families, especially if those families feel themselves to be too little respected or misunderstood in their neighborhoods. In the histories of many families studied, one child was usually assigned a special role in increasing the prestige of the family. Designated the protector of family honor, that child was loved only to the degree to which he was able to fulfill the family demands for achievement. If such a child failed, he was cold-shouldered or thrown out of the family group, with the understanding that he had brought great shame on his family.

We may experience loss as we learn to understand the "tragic link between admiration and love," as Alice Miller wrote in her seminal work *The Drama of the Gifted Child*. She speaks of the person who confuses love with praise and, having been taught that they are the same, insatiably seeks admiration because she thinks it is love. According to Miller, the love obtained through achievement, the "Safe Love" we've grown accustomed to, becomes the substitute for our primary needs for respect, understanding, and being taken seriously. According to Miller, often a whole life is devoted to this substitute.

Miller explains that a person in the grips of Safe Love is never really free, first because she is excessively dependent on admiration from others, and second because her self-respect is dependent on functions and achievements that can suddenly fail. When we rely on Safe Love, our self-esteem lies prey to the whims of chance and the haphazard decisions of others. When we accept Safe Love, we forfeit control over our lives.

An exploration of our past is the first step to recognizing Safe Love. In Miller's experience, it is a grand revelation when we realize the love that we captured with so much effort was not meant for us as we really were, that the admiration for our achievements was aimed at those achievements and not at us for ourselves. Armed with this new insight, we may begin to ask disturbing questions of those parents, lovers, or friends on whose affections we have counted, including those that Miller suggests:

- What would have happened if I had ever showed you that I was doubtful, or sad, or confused, or that I disagreed with you?

- Would your love have been there for me if I did?

- Could it be that it wasn't really me that you loved, but only what I represented to you, or strove to be in order to please you, to be desirable in your eyes?

- I am your link to the outside world. How much of your love is linked to that dependence?

- Is it possible that you may love me less if I choose not to heed your advice?

These new questions may be accompanied by much grief and pain, but the result is a new authority that comes from a different centering of our self-worth. Our actions become choices as opposed to assignments. We can express vulnerability, reach out for support, and question the competitive streaks that were once necessary for us to win at any cost. The voices of parents, teachers, bosses, and friends are suddenly cast in a different light, audible, but no longer as important. *Living with power means recognizing conditional love and saying, "I no longer want it or need it." To define a powerful self, we let go of old ways of gaining affection.*

It can be a great relief to see that our intuitions were correct—that life can be so much more fulfilling. By examining the past, we can begin to understand that, as young girls, we were acting in the only ways we thought would bring us love. Now we can realize that we tried to persuade ourselves that we were not afraid when in fact we were, or that we belittled our feelings in order to project ourselves as strong and unassailable. When we lose Safe Love, approval becomes less motivating and rejection less terrifying.

Accepting the loss of Safe Love allows us to shed our armor. We no longer have to be strong or clever or attractive or well positioned in an outward sense. Loss of Safe Love means giving up the stiff upper lip. It means collapsing in on our sadnesses and allowing ourselves to feel and be in the moment. It means that we no longer have to try to be perfect, because love of our "perfect" selves is not true love at all. Shedding our hunger for Safe Love means that we can finally begin to love ourselves.

When Kim decided to leave her job without any idea of what she wanted to do in its place, family and friends reacted in disbelief. Her father flew into rages, her mother cried, her brothers and sisters who had followed similar professional paths told her she must be having a nervous breakdown. Kim questioned herself as well. She had a feeling that nothing made sense anymore, that every system in which she had believed had somehow fallen short of the promise to deliver her into some notion of "happiness." Against the wishes of most of whom she spoke to, including her partner, Kim took a year off to do what she wanted. She decided that she wanted to paint—not to become a renowned fine artist, or to have her work shown in major galleries. Kim was going to paint just because she wanted to. After working for six more months and saving every penny of her earnings, Kim did just that. For a year Kim and her husband lived sparingly on his salary alone. It was a year that gave her a gratification that she had never felt. Realizing that her world hadn't fallen apart, that her partner truly loved her and therefore eventually supported her choice, and that her family would not shut the door on her, Kim realized that she was and *always had been* free.

WE LOSE SAFE DESTINY

What does it feel like to leave your father's house? Or your father-husband's house? How does it feel to look into his eyes and see yourself as the betrayer of the one man who has always trusted you? How does it feel to leave the security of his love even if he never cared who you were? How does it feel to say no to a man to whom you have always said yes? What happens in your body when you stand up to a beloved professor and reject all the standards that he has never questioned? And when he calls your feminine approach rambling, lacking in clarity, coherence, and emphasis, do you wonder if you are stupid? And when you find yourself alone in your empty apartment, hearing voices inside you previously thought were outside, do you wonder if finding yourself is all it was cracked up to be? Can you be the person you have always denied?

—Marion Woodman
Leaving My Father's House

One of the most profound sacrifices we make in the search for the center of our power is that of our firm sense of destiny. The Loss of Safe Destiny comes from a refusal to lean on old hierarchies—status, income, family name—all powers we perceive as greater than ourselves and that are supposed to provide and support. We may be trained to be independent American women, but the tendency to find power in marriage partners, fathers, job descriptions, and other exterior notions of power remains strong. Who has the power that we want? Those who are wealthier? Those in elite circles? Husbands? Fathers? Our gray-haired boss who looks like every figure of authority and privilege that we can recall? What and who determine our desires? Is it our families? Our friends? The unspoken norms that we hold on to almost against our wills?

Letting go of the seemingly predestined future often means recognizing that the basic tenets of life as we have learned them are not working as they should be. We work hard and score well on our exams because we are taught that doing so will allow us to succeed, yet later we may bump up against glass ceilings that no one told us about. We cultivate our pleasant dispositions because we are taught that being liked and accommodating makes a woman desirable. But we find that all of our charm and accommodation is mistaken for a willingness to do tasks that are below our qualifications. We are told that if we marry well, we will live happily, often realizing later that we are not happy at all. We strive for political power only to realize that all the conventional ways we've been taught to achieve, through credentials and elbow grease, have little to do with a political life—that what matters just as much are clout and school-day connections. The rules that we live by begin to lose their truth. They do not play out as planned, even under our own roofs. Loss of Safe Destiny allows us to pull the truths out of self-deception.

Minnie was reared in a very conservative Cambodian family that still believed that a woman only becomes acceptable upon marrying a man. She remembers being told by her mother very early on that she had to find a husband who could corral her strident nature, control her spoiled tendencies, teach her the meaning of respect, and provide for her. Her mother felt that by finding such a man, Minnie would be assured that someone would take care of her when bad times struck. Minnie recalls, "I told my mom, in as delicate a way as I could, to look at her own life instead. 'Ma, when you needed help and when you were sick, did Dad ever take care of you? The answer is no, of course, so why are you telling me to do the same?' And she has to admit that I'm right. I mean, why does she decide to live with these ideas that don't even work for her? I tell her she needs to be more realistic and that she has to have more confidence in me. When she tells me that I need a man to keep me in line, I tell her that I don't want to be kept in line."

That is not to say that Minnie wants to live her life alone forever. At twenty-nine, she is ready for a deep relationship. But knowing what she *doesn't* want hasn't given her a clue as to what *would* satisfy her. "If I don't want a disciplinarian, or a father figure, then what DO I want?" Accepting the loss of chivalrous destiny means for Minnie that she has to maneuver in undefined, uncharted territory.

When we lose destiny, we forfeit obvious markers of what is supposed to constitute a successful life. We might even begin to question the true value of our professional or scholastic achievements, or our faith in the strategies that were supposed to have earned us respect. When that happens, what remains is only the essence of who we are, stripped of camouflage. Is the person that remains someone we know? What does she stand for? What is she worth to herself?

Shedding destiny can be both liberating and daunting. Actively claiming and defending the values and lifestyle that we believe in requires that we take stands and express points of view that might not always be popular. By letting go of predestined paths, we accept the responsibility of living thoughtfully and with meaning.

Sharon recounts her dream of lost destiny. In her dream she is in China and has ventured into a dark, cryptlike bookstore. There she finds two beautiful, ancient, silk-bound Chinese dictionaries. She asks how much they are and finds that they are quite expensive, and goes away without buying them. When Sharon woke up the next morning, she was so disappointed. She regretted not purchasing them on the spot. As she came out of her sleep, she realized that she could never have had those dictionaries, no matter how real that dream might have seemed. Try as she might, she would never be able to return to that dream bookstore to find the books that could help translate the past into the present. The dream, Sharon feels, revealed a deep significance: "I didn't/couldn't buy the dictionaries, not because they were too expensive, but because ultimately they were not purchasable. I couldn't buy them. *I had to help write them.*" And write them she does, through her work as a teacher, translating her experiences as a Chinese American daughter and mother into American realities. Sharon lets go of any false comforts she may have had that roads would already be paved for her. Instead, she now understands that she'll be making her own road, by walking it.

WE LOSE THE UNBROKEN CIRCLE

Now that your mom is retired, she thinks it is a good time for you to have a baby. She'll never tell you that herself, because she wants you to have your freedom and knows that you're busy with your career. But you know, you're not getting any younger. Okay, your mom told me that you might want to adopt a Chinese baby girl, which is very great of you, but I think your mom has a point. You haven't tried to have one yourself yet, so why not have one of your own? Like your mom says, it's cheaper and safer. Come on, she's retired now, she's got time on her hands. Why not give her the grandkid you know she wants? For once, just once! Try to be a good Chinese daughter.

—My cousin, who shall remain unnamed

Although my mother has always thought of herself as independent, in her old age she's quickly reverting to tradition. Does life as a senior citizen make her suddenly feel as if she needs to protect the continuation of our clan or preserve her feeling of being needed now by hinting about grandchildren? To what extent am I to go on fulfilling promises, allowing her life and preferences to influence mine?

For many contemporary Asian American mothers, there comes a realization that the near future will not follow the same family patterns that traditionally allowed older Asian women to be comfortable—the patterns that dictated that family will provide, that daughters and sons will always be there. In effect, she loses that cultural insurance policy. No longer do we have the comfort of what Li Ching speaks of in recalling her communal childhood:

> In old-time Shanghai, I remember on hot summer nights, all the amahs, cooks, and wives came out to the common yard and just sat around and talked. Children would scream and laugh as they caught crickets; fireflies buzzed around. Some of the women played mah-jong, but that was only their excuse to pass the time. They hardly even thought about the game; they could feel the tiles underneath, so they just played by reflex. Those evenings were really about talking and about being together. On those evenings, we were all reminded that we were connected. They were part of something larger.

The past has taught us that a woman's role is as the keeper of the family bond. We support. We nourish. We maintain stability and levity. We are the wives and mothers that intuit our family's needs. We are the daughters that carry on the clan line. *Over many generations, being needed has become a primary measure of our worth.* In return, we were assured that in old age the same caring would be done for us. That is the beauty of the Unbroken Circle that has worked for generations. If we perform our roles as mothers well, the love and sacrifice will be returned when we grow old.

Yet no matter how hard we try to preserve cycles of duty within our family structures, contemporary life can make this extremely difficult. At some point, our children may venture from home in the search for individuality that is part of teenagehood. In the working world we must often travel or relocate far from our home base to keep our jobs. Unbroken Circles are also threatened when our partners are less than willing to play their assigned roles in preserving family links. In a few short generations, the extended family upon which dynasties have been built can become fractured as it becomes Americanized.

With a small, barely audible snap, my grandmother's back sprained as she lifted her fat grandson Michael up out of his stroller. For sixty years, she drank too little milk, ate too little broccoli, and her bones had turned to sawdust—osteoporosis, the doctor told my mother. Grandma came all the way from Taiwan to take care of her baby grandchildren, and what she got in return was a crooked back. Now unable to move, unable to carry out the duties that she promised, she went back home to Taiwan. Grandma died in her sleep a few years later in the family home in Shinjiu, "maybe from taking too much heart medicine," my mother explains.

Did my grandma count on an unbroken circle of family and grandchildren to keep her company in her old age? What does it take to eat five more pills than prescribed?

Sita was sixty when her husband died. She was sixteen when she married him, and he was twenty-four years her senior. It was a given that Sita would live out her old age without him, yet she hadn't known quite how hard it would be to adjust. Her children, now with their own families, didn't seem to need her. "There's no purpose for me being here anymore," she said. "I want to join my husband now." And had she done so, Sita would have become another Asian woman in America to "pull a Butterfly," as playwright David Henry Hwang referred to it. It would be easy enough to call Sita's story a romantic tragedy and appreciate the beauty of true love that compels a wife to join her deceased husband. In fact, elderly Asian women in America are fifty percent more likely to commit suicide than their white counterparts. Yet Sita conceivably has thirty years or more of life that she is willing to throw away. Not since the age of sixteen has she been given a chance to spend time with herself, to define who she is *for herself,* without needing to plug into anyone else's requirements. Is it possible for us to go through an entire life and never know what we are about, what our wildest dreams are, what we would do if our lives had been our own? Fraying circles of obligation can bring tremendous opportunity. In many cases, they can release us from the social contracts that have limited our roles to caretakers and providers, and give us the room to explore our lives in ways that were not previously possible.

How do we negotiate between American individualism on one hand and Asian family communalism on the other? How do we celebrate our individuality while still preserving connections to the family group? The two competing dynamics grate against one another, and losses are bound to occur, as Vanessa's experience attests to:

When I told my mom that I wanted to move out one day, her reaction was severe. She flew into a rage. She said to me, "Do you know what will happen to you if you move out? You'll end up worrying all the time about paying your bills, your grades will slip, you'll end up working all the time." She said to me, "Don't you ever forget. You're not American like all of your classmates. *You're Filipino!*"

Circles do not break easily, and families are not quick to throw over systems that have worked for thousands of years. This is especially true when family structures are "enmeshed," a term used by psychologists to refer to closed family systems in which every member plays a role in preserving the group dynamic. Mother may be the whip-cracker. Father may be silent or frustrated. Sister may be the peacekeeper. Brother may not live up to the dream.

In situations like these, where we fall into predictable patterns of behavior, we lose our ability to act freely—to mothers who demand too much of us or brothers who are indifferent or fathers who are distant or unavailable. We do not give ourselves the opportunity to develop emotional maturity and grounding. In enmeshed families, one doesn't separate the "I" from the "we." Parents begin to use children as a substitute for their own lives. Children, unable to build up a sense of security, grow perpetually dependent on parents. Without being able to stand on our own, we repeat the cycle of dependencies again. Like the generation before us, we become reliant on affirmation from our partners and our children. Without the ability to rely on our own emotions, we cannot sense our own needs. We become alienated from ourselves.

Breaking the circle does not mean eradicating the bonds that have given strength to our family systems—it means a compromise. It requires us to set up different formulas for interaction. Once we recognize that a family is composed of individuals, each with a unique personality and set of aspirations, we can act with each other on more open, mature ground. We can learn to give and receive from each other without the need for approval or return. Our generosity is no longer obligatory. Instead it evolves into a genuine giving and receiving.

WE LOSE THE ROMANTIC AND TRAGIC PAST

As I attempt to read and transform my memory fragments into lived narratives, as I search fading family photographs for details of the past, my (re)imagined beginnings are already dissolving. . . . On my numerous transits through Hong Kong enroute to and from China, I have always felt a strange sense of comfort, at-homeness, laced with imminent loss. . . . It is as if I were holding a photo that is dissolving even as I trace the outlines within and beyond its frame.

—Sharon Hom,
(Per)forming Law: Deformations and Transformations

The immigration experience is often accompanied by a feeling of the loss of past lives and histories. It may bring traumatic change and necessary severances. As in Sharon's case, it may feel like a dissolving picture that fades slowly, where vanishing images are replaced with more romantic memories. Whether motivated by the promise of greater opportunity, the desire to be reunited with family, or the terror of war, the immigration experience is laced with themes of awkward reconciliations in the face of necessary loss. As Joan, a Vietnamese American from Boston recounts:

When I took the oath of American citizenship, I had to renounce citizenship to the country of my origin. That was difficult. It became a philosophical consideration. Am I willing to forfeit the place of my birth and my loyalties to it in order to be American? I don't know yet what being American means, but I do know what being Vietnamese means. It takes a leap of faith to give up what you know in your heart. I do know one thing. Becoming American means taking on the heavy obligation of participating to create something new. That is a heavy responsibility to carry, and each of us, when we take that oath, has to accept that gift and burden.

Gayatri counts herself as one of the lucky few. She works for an American company in India and is able to jet back and forth from Los Angeles to her home in Bombay. A product of both cultures, she has been doing the same juggling act for fifteen years. At thirty-five, Gayatri feels that she now has to make one country her home without throwing the other away. Which culture will emerge dominant, and which one will she lose vestiges of? As she puts it, "After fifteen years, I came back to India, thinking that it was my rightful home. Even though there are parts of this culture that drive me batty, I always saw myself as much more Indian than American. I now realize that the India I remembered was an India of my imagination. How could I have forgotten how constricting and closed our societies could be? I can't make a move in India without word traveling all the way back to my family in Delhi hundreds of miles away. There's no way that I can stay in India for much longer. I'd like to move back to Los Angeles as soon as I can."

For those who find it difficult to settle in a new place, looking back at happier, less burdened times back home can be one of the few comforts available to us, as Malini describes:

It was easier in Calcutta. Even though there weren't the same conveniences—no big supermarkets, no shopping malls, the electricity would go out during the monsoon— at least I could understand the culture. There is a way I could act with my girlfriends that was easy and close, not like here, where everyone is disconnected and lives in their own little shell. In India, I didn't constantly have to explain where I was from, and where India was. My life was just assumed. I could be myself.

But Gayatri's and Malini's aren't the only ways that we may face the loss of past places and times. For those who have had to face an immigration experience through tragedy, such as war, our loss of the romantic past is of a different nature. In these situations, there have usually been abrupt severances, often unwilling, often brutal, which have left permanent marks and lingering post-traumatic stresses on one's life, no matter where one escapes to or what one achieves from that point on.

Xuan came from Vietnam in 1975 with the first flow of refugees from Vietnam. The daughter of a privileged family, Xuan attended school in Switzerland and in America, returning to her home country right before the fall of Saigon. Although her country was in the throes of a civil war, Xuan chose to return to Vietnam because "it was home." She never thought she would live anywhere else. And her family never believed that the U.S. forces would leave. But Xuan had heard the news reports in America and in Europe, and sensed the impending North Vietnamese takeover.

Xuan's family was lucky. Through a family connection, they secured the clearances needed to escape. "We stayed at my parents' house for the weeks before. We couldn't go to the movies, we couldn't go to market. I asked myself, 'What's happening to me?' My life was all planned out, and now I had no direction."

Xuan and her family clambered onto a barge headed for the sea, amid fighting on both sides of the river and U.S. helicopters flying above them. When they were floating on the barge waiting for a ship to take them to another shore, they heard on the radio that Saigon had fallen. Xuan remembers chaos, climbing over people like crabs, with feet and arms flying in all directions. At one point Xuan felt herself being flipped head over heels from the barge below onto the ship that would transport her to safe haven.

For three days on the overcrowded boat, there was no food or water. Xuan remembers being responsible for carrying the milk for her sister-in-law's newborn son, but they were not on her barge, so Xuan gave the milk to the other children, hoping that someone was doing the same for her sister-in-law. The ship stopped at Subic Bay in the Philippines. From there, Xuan and other refugees were ushered onto an aircraft carrier, "where everyone sat on the bare floor, tied up with one giant piece of rope, like cargo." They flew to the next destination, a Guam refugee camp for one week's stay, before being transported to Canada. Xuan watched the Vietnamese fighter pilots as they stood in line at the refugee camp. They were always important heroes at home, the handsome men who used to strut around the streets of Saigon in their American uniforms like proud peacocks:

Before leaving Saigon, those pilots were given orders to save their planes, not to wait for their families. They all followed their orders. And when they landed, they found out that in being so loyal, they had lost their families, and they had lost their country. Now they stood silent as the U.S. soldiers cut away their hair and cut away the stripes on their uniforms. Everything that made them proud was being taken away from them in front of all of us in the most humiliating way. They just stared straight ahead. I hurt for them.

The only way that I could face my own situation was to feel the pain of other people, like these pilots. What can my pain be compared to what these soldiers had to go through? That's when I told myself that I had to give up memory. I told myself that I had to start a new life, block the sadness out, because that was the only way I was going to be able to go forward.

Xuan cannot tell this story without breaking down in sobs that make me swallow back my own sadness with her. For over twenty years, Xuan has transformed her loss into hope, using her memories to inspire her work in America, assuring that at least here, her community will thrive.

WE LOSE HOPE FOR A MAGIC WAND

As we come into power, we acknowledge that all meaningful goals in life require great tenacity and tremendous patience. We let go of lottery ticket wishes that leave us dreaming of quick, effortless solutions that cast our fate to chance. All of a sudden, fantasies take a backseat, as we begin to work toward real goals. Tossing out the Hope for a Magic Wand enables us to understand that transformation requires tough choices.

We hope so desperately for easy solutions. How we search for the perfect set of circumstances, the ideal job, the ultimate partner, the meeting of goals that, once achieved, might deliver us into a life free of worries. When we lose the Hope for a Magic Wand, we accept that we must fight for the mere privilege to be who we are and who we dream to be.

Leslie was idealistic when she decided to run for elected office. She was an excellent advocate and was respected as someone who always played by the rules. An elected office was the natural next step in her career. "Play it straight as always," she told herself, and she'd have a good shot at winning. She had the right team of counselors to back her up, and a long track record of community service. Now all that had to happen was the follow-through of the voting public, a significant number of whom were Asian Americans, just like her. Unfortunately, Leslie began to realize that she had entered a nightmare. The next few months of campaigning were absolutely harrowing. The support she counted on from her community was nowhere near what it could have been. To add insult to injury, a member of her own Asian community began to spread rumors about Leslie that maligned her professional integrity, a low blow since Leslie depended heavily on the spotless reputation she had worked so hard to achieve. Leslie was hurt. She began to take it personally, wondering if she was really fit for this kind of work.

In the end, Leslie fought tooth and nail to deflect all of the accusations that came flying at her. In fact, they were the same kind of challenges that we all go through when we start to claim our power. She held on. And won. Leslie could see that as she entered into new realms of political power, it would be a different kind of game. Savvy and a thick skin were now just as important as one's credentials. Old rules would be replaced by new ones that were subtle and more complicated.

There are no easy solutions for Leslie, or for any of us. That is the lesson we learn when the Magic Wand is tossed away. The rules of the game aren't as simple as we thought they were. By recognizing what we have lost, we allow ourselves to roll up our sleeves and get down to the hard, real work of building.

Lesson Twelve

SHE MOVES HER WORLD

If you want one year of prosperity, grow rice. If you want ten years of prosperity, grow trees. If you want one hundred years of prosperity, grow people.

—Chinese proverb

Enough looking in. Power is also about looking out. What good is "finding ourselves" if we can't plug that knowledge into something bigger? Let's go beyond mirror work and begin to link with others.

Come with me on a road trip across America as I show you that power can be an act of connection. Along the way, there will be encounters with women who move their worlds, create, take chances, and build across communities.

Mothers, take note: As you'll see in these next pages, your daughters have indeed arrived. And guess what? You're coming with them.

A*ttention. United Flight 208 to Seattle is now boarding through Gate 12.* On hearing my flight announcement, I grab my boarding pass and my one piece of carry-on luggage, and I'm off to my next destination. It's Seattle this time. A five-hour direct flight and I gain three hours. I have time to rest and think. Over the last few years, I have averaged about sixty flights a year, usually crammed into a five-month period so that I can spend the other seven in my home in the forest. Traveling as much as I do, I can close my eyes and envision every major airport around the country—the underground neon-lit tunnel of O'Hare, the fluorescent lighting at Dulles, LAX's skydome, all the men with ten-gallon hats at Dallas–Fort Worth. I know which airports have a McDonald's—that Egg McMuffin breakfast has held me over several times as I waited to board my next flight.

This kind of traveling becomes more tolerable if one carries trinkets of home comfort, so I have my stash of luxuries: a portable tea maker that assures me a good cup of herbal tea anywhere and anytime I wish, the photos of family I place on my desk, and, for a while, a one-cup rice cooker for my mid-night snack of rice or ramen. I tossed it when I realized that it took up too much luggage space. Besides, I had faith that I could survive without rice for a few days at a time, though not for too long.

During those five-month stints, I talk. A lot. To as many people as I possibly can, about using morality as the starting point for discussions of the issues that divide us. I talk to parents about bridging communication and culture gaps with their children. I talk to the Urban League about how African Americans can build alliances with Asian Americans that can lead to greater social equity for both. I talk to students and CEOs about the concept of power as an act of connection and communication, knowing that by doing so, I must first break down their traditional notions of power. I know that many of them still see it as a means of getting one's way, forcing their opponent's hand, something outside of themselves, preserving conventional hierarchies. I tell them that what I speak of instead is the force of our collective hope and that this kind of power resides in each of us and cannot be dictated from above.

In the touring process I have also become what law professor Frank Wu calls a "Professional Asian American." I make a career out of articulating Asian American experience, and as Wu urges all PAAs to do, I have also accepted the responsibility that comes with that—to build bridges to other communities with common experience. Speaking is what I love to do, and in a very un-Asian way, I like to brag that I do it well. It's important to know where one's talents lie. That is why I often ask my audiences to think hard about their own. What do they do well and what do they enjoy? When we can put our finger on what that ability is, we move from our strength—the most viable way to express our hopes. Whether our talent lies in being a speaker, a nurse, a mother, an artist, an organizer, a taskmaster, or an executive on Madison Avenue, we can bring our humanity into all of it. Power doesn't necessarily mean we must create vast social change, or be a leader of people.

Power is about knowing what we stand for, breathing it into every activity of the day, and being clear. I have chosen to move my world by being a communicator and a connector of communities. In doing so, I have moments of trial and epiphany that become lessons in themselves. The more I encounter new people and situations, the more my ideas evolve. That state of constant learning and change is a perk of the job.

What are some of the considerations in building bridges? Join me on the road to confront them as I have . . .

MOVING FROM STRENGTH

I am onstage with Kevin Powell, a veteran cast member of MTV's *Real World*, author, and former senior editor at *Vibe* magazine. Kevin tours the country like I do, sharing his insight and experiences on race in America. On the stage there are others as well—Omar Wasow, an Internet visionary, and Tony Medina, a radical poet. We're in the company of a very diverse audience, invited by them to have a lively and sometimes contentious discussion of race issues. Each of us has pulled in a different sector of this college community. There are more African Americans and Latino Americans in this audience than I ever have when I am the lone speaker.

Kevin and I hit it off. He is a fantastic listener and is driven by a cautious optimism. When he speaks, he supports and instructs his audience without being preachy or condescending. Tony, the firebrand, the slam poet master, has a different delivery. He challenges the audience by reciting verses of his evocative and political poetry. His language riles some and excites others. Tony is extreme and adds hotness to the discussion. Learn your history, he advises, read voraciously, know your facts. Omar, of biracial African American and

Caucasian descent, is the dissident among us. He questions the idea of race as an organizing tool and tells us that he believes that race might be too limiting as a rallying issue. I tell the audience that we have to see through the media spin of our world as a chaotic, fearful place, and give them several instances of racial healing that are happening outside the view of news camera lenses. As the only woman and Asian American on the stage, I have to resist falling into the role that is easy to slip into—that of the mediator—knowing that playing the middleman among four equals could prevent me from saying what I want to say. I force myself to interject more than I otherwise would. I feel that I'm being very aggressive, and yet I am only holding my own as the discourse among equals proceeds.

When the floor opens for questions, a young African American man says that he has a statement to make. While he looks at me directly, he tells us that his people don't need anyone else to fight the fight of equity. He tells us that loose ideas like "diversity" have diluted his people's efforts to fight discrimination and that in fact his people have suffered for it. He feels that other groups reaped the benefits of what blacks fought for during the civil rights era and left blacks back down at the bottom of the ladder. "We don't need you," he says to me, and I feel the sting. "We're better off if we fight our fights alone."

He is justified in his frustration. In some ways he is right. African Americans have a history of discrimination in America unlike any other group, and poor African Americans are hit hardest. Women and other minorities have no doubt fared better in achieving some equality than African Americans after the passage of civil rights laws. Yet, while all of this is true, a comparison of oppressions will not help us to find common ground. I had to try to test the boundaries of this man's proposed solution of ethnic isolation. "Do you really feel that it would be better to battle by yourself?" I ask. "Yes," he answers.

Kevin steps in at this point, knowing that this man will listen to him with a different attention, even though Kevin and I might say the same words. Kevin tells him that he sympathizes with his points, but explains that every social change effort throughout history has required the cooperation of many constituencies. I am happy that Kevin has remedied a potentially volatile situation, and yet because the audience doesn't usually get to hear an Asian American opinion, I want them to know that I am interested in bridging divides: "Talking about these issues is difficult and painful. But realize that what's more important than *being* at the table is *staying* at the table. We have to learn to disagree and know that we can still work with each other." I have seen what has happened to too many of these well-intentioned race "workout" talks. When the going gets tough . . . everyone leaves.

So I tell them how Asian Americans, too, participated in civil rights movements. That Japanese American activist Yuri Kochiyama, a friend of Malcolm X and his family, held him close on her lap when he was shot, amid the mayhem around them. I tell them stories about Korean store owners to show them that they too suffered greatly during the Los Angeles violence of 1992. We all struggle, I tell them.

It's a lively crowd that cheers and boos at whim, so I am heartened by the wave of applause that wells up from them. They confirm my belief that there are more of us who want to talk about what draws us together rather than what distinguishes us from one another.

It is times like these when I realize my boundaries as a "race" speaker. Despite the vote of confidence from the crowd, I am reminded of how limited I am with some of the most important communities of color that I count on to hear me. It is difficult for me to admit that as an Asian American woman, I am often prejudged by the very communities of people I ally myself with. They see an Asian face and they think of privilege and honorary whiteness. To many of them, I represent the "other side." My words fall upon skeptical ears, as a representative of a people who has supposedly taken advantage of civil rights gains and given nothing back in return. In my touring I often forget that as an Asian American, I am seen as a wild card, a swing vote, a middleman. It can limit my role tremendously.

But by knowing where I am not as effective, I am able to work with others who are better suited to the task. Instead of blaming others for their inability to hear me openly, I acknowledge it and move on. I find partners—African Americans, Hispanics, gay men and women, other women of color—who can work with me in diverse audiences. In a world where race still matters tremendously, we can't be messengers for everybody.

In the Company of Community

When hit with moments of doubt, I return to the communities that comfort me most. I go to the West Coast, where fifty-five percent of all Asian Americans live, and specifically to California, a state where ten percent of the residents are Asian American. Here, Asian America and multiethnicity is a given, the backlash is strong, but so is the sense of a vigorous progressive community.

California is where some of the most forward-thinking champions of immigrant protections, bilingual education, and affirmative action have set up shop. I try to hook up with some of them whenever I come into town. While in my hotel room in Los Angeles, I call Angela Oh to catch up on what she is doing and to ask for her help on a report that I have been asked to do for a large foundation. Angela is an attorney who became a community spokesperson during the time of the Los Angeles conflicts in an attempt to explain the plight of her Korean American community to the American viewing audience. Her public views on advancing race discussions in America and her long history as a community advocate have earned her a place on the President's Council on Race Relations, where she has certainly stirred up the debate by insisting that Asian American opinions must be more fully incorporated into a race dialogue that has traditionally been one between black and white. Angela is a soulful woman, who believes in intuition and speaks from the heart. I remember her wise words when we first met in Washington, D.C., as we took part in a discussion among many Asian American women about the notion of vision and leadership in our communities: "Leadership is not a popularity contest," she told us. "It means taking a chance and sticking by it."

It must have been difficult for Angela to hold the line on that powerful White House race panel against all those established black and white names and say that the Asian American experience was just as relevant as theirs when having a race discussion. I'm sure she made a few enemies with her stridence. But leaders know that the existence of enemies can be a good sign. Some people's feathers ought to be ruffled.

The next day, I take a shuttle up to my old stomping ground, San Francisco and Berkeley, where a number of my mentors and old friends still live. In Oakland, I catch Peggy Saika on the phone. Peggy, like me, zips around the country, but she can still remain as mellow as only a Californian can.

Peggy leads a group called the Asian Pacific Environmental Network, which measures the impact of pollution on immigrant communities. Her findings support conclusions of "environmental racism"—incidences of high toxins, cancer, and environmentally induced health disorders occur most frequently among poor communities who also happen to be communities of color. Peggy's group has identified, for instance, a hub of toxicity in the Richmond area of the East Bay, where a large community of Laotians reside, and which yields some of the highest incidences of breast cancer in the nation. Recently, Peggy's group has trained Laotian girls to become community spokespersons and educators, connecting them with other communities, role models, and a national support system.

As a mentor to dozens of women, Peggy is known as a master of building processes of accountability and inclusion so that each person within a group speaks for themselves. No assumptions are ever made for anyone. In her decades of activism, Peggy has created some of Asian America's most long-lasting and respected legal and health institutions.

I am fortified by Angela's and Peggy's work, refueled and comforted to know that there are so many of us delivering these same messages of power. What I regret is that we are all so busy that we don't get to see each other often enough. Every time we meet, we meet to get a job done.

MAKING VISION TANGIBLE

On another visit to the West Coast, this time in San Francisco, I meet with a group of over twenty visionary women who are creating the National Asian Pacific American Women's Forum. Peggy is also there. Now I am with my super-sisters, and we are excited by the prospect of breaking new ground. Many of us met each other in Beijing in 1995 and found it both ironic and somehow fitting that it took an international conference on the other side of the world to finally bring us together. We are now meeting to discuss what it means to build a network of Asian American women's communities across this country and how that network will allow us to launch campaigns, conduct research, and influence government policy. We talk about how we will have to ensure that we have many different perspectives at the table—Pacific Islanders from Hawaii, Hmong from Minnesota, Koreans from Los Angeles, immigrants and American-borns.

Building this kind of diverse constituency may sound easy. At first, it seems like a task of merely creating a Noah's Ark of the Asian American diaspora—just get a few of everything, and the goal will have been met. In fact, the job is much more difficult, because once there is representation, we all then have to *work* together. To get a college-educated, American-born daughter to hear past an immigrant woman's accent is difficult. She may hear in that voice her "old-fashioned" mother instead, with all the assumptions that go along with this. And when an American-born woman talks, an older immigrant woman may hear her "know-nothing" daughter. A Vietnamese seamstress and a Filipina attorney may have little in the way of a common language. Therefore, this group understands that we must develop one. So we struggle with learning how to stay at the table. Some people may leave because the progress is slow, but others come on board to fill their shoes. All of this is part of our process.

For the next two days, we spend a lot of our time fleshing out our group philosophy. We want our decision making to be absolutely democratic, which means we will forfeit quick results for the assurance that everyone who has something to say will have a chance to say it. But our conversations can be grueling at times. Occasionally in our desire to get all the details right, we lose sight of the big picture, and there can be disagreement. We get sidetracked and tired, and fall way behind schedule. As the day progresses, it becomes clear that building something out of nothing is not easy. Keeping a national team vested in every decision requires an endless series of conference calls and consensus-building, and that, we found, was frustrating.

Some leadership gurus would predict that our way of proceeding will not work and that a consensus-driven group will run out of gas due to all the energy expended getting everyone to agree. But this is how we insist on going forth, deciding that consensus is a cultural model that suits an Asian American women's governance structure best. In our sessions, we take turns facilitating. Each of us is responsible for getting the group to agree on a set of goals. What's interesting is that this group doesn't often disagree, as other groups might. There are no ego problems. Everyone seems to participate equally. One group member sees this as a grand experiment. She says that if Asian women can't make a consensus model happen, then no one can.

It would have been so much easier to allow someone to assume the role of a benevolent dictator, the way most other organizations have. But the basic tenet of this group is that true forms of leadership emerge when we take the time and energy to build legitimacy. What would be the point of putting together yet another group that followed the old rules of leadership? There would be no use saying that we represent the viewpoints of Asian American women if we didn't first install the processes to make sure that we do. The process of creating this group is an exercise in itself, and a riskier one, with more potential pitfalls because it relies on widespread participation to keep it buoyant. It is more vulnerable to apathy and infighting. And yet hundreds of women are willing to participate in this grand experiment.

In only a few short years, this group has spawned nearly ten local chapters and has arranged meetings like this one in New York, Los Angeles, and Minneapolis. It's been a labor of love for everyone who has remained on board. Most of the work has been volunteer.

When I slump back in fatigue, I force myself to recall the words of the very wise Sunera Thobani, a South Asian woman who is one of Canada's leading feminists and the former president of Canada's powerful National Action Committee, a formidable Canadian women's organization. While building accountable leadership, she says, "we have to be cleaner than clean. We are much more vulnerable if we violate the processes that ensure participation. Our systems of accountability and decision making need to be *absolutely transparent:* How are decisions made? What is the division of labor? How are we held accountable to each other? All this has to be out in the open for everyone to see so that members feel they are being *justly* represented."

DEFINING LEADERSHIP

After a Midwest lecture one evening, a young woman from Vietnam says to me, "When I graduate, I want to do what you do. I want to be a leader, like you are. How do I do it?" Her comment silenced me and made me wonder later what leadership means. Am I a leader? I had never thought of myself as one. "Leader" for me was always a loaded word. I used to think that a leader was someone who made people jump, an overly ambitious person, someone who was arrogant. I have always questioned people in authority and wondered what their real agendas were, wary of their ability to represent my opinions.

It is a problem that "leader" has become a suspect word for those of us who try to create change. All too often we don't give each other the praise and encouragement we need to take on great responsibilities. I have seen so many well-intentioned people with noble goals get tugged back down by crab-pot mentality. I have heard too many catty criticisms of people who seemed to be genuine and honorable. Given circumstances such as these, who would want to be seen as a leader?

And yet, we must all be leaders, perhaps not of armies or of nations, but of our own destinies, in our families, and in the workplace. How can we develop a type of leadership that encourages listening and respect?

Leaders Create "Buy-in" for Their Vision

KaYing is, by all accounts, a leader. For the past several years, she has run a local organization for Hmong women, applying what she has learned in college to help them take charge of their lives. When KaYing graduated from school, she chose to remain in her community and became fluent in the Hmong language. Truly believing in self-empowerment, she told her staff one day that they would each have an equal say in the way the group was run. She opened the financial records for them to see, thinking they would feel more vested in the collective effort. She asked them for their opinions. She told them that they could use flextime in determining their schedules. But KaYing's self-empowerment principles backfired. Given the flextime option, some people seldom came to work. They began to ask for salary increases but weren't willing to attend the training sessions to justify them. Her staff just didn't know what to make of this strange way of managing and mistook KaYing's actions as an inability to lead. It didn't help that KaYing was a young, unmarried Hmong woman operating in a culture where her status as a leader would constantly be questioned, regardless. As she soon discovered, springing major change on her staff caused chaos. Without first undergoing more basic mind shifts, teaching them that freedom also implied accountability, they floundered in confusion. Great change takes time and patience. People have to know *why* they should buy into new ideas and must be allowed to do so at their own pace, KaYing learned, or even given time to decide if they want to buy in at all. Moving fast is not the same as actually getting somewhere.

When young women assume roles of responsibility in the community, power transitions from one generation to the next will not be easy, especially in Asian cultures. When homeland cultures are stuck in age-based hierarchies, as most Asian cultures are, leadership is often unwillingly or reluctantly passed along to next generations. Children will always be seen as children, no matter how old they may be, which would imply that leadership transference happens only when octogenarians become too senile to lead.

Within Asian communities in America, this is a many-sided quandary. For so many immigrant elders, their status here as community leaders is one of their few validations in a country that still seems so foreign. Leadership transition becomes even more difficult when gender is involved, as, for example, when an older Asian immigrant man is asked to pass power to a younger Asian American woman.

Jai Lee, who, like Angela Oh, became a mediator for the Korean American community after the Los Angeles conflicts, feels that young women can begin their transition into leadership by building trust. She has found workable balances that have garnered her wide respect among her Korean community's older generations. When she is with them, she is more deferential, serving them as she would never serve her Asian American contemporaries. She gains the trust and respect of her Korean first-generation community by making it clear that she has no agendas and yet is often able to persuade them to take actions that they would not otherwise take. She makes sure that elders are able to maintain their positions without compromising the potential of her community's new young leadership.

A Leader Doesn't Try to Fit Into Categories; She Creates Her Own

I met Yuan-Kwan several years ago at a Virginia college when she was only a freshman. I saw an intriguing student who, at eighteen, was well versed in Hong Kong movies and who once thought she wanted to be a concert pianist. At sixteen, she had started her own 'zine, called *Meniscus,* which was guerilla-printed on various Xerox machines and now, after five years, is a commercially produced journal. *Meniscus* is an eclectic mix of Yuan-Kwan's personal interests, carrying interviews with girl bands, Michael Chang and other tennis stars, Olympic gymnastics champions, and her friends' reviews of the latest Cantopop CDs. Alongside each story is a snapshot of a smiling Yuan-Kwan with her interviewee. Who would have thought that anyone would share Yuan-Kwan's particular set of eclectic interests? And yet by putting out this unique editorial mix of the subjects she loved, Yuan-Kwan has been able to find an audience of hundreds. *Meniscus* was part of a recent New York museum exhibition on 'zine culture. She follows her own drummer and, as a consequence, other people follow her.

I've kept a running E-mail correspondence with Yuan-Kwan over the years. The year after I met her, she became an intern at *A. Magazine.* During that summer, we would have lunch together from time to time, and she'd tell me about the newest clothes store she discovered and what her impressions were of New York City. In her junior year she went to England, and through E-mail, I would recommend good, inexpensive restaurants there to her. Now, four years later, Yuan-Kwan is sophisticated and worldly. I know she will be a leader, no matter what she does, and I bet she wouldn't be surprised to hear that.

She goes for what she wants without being overtly aggressive. She asks for help when she needs it. She has little fear, and yet, one day there may be someone who will fear her power enough to try to knock it down. The only thing she can do is know that it might happen, this trial by fire, and with the bridges she's built, there will be many of us to help her if that time comes.

Leadership Is a Tremendous Responsibility

All of us have low points when we question the roads we have taken. At those times, I ask myself why I have to travel so much. Some days, I just want to watch television at home with Zubin and eat chocolate. I want to get together with my friends at a moment's notice in a neighborhood restaurant and not have to talk to them on the phone long distance. Those are the times when I've been away for a while, when I haven't been eating well (no rice), and my throat is getting scratchy from the dry air in planes and all the talking I do for hours on end. It's inevitable, though, that at the lowest point of my whining, something will always make me snap out of my funk and remember that what I do does lead to a few good things.

And so I force myself to think about the follow-up projects that have been launched after I've visited a group and the new organizations that have been established as a result of inspiring discussions with college and community leaders. I think about the letters of support that I have written to help good people get what they wanted. And the brilliant discussions that I have had with friends whom I never would have met had I not been on the road.

Sometimes I recognize how hard this work can be and the seriousness of the possible consequences. One evening after a very personal lecture, a young Cambodian thanks me for what I've shared with the audience. "It is hard for me at home," she tells me, and she is getting choked by her words, as if she had finally found someone she could talk to and was revealing something secret for the first time. She tries to explain what the difficulty is, but then she starts to cry. I don't know what she is feeling, but my own story has triggered something in her that now hurts. I don't know if she has supportive people around her, so I try to comfort her, knowing that there is so little I can do to change things for her.

How can I introduce poignant issues in my talks, open up people's wounded places, if I will not be around to witness the repercussions of my words? Is it fair to come into cities and towns, shake up their thinking, and leave the next day? Is it irresponsible, or is it the only thing that I can do? I give myself solace by realizing that I can only be a catalyst. I can't do it all. I can't be around to make sure that every plan is followed through, or that people will interpret my words in the ways that I intended, or that anything wonderful will result from the grand promises that are made by my audiences during my presentations. The best that I can hope for is that my words and what I do can coax people to take the kernel of a story and pass it through their own lives. To be comfortable with what I do, I have to trust that people will make their own ways to their own truths.

Leaders Measure Their Progress

We can't manage what we can't measure. How will we know when we're making progress or when our actions have to be adjusted to meet our goals? The problem is that finding quantitative measurements can be difficult. "Measurement" was a topic addressed by a gathering of very special women organized by the Ms. Foundation, where they discussed how we can know when we are creating change. This is what they came up with:

We Know That Our Efforts Have Met With Success

When we feel opposition.

When what we are doing fits within our own long-term vision.

When we are reaffirmed by key allies and those whom we respect.

When what we do concretizes ideas that were previously scattered.

When our action leads to fundamental systemic change, through a ripple effect, and through a new way of voicing ideas.

BECOMING FLUENT

At eleven o'clock sharp I am picked up by a car that takes me to the headquarters of a huge telecommunications company that seeks answers to some cultural questions, including a few that have arisen in a project in the United Arab Emirates. I am there with a professor from American University, a distinguished diplomat who was part of many meetings that led to détentes in the volatile Middle East. I feel fortunate that he has agreed to come with me to talk here.

In the halls of corporate America, I speak a different vernacular. My tone changes. I wear a business suit. Here, the language of change is bottom-line oriented, a fact with which I am comfortable. As a connector, I have had to learn how to deliver messages in many different settings. In academic environments, I speak the language of hope through loftier ideas. I use pop culture references to illustrate my points and know that young audiences will know what I am talking about. To corporations, I speak the language of the bottom line.

"How will change affect our profits?" they want to know, and I show them how markets have expanded for companies that have chosen to recruit and promote a more diverse staff. I pull out charts and graphs, and cite benchmark studies, because that is the way I can make them understand. When the Department of Labor came out with a report called "Workforce 2000," they addressed the changing demographic of the American consumer, and asserted that the future growth of American companies would depend on how well they could retain and promote those with firsthand knowledge of these new consumers. The telecommunications industry was one of the first sectors to respond and diversify. Everyone calls home, they realized, and in a mobile world where generations are spread across the globe, that meant a lot of international calls. A lot of business.

As communicators, we have to express our vision in a variety of ways, and this is where the Asian American propensity for "fitting-in" may prove useful. Chameleon instincts make it easier to become fluent in many different approaches to communicating the same idea. There is nothing disingenuous about being versatile as long as one knows what one stands for and as long as we can still speak up when we ought to.

I am at this company today because a young Chinese woman, an engineer, took it upon herself to invite me—she surfed the Internet and found my name, convincing her boss that it would be a good idea if, for once, their company staff could see an Asian face talking about intercultural exchange. It takes guts to propose something like that, I think to myself, recalling what it was like to stick my neck out in a corporate environment. I ask myself why she chose to do this, or why anyone decides to volunteer an opinion that might go against the grain or jeopardize one's standing. I remind myself that some of the most courageous acts of change have happened outside of the protest lines and strikes, by people within offices who use their position to sway their management to look at things differently.

Taking Up the Gauntlet

I am staring out at a huge audience—a good twelve hundred people, the entering class of 2002. I am supposed to show them how the world is theirs to explore. I am told that the fiery minister and author Michael Eric Dyson was given this keynote position last year, and I am considerably daunted by the prospect of following in his footsteps. Michael is a preacher, perhaps one of the best in the nation, and for years, he has been one of my heroes. He rocks his audiences with references to hip-hop and healing, and he works up a sweat doing it. He understands rapture. Now, at the same place that he stood, I would have to do the same.

I am probably the first Asian American woman my audience has ever seen deliver a keynote speech. There's nothing that they can pull from their memory files to draw any assumptions. I know they don't know what to expect. I take a deep breath as my host introduces me, and I'm on. I'm glad that I asked that the houselights be half up so that now I can see my audience. And it is big. In a hall like this, the stage lights are right in your eyes. My voice echoes back to the podium, in the same way that an international phone call sometimes does. When I first began speaking, I'd need a few seconds to get used to this, but now years later, it doesn't faze me.

This next generation, brought up on Nike ads and Microsoft, assumes that the world, indeed, has no boundaries. They see a Benetton ad and assume that like those pictures, we are united in our colors, without having the faintest idea of how that might work in reality. I ask myself, "What can I tell them that will help them to understand that life is not as it is on TV and that we still have to reach out to one another—communicate with each other—to find the real stories?" I don't want their complacency to slip into apathy, as I've seen happen on so many other campuses. I want to say something to them that they will remember for the next four years.

One day, the few Asian American women who go out into the world as I do now will not feel so alone. I have to believe that I am delivering messages of hope for a reason. Within this next decade, I know there are going to be dozens of us, and then hundreds of us, who will get ourselves up before a group, with the guts to tell our own stories, linking them to the universal condition and to a message of hope. For my part, I will make sure to train a dozen of them myself, and I will tell them about epiphanies, like this one.

Sometime within the last two years, my speaking style changed. I stopped referring to notes and began to use fewer statistics and offer my heart instead. Finally, I let myself be vulnerable to audiences who cared enough to spend an evening listening to something they had not heard before. I didn't need to rely on legal theories and the backup of research studies. It no longer mattered whether pundits agreed with me. And I no longer gave anyone the right to tell me whether I did or didn't fit—there was no longer anything I felt I had to fit into. With no axes to grind, no need to sound "correct," my voice had become more lyrical—perhaps it had taken on the rhythm of a higher truth. Whether I chose to speak softly, grandly, or hold a prolonged pause, my thoughts now came from somewhere deep and strong and grounded, a place where they had never come from before.

Now I know that I am free, and no matter where life takes me from now on, I know that I will always be home.

HOW DEEPLY WOMEN PROMISE

Because she believes in herself,
she doesn't need to convince others,
Because she is content with herself,
she doesn't need others' approval.
Because she accepts herself,
the whole world accepts her.

—Adapted from the *Tao te Ching*

Puanani told me a story that I will never forget and that offers an appropriate closing to a book that I hope will bring about many new beginnings:

Puanani's mother had vowed to her, "When you have a baby, I will see her when she is born, and what a happy thing that will be! We'll have a luau at Wai'anae. I will teach your baby to sing, and show you how to feed her so that she'll grow up big and strong. She'll learn how to laugh. She'll learn *puna puna* ways."

But Puanani's mother died before Puanani had her first child. Though friends were there to help her, Puanani wanted so much for her mother to be there for the little things, especially as the baby cried and cried all night, leaving her with little time to rest. Puanani missed her mother very deeply.

One afternoon, Puanani had her baby to her breast as she walked slowly around the living room, nursing the child to sleep. As she hummed a lullaby, Puanani saw something strange, a hazy, moving shape outside the screen door. She walked toward the screen door with her baby in her arms and bent down so that the walking spirit of her mother could see the child, who also seemed to sense this cloudlike presence. "See, Mom? This is your grandchild." Puanani looked up and the light lingered as if it were gazing back, and then slowly drifted away. "Thank you, Mom, for coming back," Puanani said.

"That's when I turned my sorrow into hope," Puanani told me. "Now I knew that my mother would always be there for the baby. She would be there through me. I would pull what I could from all the things that she taught me. I would draw on her gift of power, and I would teach my child. My mother came back as she said she would, in the only way she could. And I know that it must have taken a lot of strength to get back to the living world. She did that for me. That's when I realized *how deeply women promise.*"

We make many promises to each other, and we work hard to honor our word. We promise to support, we promise to care. We promise that we will not let each other fall. Through these deeply given promises, we can hold on to hope. And hope changes worlds.

When the moon is full, I get into my car and drive to the ocean alone. There, I see the people like me, wrapped in blankets or heavy sweaters, who have also been pulled from the comfort of their warm homes toward the vastness of a shore that looks like a lunar surface, with flickers of light that skip like an electric current on the waves.

In the solitary moments of a clear, moonlit night, I stand on my own, looking upward toward the sky, and am reminded that I am part of a pattern that is tremendous and timeless. There is comfort in knowing that people have gazed at the night skies as I do since the beginning of time and will continue long after I am gone. And on this full moon night, there will be those who venture to their own coasts, to the beaches of India and Mombassa, Denmark and Thailand, and along the Mediterranean. I go to the beach on these nights to know that I am intimately connected to everything and everyone around me, forever.

As connected as we are—to friends, to family, to each other—we often feel we are ultimately on our own as we make our way through life, and that can be a frightening prospect. We can overcome this fear only by reaching out to one another, and in our shared courage, we will learn.

The lessons are numerous. We might come to understand that real power comes when we can turn rage into empathy. Or that it takes bravery to listen and act. We may finally understand that it is no longer necessary to be perfect, and that in fact, it never was. Our most gripping fears of betrayal, failure, and loneliness may loosen their hold so that we can learn to be vulnerable without being afraid. Our distrust can turn to hope, so that we can finally begin to promise.

I have found the heart of power, and it lies in a fearless-ness to be tender. It lies in the ability to open up without resistance or fear of consequences. It lies in the courage to face the world head-on, with who we are, with all of our limitations and gifts. With the understanding that we are valuable for who we are, our fear of opinions finally falls away, and compassion enters freely.

May we look inward and find the truth.

May we connect with all through the power of one.

May we give words to that which is not yet spoken.

My strength, is your strength, is ours.

Notes

INTRODUCTION:
THE NEED FOR A COMPASS

page 2 *Perhaps that need comes from* . . . Karin Aguilar–San Juan, "Forward: Breathing Fire, Confronting Power, and Other Necessary Acts of Resistance," in *Dragon Ladies,* ed. Sonia Shah (Boston: South End Press, 1997), xi.

5 *In 1976, Maxine Hong Kingston's* . . . Maxine Hong Kingston, *The Woman Warrior: Memoirs of a Girlhood Among Ghosts* (New York: Knopf, 1976).

5 *In an interview with Bill Moyers* . . . Bill Moyers, *A World of Ideas II: Public Opinions from Private Citizens* (New York: Doubleday, 1990), 17.

7 *Psychological texts* . . . Evelyn Lee, *Working With Asian Americans: A Guide for Clinicians* (New York: Guilford Press,

1997); Laura Uba, *Asian Americans: Personality Patterns, Identity, and Mental Health* (New York: Guilford Press, 1994).

7 *Collections such as* . . . Elaine H. Kim, Lilia V. Villanueva, and Asian Women United of California, *Making More Waves: New Writing by Asian American Women* (Boston: Beacon Press, 1997); Claire S. Chow, *Leaving Deep Water* (New York: Dutton, 1998); Sonia Shah, ed., *Dragon Ladies* (Boston: South End Press, 1997).

10 *By focusing solely on what sets us apart* . . . See Edward W. Said, *Orientalism* (New York: Pantheon, 1978) for a history of the intellectual construction of the "Orient" as the exotic "other," legitimated primarily for its juxtaposition to the western Occident, and Dorinne Kondo, *About Face: Performing Race in Fashion and Theater* (New York: Routledge, 1997) for a provoking interdisciplinary analysis of objectification of the Asian aesthetic.

11 *In her book* . . . Gloria Steinem, *Revolution From Within: A Book of Self-Esteem* (New York: Little, Brown, 1992), 6 (pap.).

LESSON ONE:
SHE CASTS OFF EXPECTATIONS

page 23 *In a 1987 study* . . . Robert D. Hess, Chih-Mei Chang, and Teresa M. McDevitt, "Cultural Variations in Family Beliefs About Children's Performance in Mathematics: Comparisons Among People's Republic of China, Chinese-American, and Caucasian-American Families," *Journal of Educational Psychology* 79 (1987): 179–188.

24 *As my survey responses* . . . Question 25: "What are some of the expectations that you feel your family has for you? Do you feel compelled to fulfill those expectations?"

24 *Lora remembers her mother's advice* . . . Lora Jo Foo, "Jade and Armor," *No More Frogs, No More Princes: Women Making Choices at Midlife,* eds. Joanne F. Vickers and Barbara L. Thomas (Freedom, CA: Crossing Press, 1993), 95–6.

29 *But, to the extent* . . . Harriet Lerner, *The Dance of Intimacy: A Woman's Guide to Courageous Acts of Change in Key Relationships* (New York: Harper & Row, 1989), 136 (pap.).

29 *Among Asian families* . . . See, for example, David Sue, Derald Sue, and Diane Sue, "Psychological Development of Chinese-American Children," in *The Psychosocial Development of Minority Group Children,* ed. Gloria Powell (New York: Brunner/Mazel, 1983).

30 *As psychologist and author Harriet* . . . Harriet Lerner, *The Dance of Intimacy,* 139 (pap.).

32 *Even in the most open of Asian American families* . . . N. Kibria, *Family Tightrope: The Changing Lives of Vietnamese Americans* (Princeton, NJ: Princeton University Press, 1993); Pyong Gap Min, "Korean Immigrant Wives' Overwork," *Korea Journal of Population and Development* 21 (1992): 23–36; *Invisible and in Need: Philanthropic Giving to Asian Americans and Pacific Islanders,* a report of Asian Americans and Pacific Islanders in Philanthropy (December 1992): 21.

LESSON TWO:
SHE BRINGS THE FAMILY FORWARD

page 36 *I want her to tell me* . . . Amy Tan, *The Joy Luck Club* (New York: Putnam, 1989). The success of this book gave rise to a debate among Asian American writers on an artist's responsibility in representing the whole of Asian American experience. See Amy Tan, "In the Canon for All the Wrong Reasons," *Harper's Magazine*, December 1996, 27, for the author's opinion on this matter.

37 *Stories about Asian mother-daughter relationships* . . . The tradition of the self-sacrificing woman predates American migration experiences, through movies such as *Volcano in the Blood* (1932), directed by Sun Yu, about the demise of a peasant family forced to sell their daughter, who eventually commits suicide, and *Tears of a Mother* (1937), directed by Cimu Qu, which features a suffering mother who is eventually rewarded for her selflessness.

38 *Her books include* . . . Marie Villanueva, *Nene and the Horrible Math Monster* (Chicago: Polychrome Books, 1993); Marlene Shigekawa, *Blue Jay in the Desert* (Chicago: Polychrome Books, 1993).

38 *Dan Hoang is a first-generation* . . . For a history of the Hmong people, see Sucheng Chan, ed., *Hmong Means Free: Life in Laos and America* (Philadelphia: Temple University Press, 1994).

39 *Connie Chan, a clinical professor* . . . Felicia Paik, "Say Anything," *A. Magazine*, February/March 1995, 82.

39 *Her story demonstrates how* . . . Christina Looper Baker and Christina Baker Kline, *The Conversation Begins: Mothers and Daughters Talk About Living Feminism* (New York: Bantam, 1996), 343.

40 *"I gave a speech . . . "* Ibid., 342.

43 *As Hope Edelman wrote* . . . Hope Edelman, *Motherless Daughters: The Legacy of Loss* (New York: Dell, 1994), 211.

45 *According to counselor Claire Chow* . . . Chow, *Leaving Deep Water,* 72.

46 *Sociologist Henry Trueba* . . . Henry Trueba, *Cultural Conflict & Adaptation* (Bristol, PA: Taylor & Francis, 1990).

LESSON THREE:
SHE LEARNS TO SHOUT

page 55 *"You're going to talk . . . "* Kingston, *The Woman Warrior,* 175 (pap.).

63 *In their book* . . . Mary Valentis and Anne Devane, *Female Rage: Unlocking Its Secrets, Claiming Its Power* (New York: Carol Southern Books, 1994), 2.

63 *According to Valentis and* . . . Ibid., 67.

64 *The result, the authors write* . . . Ibid., 67.

64 *In fact, the outburst of wild rage* . . . Aurora Tompar-Tiu, M.D., and Juliana Sustento-Seneriches, M.D., *Depression*

and Other Mental Health Issues, The Filipino American Experience (San Francisco: Jossey Bass Publishers, 1995), 82.

64 *In a 1990 study* . . . E. Manio, "Filipino Values in the Workplace." Paper presented to the Filipino Mental Health Resource Group, San Francisco, October 1990.

66 *In* Women Who Run . . . Clarissa Pinkola-Estes, *Women Who Run With the Wolves* (New York: Ballantine, 1992), 396 (pap.).

67 *According to Laura Uba* . . . Uba, *Asian Americans,* 17–8.

71 *Laura Uba offered this anecdote* . . . Ibid., 22.

76 *Betty, a journalist who knows* . . . Betty Wong, editor's note, *A. Magazine,* special issue "Woman Warriors," 1994, 2.

77 *Wendy Mink, a professor* . . . Baker and Kline, *The Conversation Begins,* 57.

Lesson Four:
She Questions Her Power

page 89 *University of Chicago sociologist* . . . Robert Park, "Human Migration and the Marginal Man," *The American Journal of Sociology* 33, no. 6 (May 1928): 881–93.

90 *And still after all that work* . . . M. Evelina Galang, *Her Wild American Self* (Minneapolis: Coffeehouse Press, 1996).

93 *The truth is that many Asian Americans* . . . Bill Ong Hing, "Immigration Policy," in *The State of Asian Pacific*

America: Policy Issues to the Year 2020 (Los Angeles: LEAP Asian Pacific American Policy and Planning Institute and UCLA Asian American Studies Center, 1993), 127–39; Stephen Klineberg, "First Houston Area Asian Survey Explodes 'Model Minority' Stereotype and Explains the City's Changing Demographics." Press Release, Rice University, Office of Development, March 8, 1996.

94 *Even many of America's Vietnamese . . .* For a detailed description of the Vietnamese immigration experience, see for example, Bill Ong Hing, *The Making and Remaking of Asian America, 1850–1990* (Palo Alto, CA: Stanford University Press, 1993).

95 *Second, the label of . . .* Frank Wu, "Neither Black Nor White: Asian Americans and Affirmative Action," *Boston College Third World Law Journal* 15 (1995): 225.

95 *Since the Model Minority myth . . .* See, for example, David Brand, "The New Whiz Kids: Why Asian Americans Are Doing So Well, and What It Costs Them," *Time,* August 31, 1987; David Grogan, "Brain Drain Boon for the U.S.," *People,* April 21, 1986, 30 (profiles of five Westinghouse Science Talent Search winners who were Asian American); Joel Garreau, "Capitalizing on the American Dream; Koreans and the Changing Face of Small Business," *Washington Post,* July 6, 1992.

95 *Model Minority news bites also ignore . . .* Claudine Bennett, *The Asian and Pacific Islander Population in the United States: March 1991 and 1990 Current Population Reports* (Washington, DC: U.S. Bureau of the Census, 1992);

Henry Der, "Affirmative Action Policy," in *The State of Asian Pacific America: Policy Issues to the Year 2020*; Tsukuda, "Income Parity Through Different Paths: Chinese Americans, Japanese Americans, and Caucasians in Hawaii," *Amerasia Journal* 11, no. 2 (1984): 47–60.

95 *Asian American students* . . . A. Hu, "Asian Americans: Model or Double Minority?" *Amerasia Journal* 15, no. 1 (1989): 243–57.

96 *Model Minority myths conveniently* . . . Angelo Ancheta, *Race, Rights, and the Asian American Experience* (New Brunswick, NJ: Rutgers University Press, 1998), 131; U.S. Commission on Civil Rights, *The Economic Status of Americans of Asian Descent: An Explanatory Investigation* (Washington, DC: U.S. Government Printing Office, 1988).

96 *Additionally, those higher income* . . . Yen Le Espiritu, *Asian American Women and Men* (Thousand Oaks, CA: Sage, 1997), 65–71.

96 *The portion of Asian Americans* . . . U.S. Department of Health and Human Services, *Asian American and Pacific Islander Initiative Summary* report from the Departmental Working Group (1998), 4.

97 *Recent federal studies reveal* . . . U.S. Bureau of the Census (1996 Statistical Abstract, Vital Statistics).

97 *Model Minority myths have contributed* . . . Justin Shiau, "Anti-Asian Violence Continues to Climb," *The NAPALC Review* (a publication of the National Asian Pacific American Legal Consortium) 3, no. 2 (Summer 1997).

99 *In her 'zine . . . BambooGirl,* Editor's note, First Anniversary Issue, no. 5 (Mutya Publishing, 1996), inside front cover.

100 *Working in a similar vein . . .* For sample cartoons on the Web of Angry Little Asian Girl, see www.AngryLittle AsianGirl.com.

103 *Merry White, in her . . .* Merry White, *The Material Child: Coming of Age in Japan and America* (New York: Free Press, 1993).

108 *"You have to stand for . . ."* Star Jones, *You Have to Stand for Something or You'll Fall for Anything* (New York: Bantam, 1998).

110 *Starhawk, the peace activist . . .* Starhawk, *Truth or Dare: Encounters with Power, Authority, and Mystery* (San Francisco: Harper & Row, 1987).

LESSON FIVE:
SHE TAKES BACK DESIRE

page 118 *Eye-lifts are simple . . .* See William Pai-Dei Chen, *Blepharoplasty* (Boston: Butterworth-Heinemann, 1995); Wes Young, M.D., "Taking a Second Look," *A. Magazine,* August/September 1997, 24.

119 *Eye-lifts are so accepted . . .* Todd Inoue, "Roundabout Eye," *Metro,* June 27–July 3, 1996 (Metro Publishing and Virtual Valley, Inc.), available on Internet.

119 *In 1990 the American . . .* Joanne Chen, "Before and After," *A. Magazine,* Spring 1993, 15.

120 *It isn't surprising that Asian* . . . Naomi Wolf, *The Beauty Myth: How Images of Beauty Are Used Against Women* (New York: Anchor-Doubleday, 1991). See also, Michelle Stacey, "Thin-Happy," *Elle*, August 1998, 186.

121 *In a 1995 study by the Melpomene* . . . Joanne Chen, "Through the Looking Glass," *A. Magazine,* April/May 1996, 36.

122 *A study in 1995* . . . Ibid., 36.

123 *"We're not just tall* . . . Ibid., 35.

125 *Neowhite is formulated* . . . *BambooGirl,* no. 5 (1996), back cover.

126 *Women in Thailand* . . . "The Shape of a Woman," *A. Magazine,* special issue "Woman Warriors," 1994, 7.

126 *According to a survey* . . . Ibid.

127 *As Melissa* . . . Melissa de la Cruz, "Gook Fetish," *New York Press* 10, no. 11 (March 12–18, 1997): 33.

129 *According to a 1993 report* . . . New York Department of Consumer Affairs report 1993.

129 *Insurance companies* . . . Articles describing the burgeoning Asian American market include William O'Hare, William H. Frey, and Dan Fost, "Asians in the Suburbs," *American Demographics,* May 1994, 32–37.

130 *And when media kits* . . . Introduction, *The State of Asian Pacific America: Policy Issues to the Year 2020,* citing *The New York Times,* February 2, 1992, A11.

131 *According to psychologist Judy* . . . see Slater's articles on the Web at www.thriveonline@aol.com.

133 *According to Marina Budhos* . . . Marina Budhos, "Putting the Heat on Sex Tourism," *Ms. Magazine,* March/April 1997, 12.

133 *But in 1993* . . . Ibid.

133 *Companies such as* . . . Ibid., 14.

134 *Eight of 1994's* . . . Karl Taro Greenfield, "The X Files," *A. Magazine,* August/September 1995, 34.

136 *Sociologist George Kelly* . . . Milton J. Bennett, "Toward Ethnorelativism: A Developmental Model of Intercultural Sensitivity," *Education for the Intercultural Experience,* ed. Michael Paige (Yarmouth, ME: Intercultural Press), 4.

137 *When responding to* . . . "Voices in the Dark, more survey respondents speak out," *A. Magazine,* August/September 1995, 29.

140 *In agrarian Japan* . . . Hisashi Hirayama and Kasumi K. Hirayama, "The Sexuality of Japanese Americans," *Journal of Social Work and Human Sexuality* 4, no. 3 (March 1986), 86–7.

140 *Intimate relationships based* . . . Joan Jacob Brumberg, *The Body Project: An Intimate History of American Girls* (New York: Random House, 1997), 12 (pap.).

LESSON SIX:
SHE KNOWS *WHY* SHE LOVES

page 154 *What if while* . . . ed. Geraldine Kudaka, *On a Bed of Rice: An Asian American Erotic Feast* (New York: Anchor, 1995).

157 *As Evelyn Lee* . . . Lee, *Working With Asian Americans,* 431.

157 *In* The Second Sex . . . Simone de Beauvoir, *The Second Sex* (Middlesex, England: Penguin, 1972).

159 *Fifty-five percent of Asian women* . . . Eric Liu, *The Accidental Asian: Notes of a Native Speaker* (New York: Random House, 1998), 188. For more detail about Asian intermarriage, see Larry Shinegawa and Gin Yong Pang, "Asian American Panethnicity and Intermarriage," *Amerasia Journal* 2, no. 22 (1996): 127–152.

160 *Some even interrogate* . . . de la Cruz, "Gook Fetish," 34.

161 *And in stories* . . . Mina Kumar, "Jeannie," *On a Bed of Rice,* 36–48 (pap.).

165 *"We can no longer* . . ." Helen Zia, "Another American Racism," *The New York Times* op-ed piece, cited in Rita Chaudhry Sethi, "Smells Like Racism," *The State of Asian America: Activism and Resistance in the 1990's,* ed. Karin Aguilar-San Juan (Boston: South End Press, 1994), 250.

166 *She needed to know* . . . "Focus on Racism in the Media," a special thirty-six page report published by Fairness & Accuracy in Reporting, July/August 1992.

166 *She needed to explain* . . . Elaine Kim, "Between Black and White: An Interview with Bong Hwan Kim," *The State of Asian America*, 71–75.

166 *More than two thousand seven hundred* . . . Edward T. Chang, "America's First Multiethnic Riots," *The State of Asian America*, 101.

167 *Shawn Wong* . . . Shawn Wong, *American Knees* (New York: Simon & Schuster, 1995), 229.

LESSON SEVEN:
SHE BRIDGES DISTANCE

page 171 *For those* . . . Jamake Highwater quoting from Rene Char, "China's Market Economy: A Semiosis of Cross Boundary Discourse Between Legal and Economic and Feminist Jurisprudence," *Syracuse Law Review* 45, no. 2 (1994): 832.

174 *When I think* . . . Audre Lorde, "Eye to Eye," *Sister Outsider: Essays and Speeches* (New York: Crossing Press and W.W. Norton, 1993), 159.

179 *Dances of distance* . . . Monica Sone, *Nisei Daughter* (Seattle, WA: University of Washington Press, reprinted 1979).

179 *Law professor Sharon* . . . Sharon Hom, "(Per)forming Law: Deformations and Transformations," *Chinese Women Traversing Diaspora: Memoirs, Essays, and Poetry,* ed. Sharon Hom (Hamden, CT: Garland, 1998), vol. 3, 9.

180 *According to Hope* . . . Edelman, *Motherless Daughters*, 182 (pap.).

182 *This confusion prompted* . . . Groups such as Asian Women in Business in New York City, the Asian American Journalists Association, and Catalyst gather information regarding discrimination on the job and glass-ceiling issues for Asian American women.

183 *Her first move* . . . There are several groups that deal with domestic violence in Asian American households, including the Asian Women's Shelter in San Francisco and the Asian Women's Center in New York City.

183 *Critical race theorists* . . . Frank Wu, "Neither Black Nor White: Asian Americans and Affirmative Action"; Todd Gitlin, *The Twilight of Common Dreams: Why America is Wracked by Culture Wars* (New York: Henry Holt, 1995); Jean Bethke Elshtain, *Democracy on Trial* (New York: Basic, 1995).

186 *The media had a field day* . . . Ibid., footnotes 14–19, citing "Asian-bashing" articles and incidents involving *Newsweek,* CNN, *The Washington Post,* and *The New York Times*; Frank Wu and May Nicholson, "Have You No Decency? An Analysis of Racial Aspects of Media Coverage on the John Huang Matter," *Asian American Policy Review* 7, (John F. Kennedy School of Government, 1997): 1–37, citing *The Wall Street Journal, Boston Globe,* and others for race-baited coverage of the campaign finance reform hearings in Congress.

186 *In the fall of 1997 . . . In re the Petition of the National Asian Pacific American Legal Consortium et al.,* September 10, 1997 (submitted to the United States Civil Rights Commission).

187 *We're creating a voice of influence . . .* Ariana Cha, "Mass E-Mail Strikes Back at Anti-Asian Incidents," *San Jose Mercury News,* December 14, 1997.

188 *Coincidentally at the time of . . .* "Asian Women in the Workforce: A Report by BTB Quality Solutions" (Feasterville, PA: survey of 400 Asian American women by a Pennsylvania-based management firm), 1995.

188 *Faced with backbreaking . . .* Keith Donohue, "Laboring Under the Law," *The Recorder,* no. 45, (March 6, 1996): 1, 6–7.

189 *Being part and not-part . . .* Margaret Chon, "Being Between," *Loyola of Los Angeles Entertainment Law Journal,* 17 (1997): 577.

190 *Asian American identity, like American identity . . .* Yen Le Espiritu, *Asian American Panethnicity: Bridging Institutions and Identities* (Philadelphia: Temple University Press, 1992).

190 *As a Japanese American writer . . .* David Mura, "A Sea Change in the Arts: Asian American Construction," in *The State of Asian Pacific America: Policy Issues to the Year 2020,* 202.

191 *The Institute has received . . . Connections* (the newsletter of the National Asian Pacific American Women's Forum, Denver, CO), Summer 1998, 11.

192 *Southeast Asian . . .* B. A. Miller, L. N. Kolonel, et al., eds., *Racial/Ethnic Patterns of Cancer in the United States 1988–1992: Surveillance, Epidemiology, and End Results,* National Cancer Institute, National Institute of Health Publication No. 96–4104 (Bethesda, MD), 1996.

192 *Chinese and Filipino . . . Invisible and In Need,* a report of Asian Americans and Pacific Islanders in Philanthropy (1992), 15.

192 *Preliminary findings . . . National Comparative Survey of Minority Health Care,* The Commonwealth Fund, Louis Harris and Associates, Inc., March 1995.

192 *Asian American book buyers . . .* Arundati Roy, *The God of Small Things* (New York: Random House, 1997). Iris Chang; *The Rape of Nanjing* (New York: Basic, 1997).

192 *Disney's* Mulan *. . . Variety* 372, no. 6, September 21–27, 1998.

193 *Roughly thirty-seven percent . . .* U.S. Bureau of the Census 1992 (Table 1, Internet release date Oct. 1, 1998).

193 *Books such as . . .* David Eng and Alice Hom, *Q & A: Queer in Asian America* (Philadelphia: Temple University Press, 1998); Eric Liu, *The Accidental Asian.*

194 *Leni, a Filipina* . . . From a panel discussion at First Annual Conference of the National Asian Pacific American Women's Forum, Los Angeles, 1996.

LESSON EIGHT:
SHE BECOMES A WISER FIGHTER

page 197 *Then we are forced to fight* . . . Pinkola-Estes, *Women Who Run With the Wolves.*

209 *During the yellow peril hysteria* . . . Monica Sone, *Nisei Daughter;* Jeanne W. Houston and James D. Houston, *Farewell to Manzanar* (New York: Bantam, 1983).

212 *In post–World War II Japan* . . . For more on the effect of stress on autoimmune response see Kurt Isselbacher, et al., eds., *Harrisons' Principles of Internal Medicine* (New York: McGraw Hill, 1994), and Carolyn Myss, *Anatomy of the Spirit: The Seven Stages of Power and Healing* (New York: Crown, 1996).

212 *According to psychologist* . . . Morton Beiser and Jonathan Fleming, "Measuring Psychiatric Disorders Among Southeast Asian Refugees, *Psychological Medicine* 16, (1986): 627–639; Stanley Sue and James Morishima, *The Mental Health of Asian Americans* (San Francisco: Jossey-Bass, 1982).

212 *Psychologist Laura Uba* . . . Uba, *Asian Americans,* 183.

212 *In her book* . . . Christiane Northrup, M.D., *Women's Bodies, Women's Wisdom: Creating Physical and Emotional Health and Healing* (New York: Bantam, 1994), 36.

213 *As Northrup writes* . . . Ibid.

224 *A* toronoko *believes* . . . Chogyam Trungpa, *Shambala: The Sacred Path of the Warrior* (Boston: Shambala, 1995), 200.

230 *In an ancient book* . . . Ibid., 53.

LESSON NINE:
SHE FINDS HER TEACHERS

page 233 *I taught her* . . . Amy Tan, *The Hundred Secret Senses* (New York: Putnam, 1995), 54 (pap.).

250 *In his book* . . . Steven Covey, *Principle-Centered Leadership* (New York: Fireside, 1990), 126 (pap.).

252 *Until I began* . . . See, for example, Maureen Murdock, *The Heroine's Journey: A Woman's Quest for Wholeness* (Boston: Shambala, 1990).

LESSON TEN:
SHE TAKES RISKS

page 259 *In* The Hero . . . Joseph Campbell, *The Hero With a Thousand Faces* (Princeton, NJ: Bollingen, 1949), 51.

265 *They were unionizing* . . . Foo, "Jade and Armor," 96.

265 *Even though she was only* . . . Hom, "(Per)forming Law: Deformations and Transformations," 9.

268 *In* A Path . . . Jack Kornfield, *A Path With Heart: A Guide Through the Perils and Promise of Spiritual Life* (New York: Bantam, 1993), 84 (pap.).

272 *"It's okay to be wrong . . ."* David Henry Hwang, in his William Abramowitz Guest Lecture, April 15, 1994, Kresge Auditorium, Massachusetts Institute of Technology.

273 *Congressional representative* . . . Baker and Kline, *The Conversation Begins,* 52.

275 *The effort, one of the first* . . . Felicia Lee, "Law Students Rally Against Race Bias," *The New York Times,* March, 3, 1989, B1.

283 *In his book* . . . Kornfield, *A Path With Heart,* 113.

LESSON ELEVEN:
SHE MOURNS HER LOSSES

age 290 *"When we think of loss . . ."* Judith Viorst, *Necessary Losses: The Loves, Illusions, Dependencies, and Impossible Expectations That All of Us Have to Give Up in Order to Grow* (New York: Ballantine, 1986), 15.

291 *As she explained* . . . Foo, "Jade and Armor," 97.

298 *When the pressures to perform* . . . Peter G. Bourne, "The Chinese Student—Acculturation and Mental Illness," *Psychiatry* 38 (1975): 269–77; Morton Beiser, Jay Turner, and Soma Ganesan, "Catastrophic Stress and Factors

Affecting Its Consequences Among Southeast Asian
Refugees," *Psychological Medicine* 16 (1988): 183–95.

298 *Psychologists have found . . .* For Asian Americans, see
John Moritsugu and Stanley Sue, "Minority Status as a
Stressor," *Preventative Psychology: Theory, Research, and
Practice,* ed. Robert Feldner, Leonard Jason, John
Moritsugu, and Stephanie Farber (New York:
Pergamon, 1983), 162–174; Jeong-Hwa Moon and
Joseph Pearl, "Alienation of Elderly Korean American
Immigrants As Related to Place or Residence, Gender,
Age, Years of Education, Time in the U.S., Living With
or Without Children, and Living With or Without
Spouse," *International Journal of Aging and Human
Development* 32(2) (1991): 115–24.

299 *We may experience loss . . .* Alice Miller, *The Drama of the
Gifted Child* (New York: Basic Books, 1997, revised edi-
tion), 35 (pap.).

299 *In Miller's experience . . .* Ibid., 14 (pap.).

302 *What does it feel like . . .* Marion Woodman, *Leaving My
Father's House: A Journey to Conscious Femininity* (Boston:
Shambala, 1992), 16.

305 *The dream, Sharon . . .* Sharon Hom, "(Per)forming Law:
Deformations and Transformations," 22.

308 *In fact, elderly Asian . . . .* http://www.census.gov/prod/
3/97prbs/97statab/vitstat.pdf.

310 *as I attempt . . .* Sharon Hom: "(Per)forming Law:
Deformations and Transformations," 6–7.

LESSON TWELVE:
SHE MOVES HER WORLD

page 320 *In the touring process* . . . Frank Wu, "Providing Some Perspective: On Being a Professional Asian American," *Asianweek,* February 21, 1997, 9.

335 *This is what* . . . Ms. Foundation for Women, "Beyond Beijing Networking Meeting Report," May 1996, 14.

336 *When the Department of Labor* . . . Hudson Institute, *Workforce 2000,* a report for the U.S. Department of Labor, (Washington, DC: Hudson Institute, 1987).

The discussion of "Warrior Lessons" themes continues on www.warriorlessons.com. Visit this site for additional resources, reading and teaching guides, and information on the author's continuing lecture tour, or write to Warrior Lessons, 61 East Eighth Street, P.O. Box 277, New York, New York 10003.